Coalitions &
Political Movements

Exploring Political Behavior

Series Editor
Clyde Wilcox, Georgetown University

Coalitions & Political Movements

The Lessons of the Nuclear Freeze

EDITED BY
Thomas R. Rochon
David S. Meyer

LYNNE
RIENNER
PUBLISHERS

BOULDER
LONDON

Published in the United States of America in 1997 by
Lynne Rienner Publishers, Inc.
1800 30th Street, Boulder, Colorado 80301

and in the United Kingdom by
Lynne Rienner Publishers, Inc.
3 Henrietta Street, Covent Garden, London WC2E 8LU

Library of Congress Cataloging-in-Publication Data
Coalitions and political movements: the lessons of the nuclear freeze /   edited by
  Thomas R. Rochon and David S. Meyer.
      p.   cm.—(Exploring political behavior series)
    Includes bibliographical references and index.
    ISBN 1-55587-744-3 (hardcover   :   alk. paper)
    1.   Antinuclear movement—United States.   2.   Nuclear disarmament—
  United States.   3.   Peace movements—United States.   I.   Rochon,
  Thomas R., 1952–   .   II.   Meyer, David S.   III.   Series.
  JX1974.7.N81534   1997
  327.1'747'0973—dc21   97-10773
                                                                              CIP

British Cataloguing in Publication Data
A Cataloguing in Publication record for this book
is available from the British Library.

Printed and bound in the United States of America

      The paper used in this publication meets the requirements
  ∞ of the American National Standard for Permanence of
      Paper for Printed Library Materials Z39.48–1984.

    5 4 3 2 1

To LCR and EKR
and
To the movement activists who perversely believe
they can change the world, and who sometimes do

CONTENTS

Part 3   Demobilization and Movement Transition

Part 4   Conclusion

TABLES & FIGURES

Tables

Figures

1

Introduction: The Nuclear Freeze in Theory and Action

THOMAS R. ROCHON & DAVID S. MEYER

This book was inspired by the early 1980s confluence of parallel developments in the worlds of politics and academic analysis. The nuclear freeze
movement swept the country to become the largest mass movement in a
generation, giving voice to the unease with which many viewed the deterio-
ration of relations with the Soviet Union and the risks of reliance on
nuclear weapons for deterrence. Its substantive focus was the demand that
the United States and the USSR negotiate an end to the nuclear arms race.

At about the same time in the realm of academic theory, social scientists from a variety of disciplines contributed to a flowering of research on
social and political movements. The net effect of their efforts was to recon-
ceptualize movements as a strategic means of asserting citizen influence on
political and social change. These theoretical developments were begun in
the 1970s as a response to the movements of the 1960s, none of which fit
the earlier academic treatment of movements as desperate and poorly organized responses to misery by the dispossessed.

The freeze movement came at a good time for social scientists interested in applying these theoretical considerations to a new instance of mass
mobilization and direct action in politics. The freeze was by several measures the largest movement in U.S. history. Its most spectacular moment
occurred on 12 June 1982, when about 750,000 people marched in New
York's Central Park in what was the largest national demonstration in U.S.
history to that point. This was the visible tip of a huge movement iceberg,
for the freeze had an impact on national, state, and local politics as well as
on social institutions such as universities, churches, and the mass media.
For a time, the freeze seemed to affect virtually everything.

The dramatic trajectory of the nuclear freeze was emblematic of social
movements more generally. Following Sidney Tarrow (1994: 3–4), we can
think of movements as "collective challenges by people with common purposes and solidarities in sustained interactions with elites, opponents and

1

authorities." Movements emerge as episodic campaigns that lodge challenges against the state and mainstream society, using both conventional and nonconventional means of making claims. Because movements carry ideas and constituencies normally marginal to mainstream political discourse and decisionmaking, they are necessarily short-lived. Either their concerns become institutionalized and routinized in contemporary politics, or they are forced back to the margins. Generally, the result is some combination of both these outcomes. Thus, a cycle of protest is characterized by a growth in political mobilization. This is followed both by authoritative (usually governmental) response and by changes in the way people think about the issue area. Ultimately, movement mobilization and the specific campaign come to an end, though many organizations within the movement will carry on.

The nuclear freeze stands out among movements of the 1970s and 1980s not just because of its size but because it was conceived from the beginning as a nationally coordinated campaign to enact a specific policy reform. This makes the freeze movement unusual. Although participation in direct action politics has expanded in scope since the civil rights and student movements of the 1960s, that expansion has been predominantly of local movements trying to clean up toxic wastes, block construction of a nuclear reactor, or alter zoning rules so as to preserve communities. The women's movement after the failed Equal Rights Amendment (ERA) campaign of 1972 to 1982 also shifted most of its efforts to local issues and to the judicial arena. Even the Christian Right learned during the 1980s to broaden its agenda and to operate at all levels of the polity in order to survive (Rozell and Wilcox 1995). The freeze was therefore distinct from the vast majority of the 1970s and 1980s movements in its selection of a foreign policy goal and its coordination of local pressure with a national plan of action that focused on electoral and legislative politics.

In short, the nuclear freeze movement seemed in many respects to be a throwback to the mass movements of the 1960s—a comparison that Andrew Rojecki (Chapter 6, this book) demonstrates was not lost on media commentators. But if the freeze was unusual as a movement, its history also raises troubling questions about the viability of sporadic national mobilizations as a form of popular participation. Consider the following salient aspects of the movement's experience:

1. A failure of endurance, in which the decline of the movement was as rapid as its growth. The freeze movement went from scattered local origins in 1980 to a national clearinghouse with full-time staff in St. Louis in January 1982, to the activities organized across the nation for Ground Zero Week in April, to the massive New York demonstration in June, to the extensive campaign work and impressive impact on the congressional elec-

tions in November 1982, to a Pyrrhic victory in the congressional resolution passed in 1983, to failure in preventing a decisive reelection of President Ronald Reagan in 1984, to the end of national media attention shortly thereafter and finally a merger with the long-established peace organization SANE in 1987. It was an intense but brief lifespan.

2. A failure of institutionalization, because even at its height the freeze was unable to make itself a central part of the agenda of other progressive movements or institutions in society. Although the freeze received an impressive array of endorsements from progressive social institutions and public figures, these did not serve either to advance the cause or to reshape the ideology and goals of the left. Despite the concurrent existence of large-scale peace movements in both Western and Eastern Europe, the freeze also developed only weak ties with those movements (David Cortright and Ron Pagnucco, Chapter 5, this book).

3. A failure of policy impact. Although the freeze was an instrumental force in reviving the arms control process beginning in 1984, the movement was never able to place its proposal on the agenda of arms control negotiations between the two superpowers. The civil rights movement, the women's movement, the environmental movement, and more recently perhaps the gay rights movement could all claim to have left a permanent impact on the political agenda. The freeze movement had only an indirect impact on the arms control agenda of the 1980s.

These failures of endurance, institutionalization, and policy impact illustrate the cyclic nature of movement mobilizations and tempt one to conclude that the entire effort was in vain. And in terms of the ability to attain its immediate objectives through its chosen channels of influence, the freeze may be labeled a failure. But even a failed national movement leaves behind a changed network of supportive activists and organizations, new cultural understandings of its issues, and altered patterns of access to political institutions. In other words, when we view a particular movement as one cycle in a series of mobilizations, the criteria of success and failure change. In this book we present not just another postmortem of the freeze movement itself but also an examination of where it came from and what it has left behind. These are the benefits of examining a movement across several cycles.

We have brought together in this book ten research efforts that, collectively, subject the freeze to the kind of detailed postmortem that is only possible once the movement has decayed and the postmobilization patterns of activism and policymaking have become clear. We will examine the origins of the freeze, its short-run impact on political debate and public policy, and its long-run impact on successor movements. By analyzing the freeze movement from the perspective of contemporary theories and concepts, we hope to further our understanding of both the movement and the concepts themselves. We also expect our work to enlighten the circumstances that may give rise to the *next* peace movement surge in the ongoing cycle of mobilizing campaigns—even in the radically altered conditions of the post–Cold War era. In this opening chapter, we introduce these ten studies by presenting first a brief history of the freeze movement, followed by a review of key concepts in the analysis of movements. We conclude the chapter with an overview of the research chapters in this book.

The Freeze Movement

Despite a continuous public concern about the possibility of nuclear war, activists have always had a difficult time persuading large numbers of people that nuclear weapons issues were a threat that justified mass mobilization and political action. Nuclear weapons have generally seemed too distant, the likelihood of their use too remote, the prospects for movement influence too limited, and the weaknesses of alternative policies too overwhelming to generate a movement. The emergence of this movement in the 1980s reflected the development of an attractive alternative to nuclear deterrence based on escalating stocks of arms. To an even greater extent, the emergence of the freeze reflected real changes in political power and public policy that enabled activists to reach a mobilizable audience. In this section we first consider the emergence of the freeze, then its development and interaction with mainstream political institutions, and finally its decline.

Emergence of the Freeze

Peace activists have tried to raise the nuclear issue almost continuously since the beginning of the nuclear age. After the end of the Vietnam War, activists worked on a series of local campaigns, the most successful of which were directed against the development of particular nuclear power stations. Some groups attempted to link nuclear power with nuclear weapons under a coalition organization, Mobilization for Survival (MfS). Mobilization for Survival called for a national demonstration in conjunction with the first Special Session on Disarmament at the United Nations in May 1977, but the turnout of 15,000 people drew little media attention and seemed to spark little subsequent activity.

As peace groups sought to develop a viable focus for mobilization, the American Friends Service Committee commissioned Randall Forsberg, then a graduate student in political science at MIT, to draft a proposal for action. Grafting together several arms control proposals that had circulated for decades, Forsberg wrote the "Call to Halt the Arms Race" in 1980. The centerpiece of this brief tract was a proposal for a "mutual freeze on the testing, production, and deployment of nuclear weapons and of missiles and new aircraft designed primarily to deliver nuclear weapons" (Forsberg et al. 1983: 197–198). Forsberg saw the freeze as "an essential, verifiable first step toward lessening the risk of nuclear war and reducing the nuclear arsenals" of the United States and the Soviet Union.

In December 1979, Forsberg brought the freeze proposal to the Mobilization for Survival coalition as a strategy for political action. Forsberg's idea was that the numerous peace and arms control groups then active could accomplish much more if they would cooperate on interim goals such as the freeze. Although MfS endorsed the freeze at that point, numerous other proposals competed for attention. More moderate arms control groups such as the Union of Concerned Scientists, the Federation of Atomic Scientists, and the Council for a Livable World preferred to focus on less comprehensive but more immediately promising goals such as obtaining ratification of the Strategic Arms Limitation Talks II (SALT II) agreement that had recently been reached between U.S. and Soviet negotiators.[1] Virtually all activist and lobbying groups connected to MfS were growing increasingly frustrated with the Carter administration, but their differences on political strategies and ultimate goals prevented any unified action.

Divisions between arms control groups might have buried the freeze proposal had not Ronald Reagan emerged as a unifying force. Elected in a landslide of historic proportions in November 1980, Reagan promised a large build-up of America's armed forces through increased defense spending. The Republican Party platform in 1980 called for the United States to develop sufficient strength to "prevail" in the event of nuclear war. President Reagan also came into office as a vociferous opponent of arms control, which he viewed as a means for the Soviet Union to gain advantage over the United States.

The departure in defense policy that President Reagan represented from the outgoing Carter administration was a matter more of degree than of direction. The latter years of the Carter administration had seen increasing tensions between the United States and the Soviet Union due to the Soviet invasion of Afghanistan and the deployment of a new generation of Soviet nuclear weapons, the SS-20s. President Jimmy Carter responded by increasing military spending in real terms by 5 to 7 percent annually, and in 1979 by suspending the ratification process for the SALT II treaty.

Even so, President Reagan noticeably accelerated these trends of increased arms spending and decreased willingness to negotiate. Between 1980 and 1985 defense spending rose 40 percent in real terms.[2] To President Carter's proposed development of the MX and Trident II missiles, and cruise missiles suitable for land use and submarine launch, President Reagan added development of the B-1 bomber, two new aircraft carrier battle groups, and overall expansion of the Navy to 600 ships.

The president's stance against arms control negotiations was reflected in appointments to the administration of more than fifty members of the Committee on the Present Danger, a group whose primary focus was opposition to the SALT II negotiations and treaty. These appointees presented the public with an approach to nuclear deterrence and nuclear war that seemed at times almost cavalier. Consistent with their logic of developing a clear superiority in nuclear weapons, the president, Vice President George Bush, and top-level appointees spoke often about the need to be able to fight and win a nuclear war. Eugene Rostow, director of the Arms Control and Disarmament Agency, noted that prospects for arms control were not good but that casualties in a nuclear war could be limited to between 10 and 30 million persons. Chief strategic arms negotiator Edward Rowny, who had resigned from the Carter administration to oppose SALT II, suggested that more time needed to be spent building nuclear weapons and less on negotiating their control. Richard Pipes, a member of the National Security Council, estimated the chance of nuclear war at about 40 percent. Secretary of State Alexander Haig spoke about the possibility of firing a "nuclear warning shot" inside Europe (Meyer 1990: 70–72; also, see Scheer 1982).

President Reagan's term began at a particularly important time in arms control negotiations. The United States and the Soviet Union were then discussing reduction or removal of Soviet intermediate-range nuclear missiles, the SS-20s, in Europe in exchange for cancellation of the North Atlantic Treaty Organization's (NATO's) plan to deploy Pershing II and cruise missiles in five European countries. These negotiations came to an effective impasse soon after the Reagan administration began. The resulting wave of protest demonstrations in Europe presented the American public with images of a NATO alliance in disarray, as even allied heads of state criticized the U.S. president's intransigence. Although the Reagan administration's policies had roots in the bipartisan consensus on containment of the Soviet Union, its rhetoric and domestic political management of the issue was a fundamental departure from the détente-era policy of maintaining strength while seeking stabilization of relations.

As existing arms control negotiations slowed to a crawl, the new administration's foreign policies became the object of an unusual degree of expert criticism. Civilian strategists, former policymakers, and retired military personnel attacked both the conduct and the competence of the Reagan administration. Former Secretary of Defense Clark Clifford; Arms Control and Disarmament Agency veterans William Foster, Paul Warnke, Herbert Scoville, Jr., Richard Barnet, Marcus Raskin, and Paul Walker; former UN ambassadors Averell Harriman and Donald McHenry; and Rear Admiral

Hyman Rickover all endorsed the freeze as an alternative to President Reagan's arms buildup. Former CIA director William Colby coupled endorsement of the freeze with a call for increases in conventional military capabilities.

Other officials who did not endorse the freeze were nonetheless acerbic about the direction President Reagan had given to U.S.-Soviet relations, including the four authors of an influential article advocating a "no-first use" policy: McGeorge Bundy, Gerard Smith, Robert McNamara, and George Kennan (1982). The retiring chairman of the Joint Chiefs of Staff, David Jones, left office with the declaration that "it would be throwing money in a bottomless pit to try to prepare the United States for a long nuclear war with the Soviet Union" (cited in Meyer 1990: 100). Media attention followed this expert criticism and amplified it, keeping nuclear issues in the forefront of public attention. CBS, for example, ran a five-part documentary shortly after President Reagan took office, in which the central theme was to question the administration's premises of Soviet military superiority, the need to increase armaments, and the wisdom of stalling all arms limitations talks. All told, the public was faced with a breakdown of elite consensus on U.S. foreign policy that dwarfed anything seen since the Vietnam War.

By no means was all criticism of President Reagan's defense policies supportive of the freeze. But as sponsors of the leading alternative proposal, one that had an intuitive appeal and balance, the freeze movement was the ultimate beneficiary of the growth of elite, mass media, and public concern about nuclear weapons. The bilateral freeze proposal articulated opposition to the nuclear arms race without entering into divisive debates on the causes of the arms race or on Soviet intentions. Framed as a nonpartisan, good sense solution to the arms race, the freeze proposal had by 1980 already demonstrated its potential when three state senate districts in western Massachusetts, all of which voted for Reagan, endorsed a nonbinding nuclear freeze resolution placed on the ballot by local peace activists. This highly localized effort expanded to hundreds of town meetings in New England in March 1981 and 1982 and then to city- and statewide referenda in the fall of 1982. The ensuing flurry of survey probes of public opinion consistently showed levels of support for the freeze that ranged from 70 to just over 80 percent, with strong support in all regions of the country, across all demographic categories, and even among supporters of the Republican Party (Milburn, Watanabe and Kramer 1986; Thomas R. Rochon and Stephen P. Wood in Chapter 2, this book).

Public support for the freeze was readily translated into action as organizers formed local peace groups across the United States by drawing on professional, political, and religious organizations (Conetta 1988). These smaller groups participated in national demonstrations and electoral campaigns. Some of them also engaged in locally organized direct action tactics such as blocking the transport of nuclear weapons or breaking into the offices of defense contractors to smash computer keyboards. Most groups took the more conventional route and lobbied state or national officials to support freeze referenda, but others staged symbolic activities such as peace vigils, street theater, die-ins, and teach-ins. The greatest amount of activity may have been in schools across the country, as students and teachers in high schools and colleges found ways to incorporate nuclear issues and peace studies into their curricula.

The gathering protest was made to order for the journalistic and entertainment requirements of the modern mass media. Figure 1.1 traces the extent of attention given to opposition to nuclear weapons in the *Reader's Guide to Periodical Literature,* beginning at the dawn of the nuclear era. Media coverage of the freeze dwarfed anything that had been seen before. Although there are a number of parallels between the freeze movement and earlier cycles of peace activism (see Robert Kleidman and Thomas R. Rochon, Chapter 3, this book), the freeze stands alone in its sheer magnitude. At the same time, the pattern of rise and fall in freeze coverage is similar to that of the test ban movement in the late 1950s and early 1960s.

The appetite of the media for the freeze story and the need of the movement to demonstrate its wide support led to an active and successful search for endorsement by progressive political and cultural organizations. Following the supportive statement by the American Roman Catholic archbishops in 1983, virtually every major religious denomination issued a pastoral letter endorsing some version of a nuclear arms freeze. The freeze also won endorsement from the National Council of Black Mayors, the League of Women Voters, and a variety of other political organizations not normally concerned with nuclear weapons issues. Entertainers held fund-raising benefits or even became involved in civil disobedience. The horrors of nuclear war became a popular theme in Hollywood, as special episodes of prime-time shows like *Lou Grant* and *Family Ties* took up related themes. The height of "freeze-mania" came in November 1983, when ABC broadcast a drama called *The Day After* about life in Lawrence, Kansas, after a nuclear war. The program was watched by 100 million people, including more than half of all adults in the country. In the weeks following *The Day After,* thousands of local discussion groups came together to debate the policy implications of the film (McFadden 1983). As Henry Kissinger exclaimed in dismay during a discussion program aired following the broadcast, "We are scaring ourselves to death!"

Expert criticism, grassroots protest, mass media coverage, and high-profile endorsements summed together to spark a movement. But protest alone does not make a movement, nor does the generation of mass mailings for fund-raising, efforts to lobby Congress, or even a spike in media

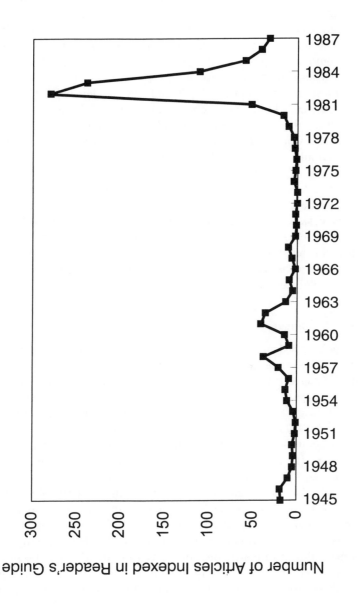

Figure 1.1   Periodical Coverage of Nuclear Weapons Opposition, 1945–1987

Number of Articles Indexed in Reader's Guide

Source: Reader's Guide to Periodical Literature.

attention to some issue. The freeze campaign can only be understood as a political movement because it generated the simultaneous presence of all these activities. Radical political groups, electoral activists, lobbyists, a wide variety of religious and educational groups, and an uncountable number of ordinary people all shared a concern that not enough was being done to prevent nuclear war. Even the least attentive portion of the American public could not help but see the flurry of controversy and become uneasily aware that something was amiss.

For a short period between 1980 and 1984, an uncommonly large number of Americans became concerned with the state of relations between the superpowers, the continuing arms spiral, and the possibility of nuclear war. Robert Jay Lifton and Richard Falk (1982) claim that the horrors of nuclear war that would follow a breakdown of deterrence are repressed from consciousness by a process they call "psychic numbing." That may normally be true, but during the height of the freeze the repressed vision of the holocaust became a very conscious possibility. The outpouring of meetings, marches, canvassing, letter writing, phone calls, discussion groups, petition signing, and other activities in conjunction with the freeze was the startling result of this burst of consciousness. The freeze was established as a national movement. The question was now: to what political use would all this social energy be employed?

The Freeze Campaign in Washington

Creating a social movement enabled nuclear freeze advocates to make political inroads that the merits of their ideas alone had not been able to bring them. Activists tried to incorporate a freeze plank in the 1980 Democratic Party platform, but President Jimmy Carter and his main rival Senator Edward Kennedy agreed to keep it off the party platform. All that changed by 1982, when increased media attention and public support made it advantageous for Democratic politicians to embrace the freeze idea.

On 10 March 1982 Senator Kennedy and Representative Jonathan Bingham (D, New York) held a joint press conference to announce their plan to introduce a nuclear freeze resolution in Congress. Kennedy introduced the resolution in the Senate with Republican colleague Mark Hatfield (Oregon) and eighteen cosponsors. Bingham and Edward Markey (D, Massachusetts) initiated the resolution in the House, with over 100 cosponsors drawn primarily but not solely from the Democratic side of the aisle. Speaker of the House Tip O'Neill became a cosponsor, signaling unmistakably the Democratic Party's intention to promote a freeze resolution.

Congressional Democrats and not a few Republicans saw political advantage in supporting some version of the proposal. Within weeks both

Randall Forsberg (author of the freeze proposal) and Randy Kehler (executive director of the Nuclear Weapons Freeze Campaign) would testify before congressional committees on the proposal. Even as the proposal entered Congress, however, activists were losing control of its meaning. Congressional sponsors insisted on making the proposal a nonbinding resolution. When freeze leaders suggested they might not support the proposal in this form, Kennedy's aides told them that the senator planned to go ahead regardless of their preferences. Randy Kehler told reporters, "I feel like I'm on a comet, but I don't know whether I'm leading it or on its tail" (cited in Meyer 1990: 128). Freeze advocates had set into motion a chain of events over which they had less and less control.

In 1982 Congress considered thirty-two separate legislative proposals on nuclear arms control in addition to the Kennedy-Hatfield freeze resolution. In this fog of contending proposals, many of them carefully crafted so as to have no actual impact on the arms race, the freeze resolution ultimately failed by a single vote. Supporters of the freeze movement were more successful on some specific weapons issues, as the House suspended funding for the MX missile. Such successes, combined with the narrow margin by which the freeze resolution itself was defeated, confirmed for many activists the feasibility of a congressionally oriented strategy. Freeze leaders entered the fall 1982 elections determined to help elect a Congress more sympathetic to the freeze proposal.

The elections of November 1982 came just after the peak of movement mobilization that occurred with the June demonstration in New York. The election itself appeared to reward handsomely the efforts of freeze activists. Freeze organizations worked on the election in forty-three states, passed eight statewide and innumerable local referenda supporting the measure, and won in thirty-eight of forty-seven congressional seats targeted as key to the passage of a freeze resolution in 1983. After the election, Markey's office estimated that the new House would have between twenty and thirty new profreeze votes (Waller 1987: 165).

The House did indeed pass a freeze resolution by a comfortable majority the following year, though it was a resolution burdened by twenty-six amendments that weakened even the symbolic significance of this nonbinding legislation. The softness of freeze support in Congress was demonstrated just three weeks later when key Democratic supporters of the freeze resurrected funding for the MX missile, which was recognized by everyone as a qualitative step forward in nuclear armament. According to Elizabeth Drew (1983), votes for the MX were procured by administration promises of a more active arms control policy. MX opponent Les AuCoin spoke caustically to his colleagues on the floor of the House: "The President gets an MX missile, and the country gets a statement of sincerity about arms control" (Drew 1983: 69).

But there was more to it than a simple trade. Congress was simply not prepared to endorse a clear shift in nuclear weapons policy. In policymaking circles, support for the freeze was largely a lever to revive the arms control process. Support for the MX, however, was an expression of determination to obtain arms control agreements from a position of strength. As Representative Norman Dicks (D, Washington) put it, "I'm getting identified as a freezie, and I've got to get back." Representative Les Aspin (D, Wisconsin) even claimed to have scheduled the MX vote shortly after the freeze vote precisely in order to enable members to balance a symbol of arms control with support for new weapons development. Although movement organizations opposed to nuclear weapons continued to grow across the country for some years, the proposal died in Washington once it had served its symbolic purpose.

Movement Decline

Paradoxically, the freeze movement foundered precisely because of the extraordinarily broad popularity of the freeze proposal among the American public. The results of polls and statewide referenda suggested the viability of a majoritarian political strategy. Freeze leaders sought increasingly to frame the issue in ways that would allow them to maintain or even increase this broad support. This meant deemphasizing the rapid movement from freeze to disarmament that Forsberg initially envisioned. It meant refusing to address other aspects of the Reagan administration's foreign policies that activists found troubling, such as U.S. involvements in Central America. It meant, finally, accepting a weak congressional freeze proposal in order to obtain the support of centrist and even conservative politicians. As leaders of the freeze became more and more single-minded, many of the original activists in the movement began to depart for more radical pastures.

The Reagan administration had enjoyed little success in marginalizing the movement by attacking it as a conduit for Soviet interests. As the freeze grew broader and more amorphous in its statements, however, the president was able to neutralize the movement by jumping on the anti–nuclear war bandwagon. Administration officials continued to condemn the freeze while simultaneously beginning to echo its major concerns. This response to the worries of the American public accelerated the hollowing out of true substantive meaning behind the freeze proposal.

In March 1983 President Reagan delivered a speech written with the express intent of stealing the movement's fire. Accepting public fears about nuclear war, Reagan criticized the freeze movement for not going far enough to break out of the logic of mutual assured destruction. He proposed instead a space-based ballistic missile defense system, the Strategic Defense Initiative (SDI), soon known popularly as "Star Wars," that would shoot down enemy missiles before they could reenter the earth's atmosphere. Such a system could be shared with the Soviets after its completion, thus ending forever the nuclear threat to both countries. "Isn't it better to save lives than to avenge them?" the president asked.

The Star Wars initiative allowed the president to shift the terms of the debate and to meld his weapons R&D program to concerns about nuclear war. The president also shifted his stance on arms control by proposing renewed negotiations with the Soviet Union. The flow of apparently casual remarks about nuclear war with the Soviets was staunched by preventing lower level appointees from conducting interviews with the press. President Reagan personally acknowledged the general concern about nuclear war by reassuring the public that "nuclear war cannot be won and must never be fought."

Faced with a transformed issue, the freeze coalition came apart. Institutionally oriented groups tempered their rhetoric further in the hope of continued access to members of Congress. Fully engaged in the legislative process, they worked to maintain congressional pressure for arms control and to lobby for reduced weapons development budgets. Other early endorsers of the freeze proposal, such as MfS, grew increasingly frustrated with the temperate politics of the mass movement. A number of freeze groups began to press for more specific stances against particular weapons systems like the MX, Pershing II, and cruise missiles. Some moved to a campaign of civil disobedience and tax resistance, citing as their cause not only nuclear weapons but also military spending and U.S. foreign policy more generally. Still other people shifted their focus to U.S. interventions in Central America, publicizing covert military operations in that region and providing shelter for war refugees who had entered the United States illegally (Wiltfong and McAdam 1991; Smith 1996). These groups were increasingly distanced from the freeze proposal, arms control issues, and the Washington policy process. By 1986, there was no longer a unified freeze campaign.

Although some groups left the freeze because it had become impotent as a way of curbing nuclear weapons, others entered the movement with an even less focused opposition not to nuclear weapons but to nuclear war itself. One group assembled a "peace ribbon" composed of fabric segments depicting people and things that participants would not want to lose in a nuclear war. Ten miles long, the ribbon was wrapped around the Pentagon and extended to the Washington Monument. The Beyond War group transferred the issue of nuclear war from the political to the personal realm, suggesting that war would not be possible if people would only embrace a new mode of thinking. Freeze activists, having initially appealed to people concerned about nuclear war, found that they were now losing exclusive rights over this terrain. Proponents of every conceivable defense policy sought to present themselves as minimizing the chances of nuclear war. The editors of the *New York Times* could justly conclude that the freeze was nothing more than "a primal scream against mankind's atomic predicament."[3]

Freeze groups were fully engaged in the 1984 election, endorsing candidates, campaigning, and contributing money. A political action committee named Freeze Voter '84 had 200 paid organizers, 25,000 volunteers, and 3.4 million contributors. The freeze organization was in some places larger than that of Democratic presidential candidate Walter Mondale, and the freeze campaign lent staff to the Mondale campaign in ten states. But these efforts were to no avail: the 1984 campaign did not become a referendum on the freeze. Mondale endorsed the nuclear freeze but also called for annual increases in defense spending of 5 percent over inflation and the development of several new nuclear weapons systems. The freeze movement had managed to alter the rhetoric of mainstream politicians, but it had little to show in the way of altered policies.

Contending Perspectives on Movements

At the same time the nuclear freeze was sweeping the country, developments in social scientific thinking about movements added a trove of new concepts and theories for understanding problems of movement mobilization, organizational and strategic dilemmas, the potential impact of movements on society and politics, and movement traits in the phase of decline.

A breakthrough occurred in the 1970s with development of the resource mobilization approach to movements (Lipsky 1968; Oberschall 1973; McCarthy and Zald 1977). This approach supplanted an earlier generation of theorizing about movements by emphasizing the strategic aspects of social protest and movement development. Movements are interpreted as a coalition of political resources and opportunities put together in order to mount campaigns for reform. Social movement organizations and their leaders stand at the center of the theory. Their role is to phrase the movement's goals, design a strategy, and develop tactics that will attract support both from a popular base and among politically influential people and institutions.

From the resource mobilization (RM) perspective, the driving force behind movement mobilization is the meshing of political resources (such as an aroused public, sympathetic allies, and mass media appeal) with political opportunities (such as a divided or closely competitive elite and open access to political institutions).[4] This perspective focuses our attention on the ability of movement organizations to put together resources and opportunities and to meld them to movement goals.[5] Movements, then, are analyzed in much the same terms one would use to understand any other policy coalition: they are a loose grouping of political forces behind a particular political goal.

The dominance of the resource mobilization approach to studying movements was challenged in the early 1980s, just as the nuclear freeze movement was developing. The chief rival perspective on movements, the new social movement (NSM) approach, is less a rebuttal of the resource mobilization perspective than a focus on different traits of movements. The new social movement perspective views ideological claims rather than resource coordination as central to movements.

Rather than being coalitions for reform (the resource mobilization perspective), new social movements are the vanguard of a revolution in social and political thought that will eventually result in alteration of the fundamental principles of democratic capitalist systems. The (largely European) advocates of the new social movement approach point to the ideas of deep ecologists, radical feminists, urban squatters, and other communal movements as examples of the emergence of a critique of the materialism, hierarchy, and spiritual impoverishment of life under "late capitalism" (Offe 1984 and 1985; Cohen 1985; Eder 1985). This is the struggle against the tendency of the political and economic systems "to colonize the life world," as Jürgen Habermas (1981: 33–37) has phrased it. The means to achieving this end is to democratize decisionmaking in areas now dominated by bureaucratic, corporate, or technically trained elites. New social movements, in short, seek a fundamental reshaping of power relations in society. The specific issues they champion, whether reducing the use of packaging materials in product marketing or creating shelters for battered women, are merely symptomatic of that broader critique.

Clearly, the new social movements approach does not fit easily with the unabashedly reformist goals of the U.S. freeze movement.[6] U.S. movements typically work closely with political institutions to press for a specific and bounded reform in policy. This is precisely what the resource mobilization perspective would lead us to expect, for U.S. movements operate in the inclusive political environment created by federalism and the separation of powers (Kitschelt 1986; Tarrow 1989a).

Despite the close fit between the experience of U.S. movements and the perspectives of the resource mobilization approach, the new social movement theory mounts a cogent challenge to some of the ways in which the resource mobilization approach interprets the freeze movement. We draw three major lessons from the NSM challenge.

First, the new social movement approach highlights the fact that political context creates grievances among the public that can be exploited by movements. It is not true, contrary to an early formulation by John McCarthy and Mayer Zald (1977: 1215), that "there is always enough discontent in any society to supply the grass-roots support for a movement if the movement is effectively organized." On the contrary, public grievances are variable. That variability is analogous to the opening and closing of a window of opportunity for movement organizations to develop popular support. In the case of the freeze movement, specific grievances created by the foreign policy of the early Reagan administration opened up the opportunity for the nuclear freeze movement to flourish.

Second, the grievances that movements exploit are connected to dilemmas in the underlying values that support the social and political system. In the case of the nuclear freeze movement, the essential contradiction is captured by the phrase "peace through strength." Nuclear deterrence requires of political leaders a balancing act between sufficient military armament to deter potential adversaries and sufficiently good relations with those potential adversaries to minimize the chances of actually going to war. The maintenance of peace between the superpowers rested on a delicate balance between enormous destructive capability and stable diplomatic relationships. Any development that called this balance into question revealed the fragility of the entire structure on which nuclear deterrence rests, and thereby created an opportunity for a mass movement to develop.

The third crucial insight stemming from the new social movement theory is that movements have social as well as political goals. The resource mobilization perspective draws our attention to the political arena, in which movement goals may include the reform of policy and recognition as a legitimate participant in policymaking (Gamson 1975). The new social movement approach redirects our attention to the social arena as a focus of movement activities. It helps us recognize that such activities as teach-ins, discussion groups, and even nonbinding electoral referenda are strategies intended to educate and engage the society, rather than being intended solely to influence policymakers. From the perspective of influencing national security policy, local activities are of only marginal value. But grassroots action is also intended to create opportunities to put an issue in front of people and to solidify the commitment of activists to the movement. When it comes to influencing the development of new social values, grassroots activity is more important than lobbying political officials or guiding legislation through Congress.

Most academic studies of movements over the last fifteen years have adopted either the resource mobilization perspective or the new social movements perspective, offering only a nod in the direction of the approach not employed. But some scholars have attempted theoretical synthesis between the two (Klandermans and Tarrow 1988; Kuechler and Dalton 1990; Tarrow 1994). The result of their efforts is a contemporary richness of social movement theory that surpasses the conceptual arsenal we have had at any previous time.

The key points of an integrated theory of movements can be summarized through the complementary expectations and insights of the two conceptual approaches at each of the three main phases of movement growth and decline. In the phase of movement origination, the expectation is that movements will develop in a context of

1. changing political opportunities (RM) and
2. an increased sense of grievance among the public (NSM).

In the mass mobilization phase, movements are expected to be

1. preoccupied with the development of relations with political authorities, potential allied institutions in society, and the mass media (RM) and
2. engaged in the development of claims concerning systemic injustices and the propagation of new social values that highlight injustice (NSM).

In the decline phase, the chief concerns of the movement will be

1. efforts to manage the shrinking resource base, leading to increased rivalries between competing movement organizations (RM), and
2. a changing focus on specific issues that engage movement activists, but a retention and even deepening of the broader critique of the system (NSM).

Although the freeze movement chose to place its greatest emphasis on the passage of a congressional resolution endorsing the freeze proposal, it was not simply a movement seeking specific policy reforms. The origins of the freeze, its treatment in the mass media, and its reception by public opinion all reflected deeply held views on such issues as nuclear deterrence, anticommunism, and prior generations of peace movement activity. The opportunities open to the freeze movement, including its choice of goals, strategies, allies, and activities, were all shaped by the broad cultural legacy of peace activism and superpower blocs that it inherited.

Nor did the freeze movement leave those elements of culture unchanged. Our understanding of the impact of the freeze movement must be shaped not only by its influence on the foreign policies of the Reagan administration but also by its impact on the ongoing network of peace movement organizations, on activists in the movement, and on public and elite opinion more generally. Even a movement like the nuclear freeze, which devoted so much of its effort to generating influence on Capitol Hill, can properly be viewed only from the perspective of its activities in both the political and the social arenas. The political and the social dimensions of movement activity are mutually reinforcing, and neither can be understood in isolation from the other.

The contributors to this book have written analyses of the freeze movement in its stages of formation, mass mobilization, and decline. In each phase the merits of the resource mobilization and new social movements theories for understanding the freeze movement cycle will be considered. These are themes to which we will also return in the concluding chapter.

What's Ahead

The theoretical terrain mapped out for this book is to apply the body of emerging theory on movements to the single case of the nuclear freeze. We seek to understand the freeze movement in its political and societal manifestations, but we also believe that the findings of our studies are applicable to other movements, particularly those that mobilize on a national basis to achieve goals in both the political and the social arenas.

The contributors to this book have spent the last decade studying the freeze movement. Their academic training is in sociology, psychology, political science, journalism, and peace studies. By bringing together their research on the freeze movement, we have fashioned a book that could not have been written by a single scholar. No one author embraces a research tradition wide enough to capture all the facets of a movement as diverse as the freeze. The contrast between different types of movement research shows that the whole movement is indeed different from and greater than the sum of its parts. The freeze campaign was both a grassroots movement and a lobbying organization. Its organizational characteristics, major activities, and legacy all look very different depending on whether one is looking up from the local level or down from the national level and depending on whether one is examining the movement from inside the political system or outside of it. No single study can adopt all of these perspectives, but the chapters to follow, among them, touch on each one of them.

The first part of the book contains four accounts of the freeze movement in its developmental phase. Thomas R. Rochon and Stephen P. Wood demonstrate in Chapter 2 that the freeze movement capitalized on public fear of nuclear war as well as public desire to maintain a stable relationship with the Soviet Union. Rather than foster new values in the public, the freeze movement heightened the salience of values that had long been present. In Chapter 3, Robert Kleidman and Rochon interpret the cyclic reappearance of peace movements in the United States as a function of the dynamics of coalition building, maintenance, and decay. In Chapter 4, Will Hathaway and David S. Meyer distinguish between the push and pull forces in coalition building, which are expressed in the balance between competitive differentiation and cooperative collaboration between movement organizations. David Cortright and Ron Pagnucco extend this analysis of the freeze coalition to the international level in Chapter 5, where the freeze wrestled with the problem of defining its relationship to European peace movements and to the Soviet Union.

Taken together, these chapters disaggregate that misleading phrase "the freeze movement." They make us aware of diversity within the movement; the tensions between its several parts; and the ways in which these tensions created a particular history of cooperation, division, and strategic choice.

The second part of the book provides three perspectives on the social and political impact of the freeze. Andrew Rojecki shows in Chapter 6 that media coverage of the freeze movement, although copious, failed to address the freeze itself as a serious policy proposal. Treatment of the freeze as a throwback to the 1960s and as the expression of a diffuse public desire for security set the stage for the movement to be derailed from its original purposes.

The freeze movement was, of course, a failure in its attempt to generate momentum for a freeze treaty. However, evaluating the political impact of a movement involves more than looking at superpower summits and congressional votes. Jeffrey W. Knopf specifies three paths to political influence in Chapter 7: mobilizing the electorate, finding sympathetic allies in Congress, and generating ideas that are used in formulating policy alternatives. Knopf shows that the freeze movement was able to activate the first two mechanisms of influence, resulting in a successful effort to revive the arms control process. In Chapter 8, Rochon places more emphasis on the lost opportunities for influence, particularly the opportunity to widen the scope of participation in setting the direction of arms control policy.

The issue of movement impact rests ultimately on an understanding of its ideological, organizational, and activist legacy. Did the freeze movement simply fade away or was it transformed into activism on other fronts? This is the issue addressed in the third part of the book. In the ninth chapter, Sam Marullo and Bob Edwards examine the death rate among peace movement organizations after the freeze mobilization. They compare the importance of strategic adaptability with the size of the resource base in aiding the survival of movement organizations and find that there are distinct prerequisites for survival among organizations of different size and scope. John MacDougall provides a case study of adaptation to movement decline among freeze organizations in Maine in Chapter 10. He finds a flexible pragmatism among Maine peace movement organizations that enabled them to thrive longer than freeze organizations in other parts of the country. Finally, in Chapter 11 Todd C. Edwards shifts the focus from organizations to activists with his contrasts between the careers of those who maintained a high level of activity for an extended period versus those who withdrew after a shorter period. Edwards's study highlights the importance of ideological evolution, level of personal efficacy, and a supportive network of family and friends in maintaining activism over the longer haul.

Taken together, these studies help us examine hypotheses generated by the resource mobilization and new social movement approaches. Until now, these hypotheses have generally been tested as mutually exclusive alternatives to each other. The result of past efforts has been predictable: some movements are considered to be resource-oriented in their character, whereas others appear to conform more to the new social movement approach. The research collected here begins from the obvious point that both ideology and resources matter in the same movements at the same time. In the polarity articulated by Jean Cohen (1985), "Strategy or Identity," the answer is "both." But such an answer raises a host of new questions. How do strategy (resource coordination) and identity (articulating broad ideological dissent) interact with each other in a movement? Does this interaction change through the phases of coalition formation, mobilization, and decline?

In our concluding chapter, we will return to these questions, bringing to them the lessons of the research reported here. The answers are significant not only for the freeze movement itself but also for our understanding of the challenges likely to be faced by national movements in the future.

Notes

We would like to thank Jeffrey Knopf and John MacDougall for their helpful comments on an earlier draft of this chapter.

1. See Steven Miller (1984b) for a collection of brief position statements by a wide variety of arms control organizations on the freeze and related proposals.

2. *Statistical Abstract of the United States, 1993,* Table 513. The cumulative five-year increase in nominal terms was 89 percent.

3. *New York Times* editorial, 19 April 1983, p. A22.

4. The "political process model" offered an important corrective to earlier iterations of resource mobilization theory by emphasizing the interplay of movement resources and external political opportunities (McAdam 1982; Tilly 1979; Tarrow 1989a). Earlier versions of resource mobilization had neglected the political arena in which activists work and had focused almost exclusive attention on the resources controlled by movement organizations. Political process models nonetheless adopt the general logic of the resource mobilization approach, and we treat them together here.

5. The leaders of movement organizations are sometimes called "entrepreneurs" in the resource mobilization literature. This is a telling analogy, for the main contribution of leaders is to bring together into a productive relationship all the different resources that make the movement possible.

6. Some West European peace movement organizations in the early 1980s, by contrast, adopted a far-reaching critique of nuclear deterrence and the two-bloc sys-

tem of military alliances dominated by superpowers. Many peace activists in Europe linked militarism to the pervasiveness of social inequality, the disempowerment of citizens, and the extent of domestic violence in Western societies (Rochon 1988). These ideas conform closely to the expectations of the new social movement theory. Despite the existence of a similar critique in parts of the U.S. freeze movement (Epstein 1991), the U.S. movement was generally more reformist and pragmatic in its issue positions.

PART 1

Development of the Freeze Coalition

2

Yodeling in the Echo Chamber: Public Opinion and the Nuclear Freeze

THOMAS R. ROCHON & STEPHEN P. WOOD

Once in a great while, public opinion seems to rise up with a singular message, as if a great revelation had come to the common imagination. Something on that order may be occurring now . . . as a grass-roots campaign is spreading in support of a bilateral freeze on nuclear weapons.

—*Bill Moyers, April 1982*

The freeze campaign came into existence in March 1981, just months after President Ronald Reagan's inaugural signaled a significant shift in U.S.-Soviet relations. Over the next three years the fates of the freeze movement and the Reagan administration seemed to be closely—and inversely—bound together. Indeed, although freeze organizations continued to operate through the late 1980s, the end of the national movement can in many respects be tied to the reelection of the president in November 1984.

The rise and fall of the freeze in tandem with the presidential electoral cycle is no coincidence, for the freeze movement chose to link its fortunes to its ability to influence the political process through the electoral system. From the very first district referenda in western Massachusetts in 1980, the freeze movement counted on and for a while received the kind of electoral support that gave it considerable power. Even while public support was the primary resource that gave the freeze movement its leverage in national politics, public opinion was also the Achilles' heel of the movement. Although large majorities of the public pronounced themselves in favor of a nuclear freeze in each of the many polls conducted on the issue between 1982 and 1984, only a small proportion were prepared to take the issue to heart. The result was a pattern of public support characterized even by movement leaders as "a mile wide and an inch deep" (Solo 1988: 24). Or, as Nuclear Weapons Freeze Campaign (NWFC) national coordinator Randy Kehler mourned in the wake of the November 1984 elections, "The impor-

25

tant message is that the American people are in favor of a freeze but they don't feel the freeze is an urgent necessity. To them it's not more important than short-term economics or personalities" (cited in Waller 1987: 294).

In this chapter we will demonstrate that the characterization of public support for the nuclear freeze as weakly committed is misleading. Support for the freeze was resistant to all efforts by the Reagan administration to introduce counterarguments to the effect that the freeze was bad policy. Nonetheless, the freeze failed to have a significant impact on the 1982 and 1984 elections, and concern about nuclear weapons proved to be a temporary phenomenon. We will explain the rise and fall of support for the nuclear freeze in light of the conflicting values in the area of arms control held by a large portion of the American public. Issues related to nuclear weapons and arms control activate one or another of those conflicting values, and support for those issues endures only so long as one value remains more salient than its rivals.

Our explanation of the fickleness of public opinion, then, stands in contrast to conventional accounts that portray the public as vacillating because of its lack of information on the subject or because of its lack of commitment to foreign policy issues. We will present instead a portrait of a public steadfast in its commitment to certain foreign policy principles and wavering only in its assessment of which principle deserves the most emphasis at a given point in time.

The Bandwagon of Public Opinion

Public opinion polls presented the American public with a great deal of evidence about its beliefs on the nuclear freeze between 1982 and 1984. Representative is a Gallup Poll conducted in September 1984, shortly before the presidential and congressional elections. In response to the question of whether the respondent is generally in favor of or opposed to "An agreement between the United States and the Soviet Union for an immediate, verifiable freeze on testing and production of nuclear weapons," 78 percent of the public answered that they were generally in favor. Note, however, that this (typical) formulation of the question assumes one key argument in favor of the freeze, namely that a freeze on testing and production of nuclear weapons would be verifiable. At the same time, a number of common objections to the freeze proposal are not raised in the question. The possibility that a freeze might lock in Soviet superiority in nuclear weapons is not mentioned. Nor is there any mention of the possibility that a freeze would ultimately be dangerous because it would prevent the testing and renewal of an aging arsenal of nuclear weapons.

The specific elements of inclusion and exclusion in question wording make little difference among those who are most attentive to politics. For those who followed the debates over arms control generally and the freeze proposal specifically, simple mention of the words "freeze" and "nuclear weapons" in the same question would have been sufficient in 1984 to conjure up a host of mental associations and to elicit an opinion that would be relatively impervious to influence from the specific question wording. Among the wider public, however, mention of the nuclear freeze did not evoke specific associations in support of and opposed to the measure. That wider public must look to the question itself for the elements of context that will enable them to formulate an opinion.

A question like that of the Gallup Poll cited above evokes support from all groups within the population because it provides an immediate context favorable to the freeze proposal. The Gallup Organization found in September 1984 that 82 percent of the Democrats supported the nuclear freeze, as did 74 percent of Republicans.[1] This is a remarkable lack of partisan differentiation, particularly in the midst of a presidential campaign in which the candidates took contrasting positions on the freeze. It suggests the imperviousness of the freeze even to opposition by a popular incumbent president on his way to a landslide reelection.

There was good news for the freeze movement in such results: they meant that the core demand for a bilateral and verifiable freeze on testing and production of nuclear weapons was very close to being a consensus desire among the American public, at least when the issue is considered on its own. In the real world of politics, however, particular issue stances are never considered in a vacuum. Some politicians and nuclear weapons experts would argue that a *verifiable* ban on testing and production is an oxymoron. Others claimed that while the freeze might be a good objective, an even better strategy would be to increase U.S. nuclear strength in order to force the Soviets into greater concessions at the negotiating table.

Members of the public who are attuned to political debate are able to supply for themselves the elements of political context that tend to be missing from most survey question formulations. Consider the results of Figure 2.1, which shows the relationship between partisanship and support for the nuclear freeze at varying levels of attentiveness to politics.[2] The American National Election Study conducted after the 1982 congressional elections included the following question:

Do you think that the United States should freeze the production of nuclear weapons ON ITS OWN, do so ONLY IF THE SOVIET UNION AGREES, or do you think that the United States should NOT FREEZE the production of nuclear weapons AT ALL?

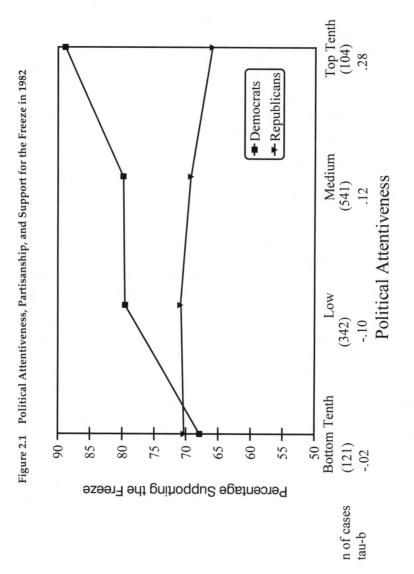

Figure 2.1 Political Attentiveness, Partisanship, and Support for the Freeze in 1982

Source: American National Election Study (1982).

Note that this question formulation is devoid of language incorporating assumptions about whether a freeze would be verifiable. This unadorned offering of alternatives leaves it entirely to the respondent to make a connection between the freeze and other beliefs about nuclear weapons, deterrence, and the Soviet Union. Since the first two response options offered in the question—a unilateral U.S. freeze and a bilateral U.S.-Soviet freeze—are both within the spirit of the freeze movement, we count both responses as being profreeze in orientation.[3]

Figure 2.1 shows that partisan differentiation in support for the nuclear freeze increases with political attentiveness. At the lowest levels of attentiveness, Democrats and Republicans are indistinguishable from each other in freeze support. Support for the freeze increased steadily at each increment of attentiveness among Democrats. Among Republicans, on the contrary, higher levels of political attentiveness meant a slightly lowered degree of support for the freeze. While there is no relationship between partisanship and freeze support among the 10 percent of the population lowest in political attentiveness, among respondents in the top decile the correlation is $r = .28$.

Respondents at higher levels of political attentiveness are as a general rule more likely to pick up partisan cues (Zaller 1992). As Figure 2.1 shows, however, the development of partisan outlooks was not symmetrical in the case of the nuclear freeze. The gradient of increasing support among Democrats is sharper than the rate of decline among Republicans. Even in the top decile of political attentiveness, two-thirds of Republican partisans defied their president and their congressional leaders—most likely knowingly—to endorse a nuclear freeze.

The characterization of public opinion as broadly but weakly supportive of a nuclear freeze may be a fair assessment of those in the nether regions of political attentiveness. To those who can supply no contextual information beyond that given in the survey question itself, the idea of a nuclear freeze sounded fair, balanced, likely to stabilize the arms race, and likely to save tax dollars. Among those at low levels of attentiveness, however, such self-evident advantages might be expected to be readily overcome by exposure to counterarguments that a freeze would not be verifiable, that it would lock in Soviet advantage, and that forbidding the testing and replacement of existing nuclear weapons would be dangerous. Indeed, a CBS/*New York Times* survey in May 1982 showed that support for the freeze fell off sharply if the survey question mentioned that it might not be verifiable or that it could lock in greater Soviet capability in nuclear weapons (cited in Finn 1985: 166). This is the operational meaning of the claim that public support is wide but shallow.

However, we find no such pattern of weakening support among those who are most attentive to politics. Such people have already heard the counterclaims against the freeze proposal, but they support it anyway. For attentive Republicans, in particular, those counterclaims came from credible and respected sources. The most impressive fact to emerge from Figure 2.1 is that those respondents who supported the Republican Party and whose exceptional political attentiveness exposed them to these (largely Republican) counterarguments were nonetheless overwhelmingly likely to support the nuclear freeze. The image of freeze support as "a mile wide but an inch deep" is therefore misleading. Support for the freeze was certainly wide, and it was certainly shallow (as are most political beliefs) among the least attentive portion of the population. But support for the freeze was also able to withstand partisan scrutiny and counterarguments even among the most attentive tenth of the population. Support for the freeze may thus be compared to the water level in a swimming pool: shallow at one end of the public spectrum but quite deep at the other.

Rise and Decline in Salience of the Freeze

We have seen that support for the freeze was resistant to the counterarguments of a president who was both popular (particularly among supporters of the Republican Party) and effective in communicating his views to the public. Yet support for the freeze also proved to be a temporary phenomenon, and within a few years it was dead as a public issue. How can we reconcile these two seemingly contradictory facts?

Tracking public support for the freeze through survey questions is complicated by the fact that such questions were not asked before 1982 or after 1984. The 1984 American National Election Study did not ask a question about the nuclear freeze, and commercial surveys such as the Gallup Poll also stopped asking freeze questions in that year. Ironically, support for the freeze as measured by the Gallup Poll reached its peak—78 percent—in September 1984, when the final question on that issue was posed by Gallup. After that date the Gallup Organization began to ask instead about reactions to the Star Wars program—a shift that reflects President Reagan's successful redefinition of the nuclear weapons issue.

Although the time series of public support for the nuclear freeze is limited to less than three years, we can locate the freeze movement in the context of wider trends in public opinion on security issues. The freeze rose and fell in tandem with a cycle in the extent of public concern about nuclear weapons and relations with the Soviet Union. This cycle of concern is depicted in Figure 2.2, which tracks the percentage of the public who mentioned either nuclear weapons or détente with the Soviet Union as being among the three most important national problems. The rise of détente as a public concern may be attributed to the worsening of relations

Figure 2.2 Nuclear Disarmament and Détente as Most Important National Problems, 1976–1990

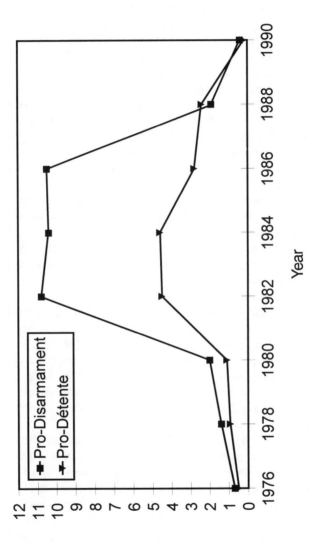

Source: American National Election Studies.

between the United States and the Soviet Union that began with the 1979 Soviet invasion of Afghanistan. This period also saw a series of new nuclear weapons deployments by both the United States and the Soviet Union, along with a decision by President Jimmy Carter, later confirmed by President Reagan, not to seek ratification of the recently negotiated Strategic Arms Limitation Talks II (SALT II) treaty. Each of these events gave the public reason to feel elevated concern about arms control and the U.S.-Soviet relationship in the early 1980s.[4]

Although external events surely provided the context for this heightened public concern, the freeze movement appears to have shaped the specific content of those fears. Prior to 1980, public concern about nuclear weapons and détente track each other quite closely, as one would generally expect to be the case. From 1980 through 1986, however, the extent of concern about nuclear weapons and disarmament greatly outpaced concern about the state of U.S.-Soviet relations, which grew at a slower rate. This increase in concern about nuclear weapons and détente was especially striking among those at the highest level of political attentiveness, 23 percent of whom mentioned nuclear weapons as being one of the most important issues facing the country in 1982.[5] The freeze movement, in short, existed in a context in which nuclear diplomacy was unusually salient and in which concern was skewed in the direction of better relations with the USSR and a reduction of nuclear weapons.

The decline of the freeze movement's influence on public opinion begins to show in Figure 2.2 in 1988, when there is an extraordinarily rapid fall in the salience of nuclear weapons as a national problem. That decline reestablished the close correspondence between concern about nuclear weapons and concern about détente. In 1990 concern about nuclear weapons and détente virtually disappeared from the public's list of most important national problems. The cycle of heightened concern about nuclear weapons had come to an end.

The puzzle we address in this chapter is captured by the contrasting images of public opinion that we get from these data. Figure 2.1 shows that support for the nuclear freeze was both extensive and largely bipartisan, even among the most attentive tenth of the public. Public support for the freeze remained high despite counterarguments advanced by the Reagan administration. The evidence from Figure 2.1 would lead us to expect that support for the freeze would be resistant to change. At the same time, Figure 2.2 shows that the public's concern for the issues of détente—and even more so for nuclear weapons and disarmament—were temporary. And this creates our puzzle, for the evidence suggests the existence both of a public whose support for the freeze was resistant to counterarguments in the early 1980s and a public that was quite prepared to jump off the freeze bandwagon by the end of the decade.

Competing Principles in
Public Opinion on Nuclear Weapons

How can we account for the coexistence of steadfastness and inconsistency in public opinion toward the freeze? Our approach draws upon the idea that people's issue positions are deeply conflicted on many enduring political problems. The source of these conflicts lies in the inconsistency between certain basic values that are widely shared and are generally stable in the American culture. When called upon to take a stance on a particular issue, people form an attitude after asking themselves which of their basic values are applicable to that issue. Rather than canvass all possible linkages between enduring values and the issue at hand, people will draw upon whichever values first come to mind. The statement of an issue attitude, then, depends to an important degree on the underlying value with which it is associated at any given moment (Zaller 1992; Chong 1993).

A case in point is the issue of abortion: the great majority of the American public believe that women and unborn babies each have rights. Whose rights come into play depends on how the issue of abortion is framed. If a total ban on abortion is proposed, then the rights of the preg-nant woman become salient. If legal restrictions short of a total ban are dis-cussed, then the rights of the unborn are more likely to be evoked as a crite-rion of judgment. If other aspects of the issue are stressed, such as public funding of abortions, then still other values (e.g., the role of government in society) may be brought to bear. What appears to be contradictory or incon-sistent in public opinion, then, is simply a reflection of ambivalence about which fundamental values one should draw upon to evaluate abortion poli-cies. This approach to public opinion is a specific application of the general model outlined by John Zaller (1992: 118), who concludes that "attitude change, then, cannot be understood . . . as a conversion experience, the replacement of one crystallized opinion structure by another. It must instead be understood as a change in the balance of positive and negative considerations relating to a given issue."

A flux in the considerations brought to bear in evaluating nuclear weapons policy may be behind the rise and fall in the salience of détente and disarmament in the 1980s. We posit two stable but antithetical princi-ples underlying Americans' attitudes toward nuclear weapons. During the Cold War era, Americans were conflicted by two basic principles of foreign policy: (1) mistrust of the Soviet Union and (2) avoidance of nuclear war.

The first of these two principles demands that the United States main-tain a strong nuclear capability, one that is at least equal to the Soviet capa-bility. A Soviet Union that believes itself able to dominate the United States would be expected to attempt to do just that. The military strength of the

United States was all that prevented Soviet expansionism from running unchecked.

The second principle demands that nuclear weapons be thought of as a means of containing Soviet expansionism rather than as a means of fighting a war. Nuclear weapons are viewed as being quite distinct from other forms of military weaponry—they are built so as *not* to be used. Nuclear war is viewed in apocalyptic terms; even those who could support an extensive conventional bombing campaign are likely to place the nuclear threshold at a much higher level. Fischhoff (1983) conducted a study of public attitudes toward types of risk stemming from sources ranging from home appliances and pesticides to nerve gas, warfare, crime, and terrorism. Of the ninety types of risk evaluated, nuclear weapons elicited the most dread, the greatest sense of lack of personal control, the strongest connection to global catastrophe, and the greatest fear of risk to future generations. Similarly, a survey of Pittsburgh residents in 1982 found that nuclear war was associated with widespread death, destruction, and the end of civilization, an act presaging the lapse into chaos (Fiske, Pratto, and Pavelchak 1983). Nuclear war is to be avoided at almost any cost.

A potential contradiction always existed between the principles of mistrust of the USSR and the desire to avoid a nuclear arms race. Members of the American public were forced constantly to weigh the relative merits of a hawkish stance toward the Soviet Union (to contain expansionist tendencies) and a more conciliatory approach (to minimize the likelihood of nuclear war). Thus, attitudes expressed about arms control and the development of new nuclear weapons could fluctuate depending on which of these two principles was invoked at any given time.

The equilibrium form of the reconciliation between these principles is nuclear deterrence or "peace through strength"—a resolution that combines the principle of distrust of the Soviet Union with the principle that overwhelming second strike nuclear strength is meant to prevent war (Ladd 1982; Harris 1984). That equilibrium may be disturbed in either of two directions. If the Soviet Union is seen as making efforts to become militarily stronger than the United States, there will be support for expansion of U.S. nuclear capability. If, however, the possibility of nuclear war seems to increase, there will be a surge of support for some means of strengthening the arms control process. In the early 1980s it was apparent that U.S. policy had moved in the direction desired by nuclear hawks, using mistrust of the Soviet Union as its justification. The public response among Republicans and Democrats alike was to support movement back in the direction of arms control.

Existing survey data tell us little about the relative salience of mistrust of the Soviets and fear of nuclear weapons over long spans of time. But it has been clear that the trade-off between the two principles became sharper as the nuclear armaments of the two superpowers grew in size and destructive potential. Figure 2.3 tracks the development of three beliefs about nuclear weapons, based on questions asked periodically since the dawn of the nuclear age. The belief that the Soviet Union has a stronger nuclear arsenal than the United States is heavily dependent on elite discourse on the subject. More than a fifth of the American population believed (erroneously) that the Soviet Union had an advantage in nuclear weapons in 1961, in the wake of the controversy over the "missile gap" during the 1960 presidential election. Again in the early 1980s, faced with persistent claims of Soviet superiority, the proportion of the population believing in Soviet nuclear superiority climbed steadily. By January 1983, fewer than 15 percent of the American public continued to believe in U.S. nuclear superiority.

Belief in the superiority of the Soviet nuclear arsenal, combined with the growth of both Soviet and U.S. nuclear weaponry, meant that the anticipated consequences of a nuclear war became more dire. In 1955, 27 percent of the public believed that "mankind would be destroyed in an all-out atomic or hydrogen bomb war" (Yankelovich and Doble 1984: 36). That proportion has increased steadily since then. Already in 1963, just over half the population said their chances of surviving a nuclear war were "poor." We know nothing about the trend line between 1963 and 1980, but in the early 1980s there was a sharp increase in the proportion of the population who regarded a nuclear war as not being survivable. A 1984 survey by the Public Agenda Foundation found overwhelming majorities, on the order of 85 to 90 percent, saying that "both the United States and the Soviet Union would be completely destroyed" in an all-out nuclear war and that "we cannot be certain that life on earth will continue after a nuclear war" (Yankelovich and Doble 1984: 33–34).

Such views are bound to have consequences for the way people think about nuclear weapons. It is hardly surprising that the proportion believing the United States should not respond with nuclear weapons in the event of a Soviet invasion of Western Europe has increased steadily. Figure 2.3 shows an especially sharp rise between 1982 and 1984 in unwillingness to use nuclear weapons in defense of Europe, just as belief in Soviet nuclear superiority and the expected casualties of a nuclear war also peaked.

These trends, in which the Soviet nuclear capability is seen as ever more threatening and yet nuclear war is also seen as ever more dangerous, represent a long-term growth—responsive to a changing reality—in the tension between two underlying principles that structure attitudes toward nuclear arms control. The belief that nuclear parity with the Soviet Union was the best achievable outcome, combined with increasing apprehension of the destruction that would accompany an exchange of nuclear missiles, meant that there was less and less room for nuclear brinkmanship. The

Figure 2.3 Beliefs About Nuclear Weapons, 1949–1984

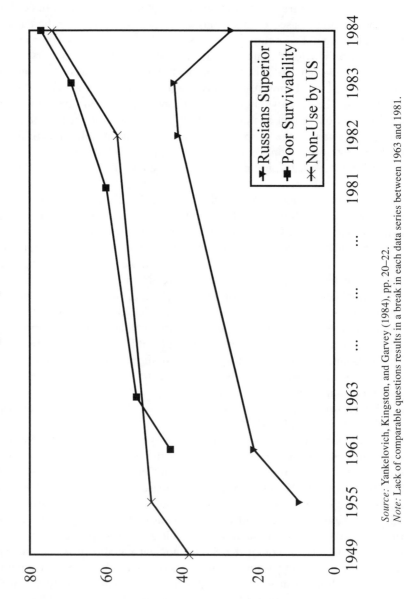

Source: Yankelovich, Kingston, and Garvey (1984), pp. 20–22.
Note: Lack of comparable questions results in a break in each data series between 1963 and 1981.

reassurance offered by an active arms control agenda, preferably accompanied by regular summitry between the U.S. president and the Soviet premier, was the only way to reconcile the need for a nuclear deterrent with the horror of nuclear war. Nuclear deterrence within the confines of an arms control dialogue became the least bad solution to a terrible predicament.

The dilemma created by mistrust of the USSR and fear of nuclear war continued to exist during the freeze movement era. The same Gallup Poll that found upward of 70 percent support for the freeze also discovered that 60 percent of the public believed that the USSR was "not at all likely" to abide by a freeze agreement (*Gallup Reporter* May 1981: 8). Louis Harris (1984) reports that dissatisfaction with the Reagan administration's efforts at negotiating a reduction in nuclear arms was found together with a deep distrust of the Soviet Union. Harris (1984: 39) further found that antipathy to the Soviet Union in the early 1980s reached its highest recorded level since the late 1950s, and he concluded that there "is growing public hostility and suspicion of [both] the Soviet Union, on the one hand, and of the Reagan Administration, on the other." The American public appears to have concluded that the nuclear arms race was not winnable, but also that the race must not be lost.

Though mistrust of the USSR did not disappear during the freeze campaign, there was increased salience of the fear that nuclear war might occur. Both beliefs, mistrust of the Soviet Union and the fear of nuclear war, were stably held. The rise and fall of the freeze campaign must therefore be attributed not to changes in underlying values but instead to alterations in which of the two basic principles deserves preeminence. In their 1984 survey of Massachusetts voters, Michael Milburn, Paul Watanabe, and Bernard Kramer (1986) found that those who supported the nuclear freeze gave as their top reason a fear of the consequences of nuclear war. Those opposed to the freeze (a mere 13 percent of the sample) gave as their top reason concern that Soviet cheating could not be detected. The only difference between public opinion in the freeze era and public opinion at other times, then, lay in the proportion of the population that saw nuclear war as a more immediate concern than Soviet duplicity.

In summary, the coexistence of mistrust of the Soviet Union with horror of nuclear war creates a dilemma for public opinion about nuclear weapons. Nuclear weapons are good—even necessary—to the extent that they are a deterrent to war. Nuclear weapons are bad—the greatest technological nightmare ever—should they ever be used. Both the necessity of nuclear weapons and the nightmare of their use have increased over time. It is in this context of an irreconcilable and ever-sharpening dilemma between mistrust of the Soviet Union and fear of nuclear war that we must view the rise and fall of public support for the freeze.

Elite Strategy in Managing Public Opinion

When the public has conflicting principles on some policy problem, one consequence is that the issue is likely to resurface repeatedly. If there is an equilibrium point at which the tension between conflicting principles can be managed, such as the combination of nuclear deterrence and arms control in this instance, then the issue may remain off the public agenda for extended periods. This equilibrium is the condition that V. O. Key, Jr. (1961: 553) described as the policy under which "long run majority purpose and public action tend to be brought into harmony." Under such conditions, the public has little reason to be attentive to or concerned about either U.S.-Soviet relations or nuclear strategy.

However, any attempt to move outside of the equilibrium policy space will lead to a sudden alteration of this situation. Abandonment of an equilibrium policy will generate movement in two directions. This happened in the 1980s, beginning with the chilling of the Cold War late in the Carter administration. Ronald Reagan found a ready audience for his warnings about the Soviet threat during his presidential candidacy in 1980, just as had other presidential candidates before him. At the same time, the continued stridency of those warnings after the Reagan administration took office undermined the nuclear weapons buildup sought by the president. The first warnings of a Soviet threat invoke the principle of mistrust and generate support for increased U.S. defense capacity. But repeated warnings in the context of a growing U.S. nuclear arsenal have the opposite effect by heightening the level of concern that a nuclear war might actually be fought. The acceleration of change in the early 1980s in perceptions of Soviet nuclear threat and the survivability of nuclear war, depicted in Figure 2.3, is a graphic illustration of this growing dilemma. In the charged atmosphere of the early 1980s, there was simultaneous support for an increase in U.S. military strength and for reestablishment of more "normal" relations with the Soviet Union. President Reagan's strategy of painting the Soviet Union as an Evil Empire, so useful to his aspirations for a defense buildup, also planted the seeds of its own demise.

The existence of conflicting public values on an issue means that the relative salience of each principle will affect public priorities. If a proposed change in policies appears to maximize one principle at the expense of the other, advocates of the principle that has been slighted will mobilize in defense of that principle. The slighted principle will receive a hearing from the public greater than what it might normally receive. This twinning of movements and countermovements in society is a common one. Zald and Useem (1987: 249–250) note that "each side in the conflict has an incentive to raise new issues that can recruit uncommitted bystanders; the struggle increases solidarity within each conflict group . . . polarization and mobilization increase in a reciprocal dynamic."

In this case, the principle of fear of nuclear war was evoked by the escalation of the nuclear arms race and by the tone of superpower relations, in which some of President Reagan's aides appeared to view nuclear war as a real possibility. The countermobilization took the form of the freeze movement, which put its own programmatic stamp on the heightened concern about nuclear war. Louis Harris (1984: 39) connected the freeze movement to a feeling of urgency: "The urgency of today is precipitated by the dread realization that humanity could well be wiped out in the event of nuclear war, not just at some vague point in the future, but anytime. And anytime could be now." This urgency was fed by the freeze movement, whose message in settings ranging from the state referendum campaigns to the widely viewed television movie *The Day After* were all focused on the need to avoid nuclear war.

The Reagan administration sought public support for its arms buildup by playing on public mistrust of the Soviet Union (Cole 1983). The goal of the nuclear freeze movement, in turn, was to keep the public focused on the horrors of nuclear war. The "policy dialogue" between the Reagan administration and leaders of the freeze movement took less the form of a direct confrontation on arms control than an indirect conflict over which of the two basic foreign policy principles deserved precedence. Neither side had to persuade the public of anything. The American public believed both sides; the only question was whose claims would be accorded precedence.

Of course, the Reagan administration and the Nuclear Weapons Freeze Campaign were not the only participants in the freeze debate. Others who joined in, however, had to be cognizant of the same structure of public opinion that shaped the strategies of the principals. Church leaders who spoke out against the development of new nuclear weapons, for example, stressed the immorality of nuclear war (Principle 2), rather than the nature of the Soviet Union (Principle 1). In its 1982 pastoral letter "The Challenge of Peace," the National Conference of Catholic Bishops declared that "under no circumstances may nuclear weapons or other instruments of mass slaughter be used for the purpose of destroying population centers or predominantly civilian targets." The Augustinian "just war" tradition was specifically set aside by Bishop John Bosco of Pittsburgh, who explained that St. Augustine "had never heard of the atom bomb" (cited in Van Voorst 1982: 87). The pastoral letter of the United Methodist Council of Bishops supported the freeze proposal and warned graphically that "hundreds of millions of people would be burned to death or blown away or reduced to sub-human levels of existence" by a nuclear war (cited in Dwyer 1983: 82). Physicians for Social Responsibility organized teach-ins at more than 150

U.S. colleges and universities in 1981, showing at many of them a film called *The Last Epidemic,* which portrayed the consequences of a nuclear bomb dropped on San Francisco (McCrea and Markle 1989: 106; Neal 1993).

Meanwhile, those who would attack the freeze proposal placed their emphasis on the untrustworthiness of the Soviet Union. That a freeze agreement would not be verifiable became an important point in the antifreeze argument, as was the claim that some freeze organizations had communist participation and that others were dupes of Soviet propaganda (see Thomas 1985 for a typical rendering). The most striking characteristic of the freeze debate was that everyone could cite facts, but which facts were relevant depended entirely upon which side one took.

To congressional leaders of the Democratic Party, looking for an issue with which to weaken the president, the freeze represented both an opportunity and a threat. The opportunity, of course, lay in the prospect of using the popularity of the freeze proposal and President Reagan's opposition to it to partisan advantage. This meant emphasizing the dangers of nuclear war entailed in the administration's foreign policy, something congressional Democrats were happy to do. Representative Walter Fauntroy (D, Washington D.C.), during the 1982 freeze debate in the House, announced:

> Many harbor the misconception that nuclear war is winnable, that security can result from ever increasing nuclear arsenals, and that use of nuclear weapons is a viable alternative. . . . The rules have changed; the nuclear arms race and nuclear war are not extensions of politics, they are mutual suicide. (cited in B. Schneider 1984: 6)

But embrace of the freeze proposal also contained risks for members of Congress, who had to persuade their constituents that they had not forgotten the principle of mistrust of the Soviet Union. Representative Clement Zablocki (D, Wisconsin), chair of the Foreign Affairs Committee, coauthor of the freeze resolution, and the man with responsibility for managing it on the House floor, positioned the freeze proposal as responsive both to concern about nuclear war and to mistrust of the Soviet Union.

> No element of the Reagan defense program is stopped by the freeze. . . .
> All that House Joint Resolution 13 tells those negotiators to do, or attempt to do, is negotiate with the Soviet Union and do so in the best security interests of the United States. (cited in Feighan 1983: 43, 44)

House Democrats, more concerned with their public standing than with crafting a coherent stance on arms control, stressed their support for both of the basic principles of American public opinion: mistrust of the Soviet Union and fear of nuclear war. Support for the nuclear freeze addressed the fear of nuclear war; subsequent votes to fund the MX missile, Trident missiles, Pershing II missiles, and the B-1 bomber all addressed public mistrust of the Soviet Union. Representative Les Aspin (D, Wisconsin) said later that he even advised the administration to bring the MX funding proposal to Congress right after the vote on the freeze as a way of increasing congressional support for the MX missiles. "The usual pattern of this place is that people get a little uncomfortable if they've gone too far one way and start looking for a way to pop back the other way" (Aspin, cited in Drew 1983: 55). Elizabeth Drew goes on to cite an aide to the House leadership:

> The MX provides the first opportunity for that group [of House Democrats] to try to recast the attitudes about them and explain what they think the vote on the nuclear freeze means—and interpret it somewhat differently from the way the others have. (cited in Drew 1983: 56)

The freeze proposal was used in the same way by Democratic candidates for the presidency in 1984: all embraced the freeze proposal, but all of them also articulated plans for additions to the U.S. nuclear arsenal. Walter Mondale, 1984 Democratic nominee for president, was typical in his statement of support for the freeze:

> I think it is a very useful initiative as an expression of concern. This administration has broken with the bipartisan tradition that's existed since the bomb first went off by which our leaders have solemnly sought to restrain nuclear arms buildups. (cited in Meyer 1990: 225)

The usefulness of the freeze proposal for the Democratic Party was that it permitted an expression of concern about nuclear war without impeding demonstration of a willingness to be tough with the Soviet Union. And this strategy was successful, at least during the height of freeze mobilization. In a reversal of the normal pattern of party images among the public, more people said in 1982 that the Democrats would be better at keeping the country out of war than the Republicans.[6] Among supporters of the nuclear freeze, those naming the Democrats as the party of peace outnumbered those naming the Republicans by almost two to one (22 percent to 12 percent). The freeze was, then, one of the relatively few issues on which the Democrats ran well in the early 1980s.

In the end, though, the strategies of both the NWFC and their Democratic supporters were for naught. The equilibrium policy space always combined the development of a strong U.S. nuclear arsenal with an active arms control agenda. Having failed in his attempt to leave that equilibrium policy space without public controversy, it was in President Reagan's power to return to the equilibrium at any time. And this he did, beginning with a speech at Eureka College in May 1982, at which the president proposed a new set of arms control negotiations, to be dubbed Strategic Arms Reduction Talks (START). Even more definitive was the Star Wars proposal, which entered a previously unexplored area in the equilibrium policy space. Star Wars ran the risk of being laughed at by the American public, but it was also an innovative way to appeal simultaneously to mistrust of the USSR and fear of nuclear war. The key feature of the Star Wars program was that it envisioned the United States with the strength of advanced military technology and, given the protective nature of Star Wars technologies, promised additional defenses against nuclear war. Star Wars was an entirely novel way to offer assurance on both principles, even though questions of cost and feasibility reduced public support for the program. Gallup Poll soundings in 1985 and 1986 found that between 52 and 61 percent of the public supported the program, including over 70 percent of those who had an opinion. A party politics analysis of public opinion would view the transition from support of the freeze to support of Star Wars as still further evidence of inconsistency in public opinion. Our analysis, based on the enduring but conflicting principles of mistrust of the Soviets and fear of nuclear war, instead sees these two as expressions of underlying continuity in values. With the Star Wars proposal, the Reagan administration regained command of the arms control agenda and the NWFC lost its position as articulator of the concern that a nuclear war might be fought.

Conclusion

We have seen in this chapter that two enduring principles structured American attitudes on foreign policy during the Cold War era: mistrust of the Soviet Union and fear that arms buildups could lead to nuclear war. Under equilibrium conditions of nuclear deterrence (a combination of U.S. military strength with détente and an active arms control program), the American public was content to leave management of the U.S.-Soviet relationship to President Reagan. When the public was persuaded that Soviet military power exceeded U.S. strength, the salience of mistrust increased and the public supported large defense buildups. When persuaded that nuclear war was a possibility, the public was swift to demand increased efforts toward ending the arms race and maintaining a stable, if cautious, relationship with the USSR. As U.S. foreign policy moved out of the equilibrium zone, public opinion rallied across the ideological spectrum to the support of an arms control proposition—the nuclear freeze—that promised to reestablish the equilibrium.

The central purpose of this chapter has been to establish that both the rise and the decline of public support for the freeze can be explained as resulting from continuity in public values. Despite the fact that public opinion bounced from widespread support for the nuclear freeze to almost equally widespread support for Star Wars, each of these issue attitudes reflected consistently held public values. Hogan and Smith (1991: 546) conclude that "there is no evidence of a radical transformation in public attitudes between 1980 and 1984." We could extend this conclusion to the entire Cold War era.

We have also seen that there was significant strategic maneuvering by all parties to the freeze debate, as each attempted to connect its policy goals to these public values. Thus, the freeze movement emphasized the horrors of nuclear war while the Reagan administration emphasized the untrustworthiness of the Soviet Union. Leaders of the Democratic Party appear to have been the first to recognize that the old equilibrium policy still held, and thus they supported both the nuclear freeze and significant additions to the U.S. nuclear arsenal. This may not have been a logically consistent policy, but it was the policy that promised to satisfy both of the basic principles underlying public opinion on the superpower relationship.

Ultimately, President Reagan trumped all other parties to the debate with his Star Wars program, a policy that established a new equilibrium responsive both to mistrust of the Soviet Union and the fear of nuclear war. From the perspective of the two enduring principles of public opinion, Star Wars *was* the nuclear freeze, minus concerns about whether the Soviets would retain an advantage in nuclear weapons or whether the Soviets could be trusted to abide by treaty commitments.

We conclude from this review of public opinion toward the nuclear freeze that certain public values are enduring and that these values introduce a significant constraint on policymakers. This is true even in the area of foreign policy, in which presidents are given relatively great latitude. The public is not a micromanager of foreign policy, but public opinion nonetheless introduces significant constraints into the formulation of foreign policy. Any policy that did not promise both to contain the Soviet Union and to manage the U.S.-Soviet relationship short of nuclear war would inspire a swelling public protest.

In 1966, V. O. Key, Jr., wrote that

> The voice of the people is but an echo. The output of an echo chamber bears an inevitable and invariable relation to the input. As candidates and parties clamor for attention and vie for popular support, the people's verdict can be no more than a selective reflection from among the alternatives and outlooks presented to them. (p. 2)

We have seen in the case of the nuclear freeze that the voice of the people was indeed an echo of what they had been told: that the Soviet Union had entered a particularly aggressive phase in the late 1970s, that the superiority of the Soviet nuclear arsenal had created a window of vulnerability, and that a limited nuclear war might be fought. But central to Key's image is that the echo chamber of public opinion offers a *selective* reflection of the words of clamoring political leaders. The principles of selection depend on the resonance between the claims of political leaders and the basic values that structure Americans' opinions of foreign policy. The equilibrium policy toward the Soviet Union during the Cold War era was nuclear deterrence combined with consistent efforts at arms control. When actual foreign policy falls within that equilibrium space, public opinion is a passive echo of elite debate. When the policies of the late Carter and early Reagan administrations moved outside of that equilibrium space, it was as if contending political elites were yodeling in the echo chamber. The sounds in the echo chamber became magnified, resulting in heightened distrust of the Soviet Union combined with consensus support for the nuclear freeze. Public support for the freeze movement was ultimately a signal to the Reagan administration to modulate its message.

The most striking feature of the freeze campaign, as with many movement campaigns, was the startling rapidity with which it grew and then subsided. We have shown that the presence of movement cycles can occur in a context of stable public values, particularly when the movement campaign centers on an issue that connects to conflicting value concerns. Distrust of the Soviet Union and fear of nuclear weapons and arms races were consistent public values throughout the Cold War era. What did change from time to time was the feeling that nuclear war was a near-term possibility. That sentiment led consistently to peace movement mobilizations during the Cold War era.

The fear of nuclear war today remains a powerful (if latent) element of American public values. With the breakup of the Soviet Union, however, the principle of mistrust of the USSR is no longer relevant. The absence of this counterweight to the fear of nuclear war may encourage isolationist responses to ethnic and other international tensions around the globe. It has certainly vitiated public support for further development of the U.S. nuclear arsenal. Continuity in public values, combined with changes in the international system, continue to structure the potential for peace movement campaigns to achieve widespread support.

Appendix

Coding of the Most Important National Problem Responses

The American National Election Study asks people to name the three most important national problems. The following specific references were counted as a statement that détente is one of the most important national problems:

530. Russia: general reference to Russia (USSR), Eastern Europe, détente

531. For peaceful relations with Russia/détente/Eastern Europe; for increased trade with Russia

The following references were counted as a statement that nuclear weapons are among the most important national problems.

710. Disarmament: General reference to ending the arms race; nuclear proliferation; test ban treaty (not 540)

711. For disarmament: for extension of test ban treaty; support toward ending of arms race; against (additional) expenditures on military/arms development; SALT

Notes

1. *The Gallup Poll Monthly,* October 1984 (Princeton, NJ: Gallup Organization). Support for the nuclear freeze was not only weakly related to partisanship, it varied little among *any* demographic or ideological group in the population. See Michael Milburn, Paul Watanabe, and Bernard Kramer (1986).

2. Political attentiveness is here measured as an additive index of the respondent's use of the mass media (newspapers, magazines, television, radio) for information about the campaign, the respondent's ability to identify correctly the majority party in both House and Senate before and after the 1982 congressional elections, and the respondent's professed interest in government. These items—media use, information, and interest—are all intercorrelated in the range of .33 to .50. We are confident, then, that the index is a more reliable indicator of political attentiveness than any of its component elements.

3. We do this despite the fact that the movement itself mobilized in favor of a *bilateral* U.S.-Soviet freeze.

4. The data in Figure 2.2, from the American National Election Study, are confirmed by Gallup Poll data that the threat of nuclear war was the most important problem in the eyes of the American public in 1984. Relations with the USSR had not been named as the top issue since 1960.

5. Only 10 percent of those at the lowest level of attentiveness mentioned nuclear weapons or disarmament as being among the most important issues (Tau-b = .14).

6. Twenty percent said the Democrats would be better at keeping the country out of war, compared to 14 percent who said the Republicans are the party of peace. The other two-thirds of the respondents said there was no difference between the parties on this issue, according to the 1982 American National Election Study.

3

Dilemmas of Organization in Peace Campaigns

ROBERT KLEIDMAN & THOMAS R. ROCHON

The freeze movement was the most recent instance in a cyclic history of peace activism that includes lengthy periods of quiescence and brief outbursts of extensive mobilization. Each of these periods of activism has its own characteristic issues, forms of organization, and patterns of action. Each successive movement is, as Wilhelm Bürklin (1985: 1) puts it, a "successive realization (in different form) of an identical principle."

If the principle of restricting the buildup of armaments has been identical between successive peace movement cycles, the differing realization lies in the distinctive coalition developed within each specific peace campaign. Coalitions permit member groups to increase their chances of political success by combining and concentrating their forces and by developing an efficient division of labor. Coalitions may also enable social movement organizations (SMOs) to build a continuing power base, develop new leaders, increase resources, and broaden the scope of the issues they address (Bobo, Kendall, and Max 1991). At the same time, however, coalitions create political and organizational tensions between member groups. Although the tensions are consistent, the ways in which they are managed are not. Successive waves of peace activism may therefore differ in certain crucial respects.

In this chapter, we compare the three major peace campaigns of the modern (post–World War I) peace movement in the United States. After describing the three peace campaigns, we focus our analysis on the organizational choices and tensions inherent in the coalitions supporting each of these three mobilizations. We conclude by examining the entirely distinct organizational dilemmas that exist during the long phases of quiescence between periods of peace activism. Our purpose is to learn what each of these campaigns tells us about mobilization during periods of activism and about how movement organizations sustain themselves between campaigns.

Mobilizing Structures and Organizational Tensions

In common with other movements, the modern U.S. peace movement has taken the form of a cyclic series of specific mobilizations or campaigns. Each manifestation of peace activism in this century began in a period marked by growing threats to peace, and each was composed of a mixture of pacifist and nonpacifist organizations. Putting aside their differences over long-term goals and strategies, peace organizations coalesced in each campaign around one or two simple goals with broad public appeal. They created umbrella organizations to coordinate the campaigns and to help extend mobilization beyond the usual bounds of peace movement activism.

The first such campaign, the Emergency Peace Campaign (EPC) in 1936, sought to promote U.S. neutrality and international economic cooperation in a climate of increasing international tension. In 1957, as the dangers of nuclear testing in the atmosphere received great publicity, the Committee for a Sane Nuclear Policy (SANE) and the Committee for Nonviolent Action (CNVA) launched the atomic test ban campaign. In 1979 and 1980, as Cold War tensions escalated, the Nuclear Weapons Freeze Campaign (NWFC) was launched.[1] These three campaigns turned threatening events and public fears into opportunities for mobilization. They affected policy but failed to achieve their main goals before world events, domestic politics, and factors internal to the campaigns combined to demobilize them. We will present brief histories of the campaigns and then analyze their organizational tensions.

The Emergency Peace Campaign, 1936–1937

Fearing the rise of isolationism at home and the approach of war abroad, a number of peace groups started the EPC in 1936 to promote U.S. neutrality and international economic cooperation. A coalition of peace groups led by pacifist organizations raised sufficient funding to set up a national office in space donated by the American Friends Service Committee (AFSC) in Philadelphia, with a staff of almost 200 full- and part-time paid activists.[2] The EPC moved quickly to its peak level of mobilization, which lasted for about one year. The official kickoff included a national radio address featuring a speech by Eleanor Roosevelt and a sounding of the Liberty Bell. EPC leaders used church networks and mass communications to reach most corners of the United States with their internationalist-neutralist message. The organization sponsored more than a thousand meetings in more than 500 cities and arranged for untold thousands of speeches by clergy, students, and labor leaders. There were about 1,700 local EPC chapters, most consisting of one or two volunteers helping to implement the national program. EPC staffers lobbied Congress to strengthen neutrality legislation.

The pressure generated by the campaign probably assisted in the passage of strongly worded neutrality legislation in 1936 and 1937, although these laws gave the president more discretion than pacifists in the campaign wished.

The EPC was the largest peace coalition in the United States to that date, but the coalition behind the campaign was uneasy from the start. The EPC encompassed two distinct wings, pacifist and liberal-internationalist. They agreed on the goal of promoting international economic cooperation in order to reduce a major cause of conflict. However, the internationalists in the campaign were ambivalent about neutrality. They accepted it as the second main goal of the campaign only at the insistence of pacifist leaders who controlled the EPC through their access to major donors and their greater organizing experience.

With passage of neutrality legislation in 1937, tensions within the coalition became sufficiently acute to bring about the end of the campaign. Pacifist groups feared that the EPC would compete with them for local activists and public support, and internationalists abandoned neutrality in favor of collective security. The EPC began a rapid decline, marked by staff layoffs, the closing of its regional offices, and a reduction in its public program. There was little left of the EPC after that summer, and the campaign officially ended in 1937.

The Test Ban Campaign, 1957–1963

After World War II, two distinct movements arose in response to the advent of atomic weapons. Scientists organized for international control of atomic weapons, and a world government movement emerged out of prewar liberal internationalism. Both efforts collapsed as the Cold War began. But in the mid-1950s publicity over the spread of fallout from U.S. atmospheric tests in the Pacific catalyzed international pressure for an atomic test ban. That pressure came to focus increasingly on the United States, especially when the Soviet Union proposed a test ban that was rejected by President Dwight D. Eisenhower on the grounds that it would not be verifiable. Democrat Adlai Stevenson campaigned for a test ban in the 1956 election, giving further encouragement to a domestic movement against nuclear testing.

To capitalize on the public attention being given to the issue, Lawrence Scott of the AFSC convened a meeting of peace leaders in early 1957 to plan a campaign promoting a ban on atomic testing as a public health measure and as a means to end the arms race. The CNVA started what became a series of nonviolent direct actions at nuclear production facilities and test sites. SANE began a more institutionally oriented strategy with a full-page advertisement in the *New York Times*.[3] Within weeks SANE received thousands of supportive letters and requests for reprints of the ad. By the summer of 1958 local activists had formed about 130 SANE chapters with a combined membership of about 25,000.

As occurred within the EPC a generation earlier, the liberal-pacifist coalition for a nuclear test ban fractured in 1960 when pacifists accused SANE's liberal leadership of caving in to congressional red-baiting. Pacifists who had worked through SANE—including some of its leading figures—quit the organization, and membership in Student SANE plummeted. Some pacifists and students changed the focus of their activism to other issues and movements, most notably the growing civil rights movement.

These splits weakened but did not end the test ban campaign. Activists continued to demonstrate, lobby, speak out, and take direct action in favor of a test ban through SANE, CNVA, and new organizations such as Women's Strike for Peace. The Cuban missile crisis renewed the public's sense of urgency and moved policymakers to negotiate a limited test ban. The 1963 Partial Nuclear Test Ban Treaty, signed by the United States, the Soviet Union, and Great Britain, outlawed atmospheric and outer space testing of atomic weapons. It fell far short of the goal of ending the nuclear arms race because it permitted the development of new weapons through underground testing. The treaty did, however, demobilize the test ban campaign. SANE's membership dropped, organizations such as the Student Peace Union (SPU, 1959–1964) disbanded altogether, and public attention shifted elsewhere.

The Nuclear Weapons Freeze Campaign, 1979–1986

The third campaign to be considered here is the nuclear freeze, which began in 1980 as a coalition between established peace groups and a new generation of local peace, environmental, and community organizers. The freeze movement quickly outstripped the test ban campaign in size and influence. Tens of thousands of volunteers worked through 1,800 local chapters, and a June 1982 rally drew 750,000 people to New York City for the United Nations Second Special Session on Disarmament. Inside and outside of the NWFC structure there were as many as 10 million participants in 6,000 organizations (Lofland, Colwell, and Johnson 1990). The freeze proposal also received a great deal of political attention because it was endorsed by leading liberal politicians and opposed by conservatives in the Reagan administration and outside it.

The decline of the freeze was a result of its symbolic success and practical failure. The mass media and mainstream politicians lost interest in the freeze in 1983—when Congress narrowly passed a symbolic freeze resolution but then voted funds for the MX missile—and wrote the campaign off entirely after President Ronald Reagan's 1984 reelection. By 1987 the NWFC had merged with SANE to form SANE/FREEZE and was reduced to 270 local groups and thirty state affiliates with 170,000 members.[4] The merged organization, renamed Peace Action in 1993, struggled to maintain local chapters and public interest in foreign policy in the post–Cold War era, when domestic issues dominated the political agenda.

Consequences of Goal Selection in the Peace Campaigns

Each of these campaigns was carried out by coalitions of peace organizations. As is true of all coalitions, participants in these campaigns shared some goals but not others. Even when coalescent organizations do not have conflicting goals, they often differ over what should be the most important goals of a campaign. The broader the coalition, the wider the range of goals emphasized by member groups.

There are two typical means for managing tensions that result from differing goals. Some coalitions take a "laundry list" approach, adopting one or two of each member group's key goals. However, as one organizer's manual suggests, this often results in "chaos and bad feelings" (Bobo, Kendall, and Max 1991: 72). A more successful approach, the one chosen in each of these peace campaigns, is to adopt a few common goals that most groups consider important and that the coalition may make achievable.

Each campaign centered on policies that seemed achievable in a few years: neutrality and greater economic cooperation, a test ban, and a nuclear freeze. Many coalition members considered these to be partial steps toward more fundamental long-term goals such as disarmament, though some did not. Their most effective appeals were to fear of war or atomic fallout rather than to any fundamental criticism of existing patterns of international relations based on armed might and a balance of terror.[5] There were exceptions to this: early SANE ads stressed not just survival but the immorality of atomic weapons. However, the heart of the appeal of each campaign was the avoidance of an immediate threat.

The selection of goals and the framing of appeals suggest that movement organizations planned the campaigns as a broad front door through which new activists and supporters could be recruited. Campaign choices also reflected a typical tendency in coalitions to seek least-common-denominator goals that all members could live with, even if none were fully satisfied. The goals of the peace campaigns were framed so as to generate a wide public appeal. By choosing goals shared by all coalition members and by many in the public, the campaigns were able to grow at a phenomenal rate.

However, the very popularity of these policies made them co-optable by mainstream political forces. This proved to be a problem for the movement organizations behind the campaigns because each was forced to make divisive decisions about what compromises should be made with political authorities. Thus, a limited test ban treaty seemed to many a reasonable compromise in the early 1960s, as did passage of a symbolic freeze resolution and resumption of arms control talks in the early 1980s. These measures were only first steps to many activists in the campaign, but the achievement of these first steps significantly reduced public support for both the test ban and the nuclear freeze. The lesson of these campaigns is that fear can be used to generate rapid mobilization, but that the same fear can be quickly abated by means other than those preferred by the campaign organizers. People drawn into support or activism because of fear left the campaign quickly once they believed the government was addressing their concerns.

The EPC was an exception to this pattern. Pacifists dominated the EPC coalition because they had raised the initial funding and they had more experience in public campaigns than the liberal internationalists. Neutrality divided the EPC coalition to a far greater extent than did the later campaign goals of a test ban and a freeze. Pacifists elevated neutrality to one of the two main campaign goals, even though many internationalists were ambivalent about it. Because neutrality was popular with large sectors of the public, the choice of this goal gave the campaign great early potential. Ultimately, though, many internationalists abandoned the EPC because of the neutrality plank. The two antinuclear campaigns, by contrast, chose least-common-denominator goals supported by a wide range of peace organizations. Ironically, the fact that the political establishment could *also* support a limited version of those goals contributed to the decline of the latter two campaigns.

Organizational Tensions in the Peace Campaigns

Despite differences in size, form, and duration, these three peace campaigns all faced comparable organizational tensions. Each of these tensions was composed of a pair of potentially incompatible organizational tasks: maintaining the autonomy of separate organizations while building a coalition among them, meshing volunteer activism with professional expertise, and organizing locally while lobbying nationally. How these tensions were managed depended in part on choices made by leaders and activists, particularly at key moments such as the outset of campaigns. Successive generations of peace organizations, when handled similarly, tended to produce similar outcomes. We discuss each set of tensions, both in general terms and as they played out in each of the three campaigns.

Autonomy Versus Coordination

Coalitions provide member groups with opportunities to expand their influence through joint action and to conserve resources through the division of labor and sharing of overhead costs. However, coalitions tend to produce organizational and ideological conflict. They may also drain time and money because of the additional demands on staff and leaders to maintain cooperation and coordination (Bobo, Kendall, and Max 1991; Staggenborg 1986; Wilson 1973). Coordination is achieved by forming an umbrella organization, but over time such groups tend to establish themselves as independent agents in competition with their constituent organizations. Umbrella organizations tend quickly to be identified with the campaign itself, a development that presents existing groups with a new rival for leadership, resources, and credit for campaign accomplishments.

Member groups were greatly concerned that their underlying goals and organizational integrity not be threatened by a campaign that might quickly overshadow them. They found different ways to address these concerns. The pacifist organizations within the EPC established a tightly centralized structure. Leaders of the pacifist groups dominated the EPC's decisionmaking bodies. Staff members on loan from pacifist groups ran the campaign. When regional offices were created, they were staffed and controlled by the national office. Local supporters were discouraged from forming large EPC chapters; instead they worked in small groups to implement the national program. New supporters were to be channeled into existing peace groups. This centralized structure gave the pacifists extensive control over the campaign, but it also meant that when leaders of the affiliated groups grew disillusioned—internationalists because of neutrality, pacifists because of the drain on their resources—the campaign effectively ended.

Both the test ban and the freeze campaign set up umbrella groups that were less tightly controlled by the coalition member organizations, which still had substantial influence through formal representation on the main governing bodies. The professional staff of SANE and the NWFC were hired by the umbrella group itself, rather than being on the payrolls of member groups. This structure was necessary because of the lack of constituent organization resources (particularly at the start of the test ban campaign), but it was also desired as a way to ensure that no single group or set of groups would dominate. Unlike the money-rich, professionally driven EPC, these campaigns made greater use of grassroots activists—the freeze campaign deliberately, the test ban campaign in response to unexpected grassroots support. Their relatively open structures allowed local activists to form chapters without burdensome procedures and requirements. A small national office was leveraged by extensive networks of local activists, to whom it provided leadership, information, and coordination.

These same loose structures, however, brought their own problems. Although both SANE and the NWFC continued to lead and coordinate activism for several years, certainly longer than the EPC, their base coalitions tended to fragment. In both SANE and the NWFC the demands of running the campaign and the assertiveness of local activists meant that campaign leaders paid more attention to local chapters than to the national peace groups. This caused national peace groups to feel that they had lost control over the campaigns.

In addition, the networks of local activists were themselves vulnerable to decay. Many radicals and pacifists left the test ban campaign after 1960, believing that SANE's leaders had failed to confront congressional red-baiting efforts. Members of the freeze coalition drifted apart after the 1983 congressional resolution, disagreeing over the promise of a congressional strategy and over the continued role of grassroots organizing and education.

In all three cases, coalitions generated early resources and leadership that gave the campaigns a fast start. After a period of time, however, tensions between the maintenance of separate roles for peace organizations and the campaign-as-coalition contributed to the decline of the campaigns once they encountered political setbacks.

Professionals Versus Grassroots Volunteers

Movement organizations typically rely on both paid professionals and volunteer activists. Professional and volunteer activism may reinforce each other, for example, when paid organizers recruit and train volunteer activists. But professional and volunteer perspectives come into conflict when an organization is forced to choose between hiring a lobbyist or a grassroots organizer. Professional and grassroots styles of activism and decisionmaking are also likely to be incompatible within an organization, as the case of the freeze shows most clearly.

The EPC dealt with the tension between professional and volunteer perspectives by remaining professionalized. The organization maintained more than 200 staff members while relying on only about 2,000 volunteers. This professional orientation minimized organizational tensions, though at the cost of also limiting the vitality, duration, and local impact of the campaign.

Both SANE and the NWFC were rooted more heavily in local activism. SANE developed 175 chapters, giving the organization a total of between 4,000 and 7,000 volunteer activists. At its peak in 1983, the NWFC had 1,800 chapters and some 45,000 to 72,000 volunteer local activists.[6] These activists gave the antinuclear campaigns more vigor and staying power than the EPC. Heavy reliance on grassroots activists in fact generated a cadre of activists who survived the campaigns themselves and moved into other movements such as civil rights and environmentalism. However, both SANE and the NWFC faced problems in integrating grass-roots activism and professionalism in their campaigns.

This tension was sharpest in the NWFC. In its early stages the NWFC often lacked effective leadership, in part because many activists saw strong leadership as incompatible with organizational democracy and participation. The NWFC later swung sharply in the other direction, as the support of leading politicians led to a more professionalized campaign centered on lobbying efforts in Washington.[7] The experience of the NWFC suggests the difficulty of maintaining a central role for both grassroots volunteers and professional staff within the same campaign.

SANE also experienced tensions between professionalism and grass-roots activism in the form of conflicts between national staff and local volunteer activists over strategy, style, resource allocation, and organizational structure and decisionmaking. Most often SANE maintained a middle course, with a balance of power between staff and volunteers. In one or two key episodes involving the alleged participation of communists, however, staff decisions led to major conflicts between the national SANE office and some of its local chapters, which disagreed with the national distancing of the organization from communist participation.

National Versus Local Action Orientation

Social movements representing disenfranchised groups or policies typically find much of their strength at the local level. Volunteer activism is mostly local. Local elites are often more receptive to pressure than national elites, and they may provide movements with important strategic allies. But movement organizations also operate nationally both in order to influence national political decisionmaking and in order to tap a wide resource base.

The distinction between local and national action gives rise to two kinds of tensions. First there is the problem of dividing resources between activities at the different levels. The clearest expression of this tension can be found in the NWFC, which began with a strategy of building a strong local base and later moved to the national level. Once the political focus of the campaign moved to Congress, the national Clearinghouse gave less attention to devising and spreading new local strategies.

The second national-local tension is the problem of coordination. To be effective beyond the local level, activism must be coordinated across locales. This raises the often controversial issue of centralization in movement organizations. Proponents of national action argue that tight coordination is necessary, whereas those who favor local action believe that autonomous activists will be more creative and motivated. All three peace campaigns were relatively centralized, and a certain degree of centralization is inherent in the very decision to undertake a campaign. There were, however, important variations across the campaigns on this dimension.

The most important differences involve the basic structure of the campaign organizations. Both SANE and the NWFC were federated organizations in which local chapters gained a key role in determining the direction of the national campaign. As federated organizations, they combined the advantages of local autonomy and relatively tight coordination. Even so, the need for coordination also created conflicts with the nominally autonomous local organizations. Both SANE and the NWFC constantly struggled with the question of how membership dues and other contributions should be divided between the local chapters and the national office. In 1960 there were major splits within SANE over the issue of participation by communists, and the national leadership expelled some chapters.

The EPC avoided these problems by maintaining tight central control over all local activity, but this solution carries a heavy price in the form of a lack of local initiative. When the national office stopped developing new programs, all local activism ceased. The presence of strong local chapters in SANE and the NWFC gave both organizations the capacity to endure setbacks at the national level without completely falling apart.

Summary of Coalition Tensions

Underlying these three tensions is a fundamental conflict between short-term and long-term organizing. Groups and leaders who start campaigns are committed to working for many years for fundamental changes, but they use campaigns to put forward short-term reform goals that could attract a wider base of activists and public support. When the short-term goals of a campaign prove to be more elusive than initially thought, controversy begins to emerge over whether the compromises involved in campaign politics are too costly. Sometimes, to their own amazement, the initiators of a campaign become aware that they are spending more effort building an organization than nurturing a movement. Campaigns are a bridge between short- and long-term activism, but they are not a stable bridge. This brings us to the issue of how movement organizations sustain themselves between campaign periods.

Peace Campaigns and Sustaining Structures

Most social movement organizations are created in the context of a particular campaign. Such pacifist groups as the AFSC, the Fellowship of Reconciliation (FOR), the War Resisters League (WRL), and the Women's

International League for Peace and Freedom (WILPF) were founded during or just after World War I.

In subsequent campaign mobilizations, these veteran organizations functioned similarly to the "movement halfway houses" described by Aldon Morris (1984).[8] Movement halfway houses serve as repositories of ideas, vision, strategies, and skilled activists. They lower the costs of subsequent mobilizations not only in their own field but also for organizations in other movements. Verta Taylor (1989) showed that such organizations as the National Women's Party helped sustain the movement during its period of abeyance in the 1920s and 1930s. Their specific contributions were to retain activists by providing a sense of community and continuity and to define goals that maintained high levels of purposive commitment in the absence of much public interest. Organizations may pass along historical experiences and lessons from one generation of activists to another. This occurs informally through the transmission of stories, symbols, traditions, and so forth. Continuity is also maintained formally through the creation of a pattern of organizational rules, procedures, charters, and official analyses.

The peace campaigns did not have as rich an informal and cultural heritage as did the civil rights movement, but they did have a formal heritage of organizations created during prior peace campaigns. These peace movement organizations have played a significant role in movement mobilizations, and not only on behalf of the peace movement itself. Among the movement halfway houses important in the civil rights movement, for example, were three peace movement organizations: the AFSC, FOR, and WRL. During the civil rights movement, these peace organizations helped train leaders in the philosophy and strategy of nonviolence and provided a place for multiracial discussion in the rigidly segregated South. Leaders of FOR founded the Congress of Racial Equality (CORE).

Peace organizations from prior mobilizations have also, as might be expected, played an important role in subsequent peace campaigns. They offer activists an organizational refuge when the movement is unpopular. They provide the initial infusion of leadership and resources when a new campaign is proposed. Yet we have found little evidence that peace organizations from prior campaigns are effective in functioning as a source of institutional memory on the successes and failures of previous mobilizations. Even activists with long experience in peace groups do not seem to know of or take account of the histories of earlier campaigns. Given the close parallels of the freeze movement with the test ban campaign, the continuity in some of the organizations involved, and the time lag of only twenty years between campaigns, the extent of the disconnect is remarkable.

How can we account for the lack of effective transmission of institutional memory? The simplest way for intercampaign learning to occur is directly through individuals, by maintaining continuity in personnel. Each campaign, however, was started by a group of leaders that entered peace activism after the previous campaign.

Nor have campaign organizers typically taken the time after the end of a mobilization to reflect on and compile systematically the histories of their campaigns. Even when they do so, such analyses are often seen as irrelevant by the next generation of campaigners. Each generation, moreover, defines a campaign strategy partly in reaction to the experience of prior mobilizations. Many pacifist leaders after World War II were radicalized by the failure of the EPC to prevent U.S. participation in the war. Freeze leaders turned to local organizing because of the failure of the Vietnam-era antiwar movement to establish a strong local base. The test ban campaign appears to have been a vague and irrelevant memory to freeze leaders.[9] Under these circumstances, it would appear that campaign organizers are often not willing to look to the past for lessons.

The freeze movement has generated an unprecedented number of analytic memoirs by key strategists and organizers. It remains to be seen what use will be made of this material in a future peace campaign.

Conclusion

Seen in historical context, the freeze was only the latest (albeit the largest) in a series of major campaigns for peace and arms limitation. Our understanding of the freeze and of each peace mobilization is deepened by comparisons with other campaigns. As bridges between long-term movement goals and short-term mobilizations, these campaigns are created by coalitions of peace organizations. Each coalition is a unique configuration, yet each also faces recurrent tensions.

The organizational dynamics of coalitions contributed to the rapid rise and sharp fall of each campaign. Whether tightly or loosely controlled, centralized or decentralized, the structures that were established provided leadership and coordination so long as the coalition partners gave priority to the campaigns. These campaign organizations were successful in generating money and publicity for their causes. They were also able to deploy a professional staff (in the case of the EPC) and a large base of volunteer activists (in the case of the two antinuclear campaigns). Indeed, this comparison of peace movement campaigns shows that the right combination of political opportunity and campaign strategy enables movement organizations to mobilize large amounts of money and large numbers of people.

However, an examination of the three major peace campaigns in the United States since World War I also shows that campaign coalitions experience a typical set of tensions. Once the coalitions encountered internal problems and external setbacks, these structures revealed their fragility. Division, uncertainty over goals, and a breakdown of coordination may in each case have accelerated the decline of the campaigns.

Examination of successive waves of peace campaigns helps us understand the phenomenon of movement cycles of mobilization and demobilization. Since World War I, the peace movement has been sustained by a handful of small organizations that periodically overcome their differing perspectives to coalesce on a particular issue or threat to peace. The tensions inherent in these coalitions may be mitigated by early success and by the generation of new resources that do not threaten the resource base of the existing organizations. But those tensions are never fully resolved. They appear always to resurface and limit the life of the campaign coalition. Finally, peace movement organizations have not generally succeeded in distilling, debating, and teaching the lessons of one mobilization campaign to the leaders and organizations of the next.

Notes

1. In the EPC the central organization was almost coterminous with the broader campaign. Both are typically capitalized. The nuclear weapons freeze campaign extended far beyond the bounds of the NWFC organization and is typically referred to in lowercase, but the organization name is capitalized.

2. Several top staff members were on loan from their home organizations, which continued to pay their salaries. Others served for subsistence wages, making them quasi-volunteers. See Robert Kleidman (1994) for details of staffing and organization in these three campaigns.

3. Although the test ban campaign spawned several national organizations, SANE was clearly the largest and most visible. We focus on SANE in this chapter.

4. *Nuclear Times* 8, no. 5 (Autumn 1990), p. 7.

5. Peter Sandman and JoAnn Valenti (1986) discuss the role of fear in the test ban and freeze campaigns. See also Thomas R. Rochon and Stephen P. Wood, Chapter 2, this book.

6. Grassroots activism outside the key campaign organizations was in proportion to the volunteer activism within these groups, with the EPC catalyzing the least local effort and the freeze campaign the most. The best estimates are that the EPC had several thousand local activists, the test ban had 300,000 activists, and the nuclear freeze had 10 million (Kleidman 1993).

7. One lesson of the freeze is that governmental institutions are able to incorporate and demobilize grassroots movements. Freeze leaders had wanted more time to organize grassroots activism before moving to Congress, but elected officials seeking to capitalize on the issue's popularity would not wait. See David Meyer (1990) and Thomas R. Rochon, Chapter 8, this book.

8. Bob Edwards and John McCarthy (1992) develop a similar concept in the "movement mentoring organization."

9. One key freeze leader, in a personal interview, said, "I did not spend a

minute to go to AFSC files to see what they had . . . on the test ban campaign. I never even heard of it." When an older activist did bring up that history, he ignored her. "I'm not trying to be an elitist, but it just didn't get me. I'd look at a book she'd show me and you know it just wasn't in color, the pictures were black and white and I didn't get too much from it."

4

Competition & Cooperation in Movement Coalitions: Lobbying for Peace in the 1980s

WILL HATHAWAY & DAVID S. MEYER

Social movements seek to influence government policy, but movements are rarely monolithic in their efforts to effect policy reform. Indeed, movements generally comprise a number of formal organizations, often with differing political goals and strategies. Activist choices about how to organize a movement and specifically patterns of cooperation and competition among potential allies dramatically influence a movement's emergence, development, demise, and ultimately its impact. The generally untold story of a movement concerns the political and tactical decisions groups make on the extent and content of their cooperation with each other.

Surprisingly, there is little systematic thinking about the effects of coalition participation on activists and on movement dynamics. Organization leaders and academic theorists generally seem to view coalitions as a tool for success without examining the potential negative consequences for individual organizations. There is a need for more critical analysis of coalitions and their relation to organizational success. By analyzing the forces that cause coalition formation and the factors that sustain coalitions, we may be better able to understand what functions coalitions perform and more accurately weigh the benefits and costs of particular alliances.

In this chapter we want to provide a systematic way of looking at coalitions and at the countervailing pressures groups face in choosing to participate in them. We explore a particular type of cooperative arrangement between organizations: the long-term lobbying coalition. Long-term lobbying coalitions seek to influence legislative and executive policymaking, and increasing numbers of organizations regularly enter into such

An earlier version of this chapter was published in volume 38 of the *Berkeley Journal of Sociology* and is reprinted here with permission of the editors.

arrangements (Milbrath 1963; Berry 1977; Keller 1982; Schlozman and Tierney 1986). In addition to being a prevalent form of political organization, this type of coalition offers opportunities to observe intergroup cooperation on a range of topics over an extended period of time (Tydeman 1981), thus providing an ideal opportunity to examine the internal workings of a coalition.

We begin by briefly reviewing the existing literature on coalitions and identifying three distinct perspectives within the literature: formal models, resource mobilization, and activist pleas. We suggest that despite the potential contributions of each approach, all neglect the relationship between group decisions to cooperate and the larger political environment. Drawing from this literature, we discuss the countervailing pressures on groups to cooperate in order to achieve political goals and to differentiate in order to maintain organizational autonomy and survival. We contend that coalitions can survive over a long period of time by establishing a means of ensuring *cooperative differentiation*. We test these propositions by examining two long-term lobbying coalitions concerned with arms control: the Monday Lobby Group (MLG) based in Washington, D.C., and the Coalition for Arms Control (CAC) based in Ann Arbor, Michigan. We conclude with a discussion of coalition maintenance, offering suggestions for successful coalition building.

Theoretical Background on Coalitions

The literature on coalitions ranges from formal, academic analyses to activist pleas and handbooks. A brief review will help illustrate both the diversity of approaches and the need for further study.

The earliest studies contain primarily formal or mathematical models (see, for example, Collins and Ravin 1969; Gamson 1964; Groennings, Kelly, and Leiserson 1970; Riker 1962). Generally working from formal logic but sometimes from social psychological experiments, the authors tried to develop formulas that could predict outcomes in "real world" situations. These writers were primarily concerned with the formation of legislative majorities in multiparty states (see, for example, Riker 1962; Hinckley 1972). The utility of these models in predicting actual behavior remains a contested issue (Browne 1973), and for our purposes there are other problems as well. Models based on the formation of governments, which have concrete benefits to disperse to participants and offer immediate policy impact, are of little value in understanding cooperation and competition between political organizations whose actual influence on policy is always in question and that rely on financial support from nongovernmental sources.

If the formal modeling literature suffers from lack of reference to actual politics, another portion of the literature bears the weight of practical experience far too heavily. Organizers and political activists frequently produce *activist pleas,* essentially assuming the desirability of formal alliances between relatively compatible political organizations. This work trumpets both the necessity and utility of coalition work, trying to instill in readers (presumably potential activists) appreciation of what the authors see as the inherent need to work together (Adams 1991; Kahn 1982; Sampson 1984; Tydeman 1981). This stream of work is valuable, as it reflects the conventional wisdom on coalitions in activist circles. It is limited, however, in its presumption of the benefits of cooperation while essentially ignoring potential costs. Activist pleas are reluctant to challenge the assumption that building broader, more inclusive coalitions is inherently good.

The most promising stream of writing on coalitions comes from the *resource mobilization* school of analysis. Analysts working within this tradition hold that movement activity is the product of purposive activity by activists. Organization leaders seek to obtain resources that allow for their group's survival (McCarthy and Zald 1977; Zald and McCarthy 1987). The critical assumptions underlying resource mobilization are useful to understanding coalitions—specifically, that activists play some role in creating the movements in which they participate and that organizational maintenance is an important consideration in making political decisions. The missing dimension in much of this work, however, is the constraining effect that political context has on activist choices. Using the framework of resource mobilization, several earlier case studies of the relationships between allied organizations offer valuable insights into coalitions (McAdam 1982; Staggenborg 1986).

From the resource mobilization school we take the insight that there is often conflict between the purposive or political goals of an organization and its organizational needs. To this level of analysis, we need to add the dimension of external political context. In her study of the prochoice movement, for example, Suzanne Staggenborg (1986) finds an increased likelihood of organizational cooperation when there is potential for big gains or a threat of large losses. Although these potential payoffs for the movement are important *external* environmental factors, *internal* factors also determine the durability of coalitions. Staggenborg argues that internal conflict is minimized when the coalition is kept on an informal basis, established organizations provide the coalition infrastructure, and the focus of the alliance's efforts is on activities such as lobbying. Given that working in alliances with other groups is seen as the effective method for lobbying in Washington, the move toward coalition relationships may be the culmination of the professionalization and formalization of a social movement (Staggenborg 1988).

The literature on coalitions is inadequate for several reasons. The formal models do not draw from or reflect reality, and the activist pleas reflect assumptions about efficacy and neglect real obstacles. Of the existing studies, resource mobilization is the most promising in its treatment of coalitions, suggesting that (1) coalitions can present a diversity of approaches to achieve political goals, mount successive waves of activism, and incorporate diverse constituencies within a social protest movement (McAdam 1982 and 1983; Robert Kleidman and Thomas R. Rochon, Chapter 3, this book); (2) resource competition and ideological differences form obstacles to coalition formation (Covert 1990); and (3) coalition formation reflects the external environment. Using these insights, we can generate some propositions about group behavior in coalitions.

Cooperation Versus Differentiation

Groups confront conflicting pressures to cooperate and to differentiate largely because a group must manage relationships both with the government (or another target) and with its supporters. Each audience requires different treatment and values different approaches. The incentives for groups to cooperate are greatest when groups can define their goals primarily in terms of political influence. The reasons are obvious: numbers matter in any democratic polity, and cooperation increases the resources available to pressure the government. A diverse coalition can exert pressure on several political fronts and offers activists numerous choices for political action (McAdam 1982). Political influence appears most likely when a number of groups are able to cooperate and present a united front.

Even as groups seek short-term political influence, however, they also seek long-term political survival. Thus they must maintain a stable flow of resources simply for organizational maintenance. In order to attract resources, a group must convince potential members and supporters not only of the importance of the issues it addresses but also of the unique and vital role the individual group plays. In the effort to maintain itself, a group competes for resources not with its political opponents but with its allies. Chances for individual group survival are enhanced when the group is able to define a distinct and independent identity, distinguishing itself from other groups (Wilson 1973; Zald and McCarthy 1987).

Naturally, it is simple for groups working on different sets of issues to distinguish themselves; indeed, it is fairly unlikely that the National Rifle Association (NRA) would feel compelled to draw distinctions between its work and that of the National Organization for Women (NOW). Not only do these two groups draw from different constituencies, but the issues with which they are concerned overlap little, if at all. The activities of one are unlikely to figure in the calculations of the other. Political opponents may alter the larger landscape but offer no prospects for cooperation. Thus, the NRA may have difficult decisions to make regarding a group like Handgun Control, but these decisions are based solely on effective political opposition. The most critical decisions a group makes involve its relations with potential allies and competitors: organizations that share the same basic concerns and work on the same sets of issues (Meyer and Imig 1993).

We can consider conflicting tendencies of groups in a sector with the help of a two-by-two table. The two dimensions reflect the two audiences groups must address: their supporters, members, and funders (market) and their targets (government). The incentives to cooperate increase among groups with similar ultimate ends. Groups with similar constituencies or tactics are most likely to compete (see Table 4.1).

Table 4.1   The Propensity to Intergroup Cooperation

Political Agreement	Market Overlap	
	Low	High
Low	Opposition	Opposition
High	Cooperation	Competition

Groups that address the same basic issues but seek different political goals are not competitors but opponents. For example, the NRA seeks to protect citizen access to firearms, while Handgun Control seeks to limit it. They face each other only in the context of the government, share no common support, and have neither incentive nor cause to work together.

Groups that work on the same sets of issues and seek to move government policy in the same general direction have incentives to cooperate (in order to enhance their influence on government policy) and to compete (in order to secure organizational survival). This is the realm in which difficult alliance decisions must be made. Group success in managing tendencies toward cooperation and competition reflects the relationship of the groups in a sector to the larger political environment.

Market overlap is a function of what James Q. Wilson (1973: 263) terms "autonomy," what we might describe as a secure market niche. Older organizations with established bureaucracies, professional staffs, and routinized relationships with members or funders thus enjoy a considerable advantage over newcomers, who must establish all of these things (Zald and McCarthy 1987). The dimensions of cooperation and competition include the following:

1. "Product differentiation": Groups make ideological distinctions among themselves on ultimate goals. The War Resisters League (WRL), for example, although among the earliest sponsors of the nuclear freeze campaign, sought to distinguish itself from the larger movement by criticizing the rest of the freeze coalition and identifying itself as the "only organization calling for unilateral disarmament" (Meyer 1990: 210). For such groups, meaningful cooperation is contingent upon reaching broad agreement on at least intermediary objectives, so they can forge ad hoc issue-based alliances.

When resources within an interest group sector are plentiful, groups are more likely to forge these sorts of agreements. When financial survival is less difficult, the pressures to differentiate and establish a distinct market niche are not as great as when individual group survival is in jeopardy. Because resource availability responds to the larger political environment, we expect groups to be more likely to cooperate when there is an atmosphere of crisis and political mobilization is high and more likely to differentiate when there is less general urgency and political mobilization is low.

2. Supporting constituency: The purported beneficiary constituency can overlap without creating pressures for competition as long as two organizations have distinctive support networks. As an example, Wilson (1973) notes that the Southern Christian Leadership Conference and the Urban League both focused their efforts on enhanced opportunity for African Americans. Most important, however, their sources of funding were distinct, so that neither organization threatened the other's base of support.

Potential coalition partners enhance their prospects for cooperation by carving out distinct and stable bases of financial support. Groups may cede potential supporters to allied groups by virtue of geographic territory (for example, Public Interest Research Groups, or PIRGS, which organize by state), professional constituency (physicians, lawyers, teachers), or source of financial support. For public interest groups, sources of financial support may include government, direct mail membership, funds from the grass-roots that are generated by canvassing, and grants or gifts from foundations or wealthy donors.

Some sources of funding are more stable than others, but virtually no funding source for public interest groups is immune to threat from withdrawal. Economic recession, for example, limits the availability of resources for public interest groups as a whole (McCarthy and Zald 1977). The political salience of particular issues also affects the attractiveness of funding. Cooperation is most likely when political urgency and political mobilization on an issue are both high.

3. Locus of activity: Competition between groups also depends on their intended venue for political action. A group that emphasizes electoral efforts in support of a given goal is not in direct competition with one that emphasizes either direct expressive action or litigation. The American Civil Liberties Union can work in cooperation with NOW to protect abortion rights. In addition to having distinct funding bases, such groups can pursue contrasting yet complementary means to achieve the same political end.

4. Strategy and tactics: Closely related to the locus of activity are the strategies for influence adopted by a group. Obviously, filing legal briefs is an appropriate tactic only within the legal system. The tactic of lobbying is only appropriate with legislators and executive agencies. Groups within the same sector can adopt distinct sets of tactics, thus differentiating themselves to their supporters while cooperating in the service of political ends. Within the environmental sector, Greenpeace uses direct action and civil disobedience, whereas the Nature Conservancy seeks to buy and protect large tracts of land. Allied organizations in the environment movement, with varying degrees of coordination, may press congressional legislation or executive regulatory action.

5. Authenticity: Finally, groups compete to claim the legitimacy associated with speaking for a larger movement base. Political organizations seek recognition from both the government and the public as the institutional voice of a larger public concern or political movement. These audiences, however, push groups in different directions. Government is most likely to recognize and deal with the most moderate and established groups within a sector. On Capitol Hill, "credibility" means providing reliable and sober information and working closely with government officials for achievable, incremental, and essentially moderate goals (Berry 1989). In contrast, grassroots support calls for a politics of polemic that demonizes the opponent and overstates the nature of group differences with the state (Lipsky 1968). Within a sector, groups carve out distinct balances between state and grassroots credibility.

The balance between appeals to the grassroots and to the state varies across groups and over time. Since the greatest gains of cooperation are found in relations with the state, cooperation is most likely when a sector is growing, that is, when the issue is salient, funds are increasing, and there is a growing movement. Conversely, when resources are scarce, the issue is less urgent, and a large movement is not visible, groups focus on individual survival. Thus, cooperation is most difficult and least likely during movement decline.

Of course, coalitions survive movement declines. We suggest a two-part process. Coalitions form in stages of movement growth, and when a movement begins to recede the groups can maintain their alliance through *cooperative differentiation*. In other words, they maintain a public face of solidarity toward the state while differentiating themselves in communications with their constituencies.

Data and Methods

We explore the origins, development, and maintenance of two coalitions within the nuclear disarmament movement, the MLG and the CAC. Both groups formed at the height of dissident mobilization associated with the nuclear freeze movement in the early 1980s but survived well after the peak of movement activity passed. They did so, in part, through cooperative differentiation.

Extensive and varied data are available for the study of these two coalitions. In the case of the MLG we had the opportunity for personal observation at the height of the lobbying struggle over the MX missile in 1983–1984 and again briefly in January 1990. There is documentary material on the MLG, including books by individuals who participated in the coalition (Pertschuk 1986; Solo 1988; Waller 1987). In 1990 we interviewed eleven active members of the MLG representing various groups and factions within the coalition. We were also able to piece together archival data on group membership from lists of participants in the MLG's annual planning retreats. Our studies of the CAC include even more extensive personal observations. Beginning with the initial formation of the coalition in spring of 1983 and its later heightened activities in the period from 1985 through 1988, direct involvement offered the opportunity for observing coalition dynamics firsthand. We gathered written survey responses from thirty-seven past and current members of the CAC in 1989–1990 and used extensive documentary data, including written minutes from every CAC meeting dating from 1983 (Hathaway 1990).

The Monday Lobby Group

Coalition Formation

The MLG grew from five groups seeking to coordinate lobbying on Strategic Arms Limitation Talks II (SALT II) ratification to fifty-six groups with multiple legislative goals (freeze, MX, Trident, Strategic Defense Initiative [SDI], Anti-Satellite [ASAT], Anti-Ballistic Missiles [ABM], SALT, chemical weapons, military budget, and so on). Growth in available resources had three observable effects. First, it increased the number of existing groups emphasizing peace issues, including such well-established organizations as Common Cause and the Sierra Club (Keller 1982; Lewis and Blacker 1983). Second, it added newly formed or reactivated peace groups such as Women's Action for Nuclear Disarmament (WAND), Educators for Social Responsibility, Physicians for Social Responsibility, and the Nuclear Weapons Freeze Campaign (NWFC) (Szegedy-Maszak 1989). Third, it produced tremendous growth for previously established peace groups such as Committee for a Sane Nuclear Policy (SANE), which mounted an ambitious door-to-door membership drive, and Council for a Livable World, which saw its membership climb from a low of 7,500 in 1980 to a high of 100,000 in 1986 (Hathaway 1990).

The freeze campaign galvanized the cooperative efforts of these peace groups. Earlier efforts to form alliances tended to focus on opposition to particular weapons such as the ABM and the B-1 bomber, or on Senate ratification of specific treaties. These earlier coalition efforts provided positive experiences of building diverse coalitions, lobbying on Capitol Hill, establishing working relationships with sympathetic members of Congress, and organizing grassroots activists at the congressional district level. However, other important lessons learned in these coalition efforts were the inherent limitations of arms control lobbying. As arms control proponent Representative Thomas Downey (D, New York) puts it,

> It's impossible in Congress for the opponents of the B-1 to say, "Don't build the B-1, build a hospital," because then the people making the decisions stop listening to you, stop taking you seriously. The antidote is always another weapon system that meets the same mission requirement. (Kotz 1988: 153)

The comprehensive nature of the freeze proposal allowed groups to oppose a broad range of nuclear weapons at once. Established arms control groups initially avoided the freeze, but its growing popular support and comprehensiveness made it the perfect vehicle for fighting a multifront, legislative battle. Earlier peace group alliances had involved diverse groups, but they were not all-inclusive coalitions (Paine 1985; Waller 1987). The MLG used the freeze as an initial goal and organized a broad coalition with the modest objective of avoiding duplicated or conflicting efforts by the handful of arms control lobbyists in Washington. From a membership of seven groups in 1981, the MLG expanded to thirty-five groups in 1983 and grew further to forty-one groups by 1986 (Hathaway 1990).

Coalition Maintenance

Faced with the task of achieving legislative goals, many peace groups came to the MLG with the following needs:

1. Training in lobbying: Peace organizations that drew their strength from the support of grassroots activists tended to be inexperienced in the techniques of Capitol Hill lobbying. Many of them viewed the concept of compromise and deal making with contempt. The more experienced "senior" lobbyists worked to reorient newer lobbyists to their own professional approach (Pertschuk 1986).

2. Demonstrations of tangible achievement: Perhaps in part because they found the process abhorrent and had insisted on extreme, "all-or-nothing" positions, peace groups had achieved little success in past lobbying efforts. The apparent ineffectiveness of the freeze legislation highlighted the need to demonstrate to the growing peace constituencies that the national organizations could in fact achieve results.

3. Channels for their constituencies' expectations: The pressures for action and results relate to the need for organizational maintenance. Somehow the groups had to "deliver" to hold the support of the newly activated grassroots base.

The grassroots constituencies of the various peace organizations had ideological expectations shaped in part by the groups' own past marketing efforts. Groups strove to meet these goals and thereby retain the support of their respective memberships. As a result of the groups' differentiation toward their grassroots constituencies, the coalition contained a diversity of ideological perspectives on the issues. For example, congregations supporting the work of religious groups such as the United Church of Christ's Office for Church in Society expected their lobbyists to take morally or spiritually based positions. Progressive activists with broad political agendas sought to link peace issues to the larger context of social justice. Other groups, such as Physicians for Social Responsibility and the Union of Concerned Scientists, had members who viewed the issues as more narrowly defined scientific or medical questions. Common Cause and the "senior lobbyists" sought issues on which the MLG could obtain majority votes in Congress.

These varied ideological approaches are represented by two loose "camps," or schools of thought, within the MLG—the *arms control faction* and the *disarmament faction*—a difference of opinion that has existed in the peace movement for decades (Wittner 1984). In the MLG the arms control faction is characterized by belief in incremental steps toward disarmament. They view the nuclear balance as something that can be managed through arms control and planning and see working with the leaders in Congress as the way to achieve this nuclear stability. These groups favor legislative goals that have credibility in Congress and are therefore "winnable." The establishment of direct working relationships with members of Congress, preferably members in leadership positions such as key committee chairs, is the preferred tactic of the arms controllers. The core leadership of the MLG is drawn from the arms control wing, including such groups as the Council for a Livable World, Common Cause, Physicians for Social Responsibility, the Professionals Coalition, and the Union of Concerned Scientists. Before its merger with the NWFC, SANE's lobbyists were also part of this liberal arms control leadership.

The disarmament faction is generally impatient with the slow, incremental pace of congressional lobbying. They seek more immediate and decisive action to end the arms race. Because they view the arms race as only one manifestation of a militaristic society, disarmament groups tend to have broad agendas that include military intervention and human rights issues. The MLG approach of tackling weapon systems individually is difficult for these groups, given their preference for a sweeping reassessment of the assumptions underlying national security policy. Disarmament groups tend to be closely attuned to their memberships and anxious to integrate the grassroots into the strategies of the MLG. For example, rather than focusing upon the congressional leadership, they emphasize organizing opposition in every congressional district. Disarmament groups also look more favorably on what might be considered unorthodox tactics, such as American Peace Test's occupations of nuclear weapon test sites or the White Train protests. Some of these groups engage in civil disobedience, and religious groups among them may encourage confrontational protests in which activists "bear witness." Groups in this faction include SANE/FREEZE, Greenpeace, Women's International League for Peace and Freedom (WILPF), Women's Strike for Peace, and the American Friends Service Committee (AFSC).

These factions manage to work together cooperatively, maintaining their autonomy while participating in the MLG's common-denominator strategies. The key to MLG maintenance is allowing space for conflicts between groups to be "played out" without detriment to the coalition work. It is not a matter of merely suppressing conflict but of permitting conflicts between groups or factions to occur without destroying the coalition.

By debating positions within the coalition, the groups sharpen their arguments and anticipate likely criticism or attacks on their positions outside the coalition. They can test and select the most effective arguments (Towell 1984). The organizations avoid playing out their rivalry in public and try to find ways to present differing opinions or positions to the public without tearing each other down. This results in less "blindsiding," in which the factions might publicly catch each other off guard, causing embarrassment and potentially damaging the credibility of the coalition on Capitol Hill. The conflict between factions within the coalition is used regularly to augment lobbying strategy. In putting forward their "more ambitious" agenda, the disarmament faction helps to position the moderate, majority MLG position by creating a more extreme point of reference on the left. The military budget debate is an example of this phenomenon.

There were two different MLG campaigns to cut the military budget in 1990–1991: the Budget for a Strong America (BSA) (a product of the arms control faction) and the Citizens' Budget Campaign (CBC) (a product of the disarmament faction). The BSA proposed cuts of $90 billion in the military budget spread over three years ($18 billion in fiscal year 1991, $30 billion in FY 1992, and $40 billion in FY 1993). The proposed savings would result from reductions in spending for strategic weapons such as the MX, SDI, and the B-2 bomber. Under the BSA, some of the money saved through these cuts would be reallocated to domestic programs and to reduction of the federal deficit. The CBC proposed larger cuts in military spending and reallocation of money to domestic spending, and the CBC also viewed new taxes as a necessity for meeting human needs. The BSA proposed a choice between funding the MX or Midgetman strategic missiles, while CBC rejected both.

The arms control faction viewed its Budget for a Strong America as a moderate, carefully crafted reform proposal for which they had lined up support from leaders in Congress (and therefore had a chance of winning). They saw the Citizens' Budget Campaign of the disarmament faction as an improbable legislative vehicle because of its inclusion of new taxes and the lack of adequate congressional sponsorship. The disarmament faction, in contrast, viewed its Citizens' Budget Campaign as not only the more principled of the two proposals but the more practical because of its recognition of the need for additional revenue for domestic programs. Instead of backroom courting of the congressional leadership, the disarmers focused on a grassroots letter- and postcard-writing campaign in an effort to gain congressional support.

In the end, neither of these proposals succeeded, but the existence of rival proposals did not cause antagonism between the disarmament and arms control factions. Although they may be frustrated with each other, the arms controllers and the disarmers each recognize that the other is doing what it must in order to please its constituencies. They do not seek to promote their own proposal by tearing down that of the other faction. They agree to disagree.

Coalition Survival

The MLG grew during the first half of the 1980s to a membership high of fifty-six organizations during 1986–1987. The public interest in nuclear arms issues as reflected in media coverage of peace issues peaked between 1982 and 1984 and declined dramatically by 1985 (see Figure 1.1). Given the resource mobilization hypothesis of disincentives to collaboration in times of scarce resources, how can we explain the late peak of the MLG and its continuing durability as a functioning coalition?

The following elements seem to have helped sustain the MLG even as public support and resources declined:

1. Established structure: The MLG developed informal patterns and procedures that perpetuated the coalition. Some of these included regular meeting times and locations, annual retreats, and coordinated sharing of meeting facilitation responsibilities.

2. Ongoing and past achievements: Early legislative victories generated momentum and boosted morale among MLG lobbyists. These victories may have seemed marginal in terms of the larger goal of ending the arms race (Solo 1988), but there were significant accomplishments in the "gray areas" of establishing relationships with congressional and media elites and in preventing further erosion of existing arms control agreements by the Reagan administration.

3. Solidary incentives: Through a sense of shared culture and professional association, the MLG fostered personal friendships and bonds between the lobbyists. Those interviewed spoke of the camaraderie and support they felt as a member of the coalition. Given that these individuals were often the only people in their organizations working full time on congressional lobbying, without this sense of being part of a team their jobs might have seemed lonely indeed.

4. Undesirability of the alternatives: The trend toward coalitions in Washington is strong (Smith 1988), partly because the alternative of social movement organizations working separately toward shared goals seems inefficient and illogical. When asked what they would do in the absence of the MLG, peace lobbyists said that they would still find ways to work together with like-minded groups. This determination to find ways of working in concert with other organizations makes coalition strategies on Capitol Hill inevitable.

5. Measures to mitigate competition: The MLG avoids destructive rivalry because interorganizational competition is constructively managed. MLG members recognize that participating groups will differentiate themselves to their respective grassroots constituencies, though they may simultaneously work together on the MLG's preferred legislative goals. By avoiding divisive decisionmaking procedures such as formal voting or internal leadership designations and by allowing members the flexibility to pursue alternative ideological goals, the MLG accommodates diversity within the peace community.

Members of the MLG are also conscious of the need to avoid competition with their constituent organizations. The MLG avoids this potential problem by keeping a low profile itself. For all its longevity, the MLG is an informal entity with no offices, staff, or even letterhead and, most important, no fund-raising of its own that might threaten member organizations.

The Coalition for Arms Control

Coalition Formation

At the time of its formation in 1983, the CAC in Michigan's 2nd Congressional District shared the same beneficial political opportunity structure enjoyed by the MLG. Additional factors supporting creation of the CAC include the following:

1. Local activist alignments: After intensive work on Michigan's 1982 Nuclear Weapons Freeze Ballot Issue campaign, the local freeze leadership ceased operations. Several activists sought to transfer freeze resources, primarily membership lists, to the Michigan Alliance for Disarmament, but this organization failed to hold the interest of more moderate freeze supporters. Local peace activists sought an alternative peace organization through which they could work for change within the system.
2. The Monday Lobby Group: The CAC modeled itself after the example set by the new national peace coalition. Using the MLG as a guide, the CAC fashioned a loose-knit, low-profile coalition. Local activists met regularly in downtown Ann Arbor.
3. The swing vote crisis: The evolving conservatism of the district's congressman, Carl Pursell, a Republican whose military spending votes were increasingly influenced by the Reagan administration, presented a particular challenge to the peace activists. In an important sense, Pursell's "hawkish" voting brought the national debate home to the Michigan activists ("AX MX: Demonstrators protest Pursell's switch to support for missile," *Ann Arbor News,* 24 May 1983). Loathe to completely alienate potential supporters, Congressman Pursell tried to position himself as a "swing vote," someone who could vote either way depending on the circumstances and therefore someone who required the constant attention of concerned lobbyists (Silberman 1985). Here again, resourceful activists turned an external threat into an organizing opportunity.

Pressures for differentiation between the ten to fifteen CAC member organizations were a function of their differing constituencies and had little to do with fund-raising. The groups were primarily composed of volunteers; only the Interfaith Council for Peace and Justice (IFCPJ) and SANE (later SANE/FREEZE) had full-time paid staff. Most of the groups in the

CAC had no need for any ongoing fund-raising efforts such as those mounted by the national organizations. Each CAC group held to its ideological identity and carved out its own separate role within the coalition. For example, Physicians for Social Responsibility (PSR) offered a medical assessment of the dangers of nuclear war. PSR had relatively few members willing to donate time to the coalition, but they provided money to help cover the CAC's expenses. Women's Action for Nuclear Disarmament succeeded in recruiting and involving many women in CAC projects. IFCPJ presented a religious view on peace issues and served as liaison to member congregations throughout the district. SANE/FREEZE pushed for more leftist positions while working to expand the peace constituency through its door-to-door canvassing operation. These two organizations supported the coalition's activities both with their paid staff and permanent offices.

Conflicts within the CAC were ideological, geographical, and tactical in nature. An example of the first was an ongoing tension about taking a position on U.S. military involvement in Central America. The members of PSR had agreed to focus their efforts only on nuclear weapons. Another coalition group, the Michigan Alliance for Disarmament (MAD), tried to broaden the CAC's agenda to include the issue of military intervention and move the activists toward more confrontational tactics. During debates in 1985 over whether to diversify into areas other than nuclear weaponry and defense issues, PSR members made it clear they would withdraw if the CAC made Central American intervention a priority. Though PSR had always provided significant financial support of CAC activities, it was less the loss of these funds than the potential loss of leadership skills of a particular PSR member that gave substance to this threat.

The CAC decided initially to approach Representative Pursell with letters, postcards, phone calls, and requests for meetings. They also published letters in newspapers and used any other form of communication that might impress upon him the opposition of his constituents to MX funding. In this effort the coalition was successful. Mail flowed from all parts of the district and editorial pages reflected the concerns of citizens. Although Representative Pursell's staff attempted to characterize the opposition as "just Ann Arborites," a Pursell staffer in Washington conceded that "constituent mail is running heavily against the MX" ("Pressure building on Pursell as MX funding vote approaches," *Ann Arbor News,* 1 May 1984).

Participating groups agreed that persuading Pursell to vote for arms control legislation was the CAC's primary goal. This shared locus of activity aside, however, some groups and individuals were impatient with the CAC tactics. There were factional conflicts over the CAC's "moderate, non-confrontational style and focus on public officials" (survey response). Though most respondents indicated that they were never in conflict with the coalition, five or six said that they had felt friction. The nature of this conflict was a feeling that the CAC was "over-cautious" and too willing to maintain cordial relations with Representative Pursell in an election year. Some of the activists, even within more moderate groups, became increasingly impatient with what they perceived to be Pursell's manipulative voting. By voting for some of the positions of the CAC shortly before elections, Pursell seemed to be undercutting potential CAC opposition without providing the consistent pro–arms control voting record the CAC sought.

Coalition Maintenance

The CAC, modeled originally after the Monday Lobby Group, maintained itself through much the same techniques. Groups within the coalition were free to differentiate themselves to their respective constituencies and could decide whether to work on a given CAC goal or focus their energies elsewhere. Generally, the groups found little disagreement. The exception may be the MAD, which viewed the coalition's moderate tactics and focus on nuclear weapons as overly restrictive and eventually opted out of CAC activities.

These discussions culminated in a coalition "summit meeting" in November 1985. There was a growing realization that the goals of the peace movement required a long-term struggle and that the coalition should be restructured as a permanent organization instead of an ad hoc alliance. Such moves toward more permanent structures force loosely allied groups into a very delicate situation: balancing the needs of the individual groups with the requirements of a stronger coalition (Clark 1966; Carmichael and Hamilton 1967; Staggenborg 1986).

Rather than fully commit to a new organization, the coalition decided at the 1985 summit to defer such issues as office space and staff to the future. The group decided to make a clear statement that nuclear weapons and overall defense spending were the only issues upon which the coalition would work. This was a difficult decision because many activists and their organizations wanted to pursue a broader agenda. The coalition devised rules for the use of a combined mailing that included limits on the number of mailings annually and on the ability of the groups to withdraw their membership lists from particular mailings. Another rule made clear the procedure through which the coalition would make decisions and the means by which any coalition members could ensure that their organization was not associated with a given position. The activists also agreed that the loose, consensual structure of the coalition was preferable to a more stratified or formalized format. They felt strongly enough about this to leave decision-making power with the individual organizations.

Coalition Survival

Members of the CAC recognized the need for long-term peace activism, yet they balked at a more permanent coalition structure. Shared realization of the need for an ongoing alliance may help keep the groups working together, but this is insufficient as an explanation for the durability of the coalition. What benefits do the participating activists derive from the coalition to keep them involved after nearly ten years? The answer lies primarily in the solidary benefit of friendship.

The sense of community within the CAC is very strong, but it is not a closed community or an elitist one. As PSR leader Arthur Vander states,

> Being with people I have come to respect and love for a few hours once a month just feels good! We have been incredibly fortunate in that we have attracted no egomaniacs or power-lovers, no one who might use an organization for his own agenda. The absence of officers or any real structure has helped maintain the spirit of togetherness and respect.

Like members of the MLG, members of the CAC view their coalition approvingly as a "non-hierarchical, loose, informal, consensus-building, participatory democracy in which all attendees have equal input" (survey response). As IFCPJ board member Mary Hathaway states,

> I think that the Coalition's tact and gentleness have become more than a strategy. They shape the way we deal with each other. Our meetings are friendly and we leave refreshed and encouraged. We like each other. We take note of each other's bereavements, weddings, etc. We're supportive and maybe even empowering to each other.

The camaraderie built during the early period of the coalition's efforts together with its open, flexible structure have carried it through ideological and organizational disagreements as well as frustrating political setbacks. In response to the constant pressure from constituents, Congressman Pursell eventually returned to a more dovish position on arms control votes. In the end the CAC outlasted Pursell, who announced his retirement from Congress in 1992 with the redrawing of the district boundaries.

Profile of the Successful Coalition

Coalition Formation

Nuclear disarmament groups are most likely to form coalitions when there is (1) a publicly recognized issue crisis that generates significant public

concern and (2) a common locus for the group's activities such as legislators and when (3) resources needed by the groups flow to the issue crisis
and locus of activity in a quantity sufficient to sustain the groups and
diminish organizational competition for financial survival.

Coalition Maintenance

Coalitions endure when they can provide recognizable benefits to their
members and when the tendencies of groups to compete are handled constructively. The coalitions we described provide a variety of benefits to
their members. These benefits include goal achievements that can be trum-
peted to the groups' constituencies and solidary benefits that accrue to the
participating activists. Both the MLG and the CAC accommodate differences between the member groups and view competition and conflict as a
positive, revitalizing force.

Both the CAC and the MLG survive because their member groups recognize (though some only grudgingly) that: (1) congressional elites are a
necessary locus of at least some of their activity; (2) coalition strategies
make sense and in fact may be a necessity in approaching Congress; and
(3) the coalitions are structured to allow space for group differentiation and
constructive debate. Indeed, groups frequently deemphasize coalition participation in communications with their supporters to such an extent that
most group constituencies are unaware of the importance played by these
alliances.

Effects of Coalition Participation

Coalition participation affects group strength and survival, as well as political efficacy. We have focused on the first problem. The effect of coalition
participation on groups within the MLG has been mixed. Well-established
peace organizations, those whose focus was originally on issues of nuclear
weapons and military spending, continue to work on these goals. Newly
formed groups have now either disappeared or have diversified into other
areas with more popular support (Meyer 1993a). Common Cause invested
huge amounts of resources in coalition activities during the early stages of
the MLG but gradually shifted its efforts to other issues, so that it is now
only nominally an MLG participant.

The effects of coalition participation are more apparent for those individuals who represent the groups in coalition activities. The solidary benefits of training, mentoring, professional association, support for personal
initiative, opportunity for career advancement, and friendship make the
coalitions attractive to people who attend the frequent meetings. Coalitions

provide a sense of momentum and movement cohesion to what would otherwise be the separate and scattered activities of the member organizations.

Suggestions for Long-Term Success

The histories of the MLG and the CAC offer some general rules for long-term coalitions. First, there must be a common locus of activity for the coalition member organizations in order to keep the coalition focused. Second, groups should avoid the trap of directing too much attention inward toward the structure of the coalition. Third, a balance must be struck between keeping the issue crisis alive and accentuating progress. In other words, coalitions must avoid complacency but recognize and celebrate incremental successes.

Conclusion

Political organizations are not unitary actors; they work in cooperation and competition with similarly minded groups. We have established that cooperation through coalition formation, at least in the case of arms control and disarmament groups, is closely related to the larger political environment. The Monday Lobby Group grew dramatically in response to popular mobilization for the nuclear freeze. This growth, especially in the context of the larger political environment, enhanced the members' access to Congress. The Coalition for Arms Control started in response to the challenge presented by a particular congressman. The important point here is that coalition formation was a function not only of activist choice but also of changing political opportunities.

These coalitions were able to survive even when the political winds shifted and mass mobilization faltered. Clearly, this was less a function of the external political environment than of activist management of the conflicting pressures to cooperate and to differentiate. We found that the primary way the coalitions and participating organizations coped with these conflicts was by recognizing the different audiences they faced: targets of influence and sources of support. They emphasized differences to potential supporters while emphasizing commonality and cooperation to government officials. This process of cooperative differentiation is intended to maximize the political benefits of cooperation while ensuring group autonomy. The survival of both coalitions and of most of the cooperating groups within them suggests it is a successful strategy.

5

Transnational Activism in the Nuclear Weapons Freeze Campaign

DAVID CORTRIGHT & RON PAGNUCCO

The Nuclear Weapons Freeze Campaign (NWFC) is best known for its largely successful efforts to develop a grassroots constituency across the United States to end the testing, production, and deployment of nuclear weapons by the two superpowers. The original sponsors of the proposal for a bilateral freeze believed that its evenhanded focus would have broad appeal among the American people and would allow the peace movement to reach beyond its traditional and relatively small constituency. Although the NWFC's efforts to mobilize the American people to put pressure on Congress and the president were central to its strategy, it also engaged in transnational activities that are less well known. In this essay we review several of these activities: NWFC lobbying at the United Nations in 1982, its cooperation with peace groups in Western Europe, its relations with official and unofficial peace groups in the Soviet Union, and its involvement in the transnational movement against U.S. military involvement in Central America.

Historically, transnational activism has been common in the U.S. peace movement. The liberal-internationalist wing of the movement has organized international peace conferences and organizations; worked for the establishment of the World Court, the League of Nations, and the United Nations; sent peace delegations to the capitals of nations in conflict; and brought together the citizens of different nations in the hopes of promoting mutual understanding (Chatfield with Kleidman 1992; Marullo, Pagnucco, and Smith 1996). As will be seen, however, the sociopolitical environment in the United States and the bilateral focus of the NWFC shaped and in some ways limited its transnational efforts.

The founders of the NWFC recognized the importance of transnational contacts and established an International Task Force in 1981. Terry Provance of the American Friends Service Committee (AFSC) was the first chair of the task force. Provance already had experience with transnational tactics; two years earlier he had organized a delegation to the Soviet Union to present a nuclear moratorium proposal to officials at the Soviet Foreign Ministry and scholars at the Institute for U.S.A.-Canada Studies (Solo 1988: 44–45). Though there were no concrete results from the visit, several members of the delegation were encouraged by the experience and joined Randall Forsberg in efforts to create the NWFC.

Growth of the peace movement in Western Europe also gave impetus to the NWFC to create an International Task Force. In December 1979 NATO approved the deployment of ground-launched cruise and Pershing II missiles. The thought of these weapons facing SS-20 missiles in the Soviet Union created widespread concern over the possibility of nuclear war in Europe (Rochon 1988). The NWFC believed it needed to be in contact with this growing movement. In addition, the rapid growth of the freeze movement in the United States gained it international attention. According to Randy Kehler, national coordinator of the NWFC, "we got pulled into the international arena. . . . The very size and visibility of the Freeze Campaign meant that people were contacting us from other countries, wanting to know what we were doing" (Kehler 1993). Kehler also believes that it was important for the freeze movement to "establish relationships and broaden our vision to include a global disarmament perspective." However, Solo (1988: 114) convincingly argues that the NWFC never truly adopted a transnational perspective but remained wedded to its bilateralist approach, which led it to believe that "it could stop the arms race without challenging the cold war." The U.S. sociopolitical environment made it difficult for the NWFC to move beyond a bilateral, Cold War orientation.

At the United Nations

Peace groups have played important roles in the development of intergovernmental organizations, especially the United Nations and its various agencies. Virtually from the beginning of the modern U.S. peace movement in the early 1800s, many peace groups have believed that the anarchy of the international system of autonomous nation-states is responsible for war and that the remedy lies in the development of multilateral institutions for international governance and conflict resolution (Chatfield 1997). Some U.S. peace groups worked after World War II to place all nuclear weapons under the international control of the United Nations (Chatfield with Kleidman 1992; Pagnucco 1992). And, as international organizations have in fact become more prominent, the women's, human rights, environmental, and peace movements have increasingly coordinated their efforts with them (Smith 1997).

In 1982, the NWFC attempted to work through the United Nations to promote a nuclear freeze. The NWFC used the occasion of the Second Special Session on Disarmament (SSDII) to join other peace groups in organizing the June 1982 rally against the nuclear arms race in Central Park.[1] Inside the UN, the NWFC's International Task Force launched a campaign to lobby for passage of a freeze resolution by the General Assembly. The task force hired a three-person staff to lobby national missions and coordinate lobbying efforts by other citizen groups. On 8 June 1982, as the SSDII was beginning, the NWFC delivered a total of 2,139,499 signatures of U.S. citizens in support of a bilateral nuclear freeze to the U.S. and Soviet missions to the United Nations. Randy Kehler led a delegation of peace movement representatives that met for an hour with Soviet UN officials to urge support for an immediate halt to the production, testing, and deployment of nuclear weapons. Although Soviet diplomats were willing to meet with the freeze delegation, officials at the U.S. mission, in the words of Kehler (1993), "came down the hall, took our boxes and shooed us away."

Working from mid-April through December of 1982, the task force staff distributed copies of the freeze proposal and supporting documentation to all 157 national missions to the UN, interviewed and met with groups of delegates, wrote to and conferred with U.S. and Soviet negotiators, and provided information and support for other citizen groups. A key NWFC ally in this effort was the Parliamentarians for World Order, which used its extensive network of members of national legislatures in twenty-eight countries to win support for the freeze in the UN. The Parliamentarians also introduced the freeze proposal into the legislatures of a number of individual countries, including Jamaica, Australia, Canada, Iceland, India, Italy, Kenya, New Zealand, Nigeria, and the United Kingdom (Deuce 1983). On 13 December 1982 the General Assembly approved two freeze resolutions. The resolution introduced by Sweden and Mexico, which was closest to the language of the NWFC proposal, received 119 yeas, 17 nays, and 5 abstentions, with 17 countries not voting. The United States and most Western nations opposed the resolutions, which had no binding power. Even so, its approval by a large majority showed worldwide support for ending the nuclear arms race (Solo 1993).

After the success in the General Assembly, the NWFC disbanded its International Task Force. Although it hired an international coordinator in 1983, it did not continue to work at the UN. In late 1982 and early 1983, the NWFC returned to its bilateral focus and devoted its attention to grassroots organizing and lobbying Congress. The NWFC thereby passed up any possible opportunity it may have had to increase citizen involvement in the UN.

Cooperation with the West European Peace Movement

The NWFC was in communication with a number of the major peace groups in Western Europe, including the Interchurch Peace Council (IKV) in the Netherlands, the Campaign for Nuclear Disarmament (CND) in Great Britain, and the Green Party in West Germany. Although the NWFC and these groups shared a concern over the U.S.-Soviet nuclear arms race, differences in perspectives and in sociopolitical contexts made transatlantic cooperation difficult. The bilateral approach of the NWFC was not entirely accepted by many of the West European groups, though they were not necessarily hostile to it (Kent 1995; Schennink 1994). European peace movements were much more concerned with the planned deployment of Intermediate-Range Nuclear Force (INF) missiles—cruise and Pershing II missiles—on their soil. Many of these groups held a "nonaligned" rather than bilateralist perspective on the nuclear arms race, according to Thomas Rochon (1988):

> The dominant strand of thought within the [European] peace movement [was] that the problem of the arms race is rooted in an international system composed of two superpowers who each line up their allies and prepare to confront the other. . . . Each [superpower] needs the other to justify its own domination within its bloc. A state of disarmed peace would undermine the basis of bloc cohesion and weaken the dominance of the superpowers.

The European perspective on the INF issue was articulated in an open letter to U.S. peace supporters from a group of 166 prominent scholars, peace researchers, physicians, lawyers, writers, and artists from West Germany in June 1982. The letter, which was reprinted in the *Freeze Newsletter* (1982: 9), appealed to Americans to join their colleagues in Europe "in finding a common path toward disarmament and peace."

> If we cannot prevent the installation of new nuclear missiles in Europe, the ensuing round of the arms race will also prevent the success of the Freeze Campaign. . . . Accordingly, we ask the American peace movement to unequivocally demand the reversal of the NATO decision to station new nuclear missiles in Europe. (*Freeze Newsletter* 1982: 9)

The European perspective was also delivered directly to NWFC representatives who toured West Germany in November 1982. According to Steve Ladd, field coordinator for the Northern California Freeze Campaign and a member of the delegation, the Germans expressed "major concern [about] our position on the cruise and Pershing missiles" (Ladd, Hallett, and Martin 1983: 9). Ladd tried to reassure the Germans that stopping the new missiles was "within the context of achieving a bilateral freeze," but his colleagues were apparently unconvinced. Ladd's report from the trip noted that there were still "questions about why we could not unilaterally call for a stop to the deployment of the new missiles" (Ladd, Hallett, and Martin 1983: 9).

Pam Solo was one of those who urged the freeze campaign to take a stronger stand against the INF missiles. She and Mike Jendrzejczyk worked tirelessly within the freeze movement to gain a greater commitment for a campaign against the missiles. At a meeting in Bonn in April 1982, Solo and others developed a proposal that would bridge the difference between the bilateral nature of the freeze and the unilateral demand of the European peace movement. The proposal demanded a delay in the NATO deployment to give negotiators more time to work out an agreement. At the NWFC's 1983 national conference, this proposal for a delay strategy was approved. Despite strong support for this approach at the grassroots level, however, the NWFC's national leadership was more cautious and failed to implement the strategy (Solo 1988: 121).

The reluctance of the NWFC came in part from its alliance with arms control lobbyists and legislative aides in Washington (see Pagnucco and Smith 1993). As members of Congress "discovered" the freeze in 1982 and introduced resolutions in favor of the proposal, they also sought to tame and control the movement. Senator Edward Kennedy (D, Massachusetts) hoped to use his support for the freeze to build his looming presidential candidacy. He and others were willing to back the freeze, although in a watered-down fashion, but they wanted to avoid the INF issue because it was seen as a "loser" on Capitol Hill. Arms control lobbyists agreed that opposition to the INF weapons would not garner much interest in Congress since home districts in the United States were not affected. They, too, ducked the issue. As the NWFC became a captive of conventional arms control politics in Washington, interest in the INF issue waned.

The NWFC took some steps to support the European opposition to INF weapons, but the measures were limited in scope and largely confined to lobbying in Washington. In the autumn of 1983 the national headquarters worked with the office of Representative Edward Markey (D, Massachusetts), principal sponsor of the freeze resolution in the House of Representatives, and Randall Forsberg's Institute for Defense and Disarmament Studies to cosponsor three delegations of political leaders from Western Europe. The first delegation arrived in mid-September and included Egon Bahr of the Social Democratic Party of West Germany; Denis Healey, Labour Party member of Parliament (MP) and former defense minister of Great Britain; and Thorvald Stoltenberg, former defense minister of Norway. The three spoke before a packed hearing room on Capitol Hill and argued for a delay in deployment pending further negotiations. A second delegation later that month was led by Willy Brandt, former chancellor of West Germany, and a third group in early October included additional members of parliament from Italy, Belgium, the Netherlands, and West Germany (Fine 1983). These were high-powered and impressive delegations, but one may question the strategy of focusing on Capitol Hill when lobbyists and members of Congress had already indicated their lack of interest. Although grassroots concern about INF was greater, the freeze campaign had no program for mobilizing its considerable constituency in opposition to the new missiles.

Timidity on the INF issue led to major problems for the NWFC. By retreating to an ever more narrow agenda, the movement found itself paralyzed in the face of what many considered the most critical nuclear weapons issue of the decade. The concern originally raised in the appeal from West Germany proved correct. As a major new escalation of the arms race proceeded in Europe, it was hard to argue that a nuclear freeze was possible. With the cruise and Pershing II missiles arriving in Europe, hope that the arms race might be halted began to fade.

Contact with the Soviet Government

The NWFC made several attempts to lobby the Soviet government to take initiatives for ending the arms race. Perhaps the most dramatic example of this effort was the SANE/FREEZE/European Peace Movement delegation to the U.S.-Soviet summit in Geneva in 1985. The ascent to power of Mikhail Gorbachev in March 1985 dramatically improved prospects for U.S.-Soviet relations and created White House interest in a summit meeting. As the administration prepared for the meeting, it became clear that the emphasis would be on atmosphere instead of substance. The administration would carefully avoid any agreements that might restrain the U.S. arms buildup. At the Pentagon, Caspar Weinberger and other hard-liners dug in their heels against any compromise on the Strategic Defense Initiative and other weapons systems. White House press officers labored to lower public expectations and dampen media speculation that agreement might result. This was to be just a "get acquainted" session.

As soon the Reagan-Gorbachev summit was announced in April, leaders of the NWFC and SANE met to plan a response. Since the peace movement had done much to generate public pressure for such a summit, it seemed only natural that the movement should have a role in the event. It was decided that a citizens' delegation would be sent to Geneva to seek meetings with Reagan and Gorbachev. An independent group, Women for a Meaningful Summit, came up with the same idea and also decided to send a delegation. The goal of these efforts was to raise public expectations, thereby countering White House strategy, and to build continuing pressure for concrete steps to halt the arms race.

The freeze movement cooperated closely with West European peace groups on the Geneva summit effort. Discussions were held with leaders of the NWFC, SANE, and other groups in the United States and Europe to send a joint delegation to the summit, develop common political demands, and coordinate press statements. The U.S. and European groups were able to agree on a goal of raising expectations for concrete results from the summit and worked effectively together both at Geneva and at the Reykjavik summit that followed a year later. It was also decided that the peace movement delegation would be more effective if it carried to Geneva an expression of mass support for disarmament. Accordingly, a national petition drive was launched, the "Appeal to World Leaders," with the goal of collecting one million signatures by the time of the summit in November. The petition called on Reagan and Gorbachev to achieve progress at the summit and to agree on a mutual halt to nuclear weapons testing.

The decision to focus on a test ban was motivated by several factors. In the wake of the deployment of INF missiles in Europe and the failure to pass meaningful freeze legislation in Congress, the NWFC struggled to find a new, more realistic programmatic focus that could sustain continued citizen activism. After floundering for several months with various formulas for a "quick freeze," the NWFC began to focus increasingly on the simple demand for a halt to nuclear testing.[2] A U.S.-Soviet nuclear test ban had long been a goal for the peace movement, and it was always seen as an essential part of the nuclear freeze. SANE and other groups began to revive the test ban issue in 1984 as a way of sustaining the momentum of the freeze movement and applying it to a specific, easily verifiable first step toward ending the arms race.

These efforts suddenly assumed increased importance in August 1985, when Gorbachev announced that the Soviet Union would begin a unilateral moratorium on nuclear testing. Peace activists quickly recognized the importance of the Soviet action and turned their attention to convincing the Reagan administration to accept the Soviet offer. Because of the popularity of the test ban, SANE door-to-door canvassers and local freeze organizers found an enthusiastic response when asking for signatures on the "Appeal to World Leaders." After Gorbachev announced the Soviet moratorium, public reaction became even more positive. As a result, the goal of obtaining one million signatures on the "Appeal" was reached in just a few months.

By coincidence the annual nuclear freeze conference in 1985 was scheduled for the weekend of 15–17 November, two days prior to the beginning of the Geneva summit. It was decided to turn the Chicago gathering into a rally to send off the citizens' delegation and the petitions. On the final day of the conference, a huge thermometer was displayed at the front of the hall to tally the number of signatures. A roll call of the states began, and SANE and NWFC representatives from local chapters came forward to present their petitions. When the organizers from New York stepped forward with the petitions that put the marker over the top, balloons were released and music blared, and the freeze conference turned into a rollicking celebration. In the midst of the excitement, with activists cheering, the delegation, led by the Reverend Jesse Jackson, left the stage and marched out through the hall to depart for O'Hare airport.[3] Once in Geneva, General Secretary Gorbachev met personally with the delegation and noted that "these petitions represent the hopes of millions of Americans." By contrast, a lower-level official at the U.S. embassy received the petitions but gave no indication of administration support or interest.

Much of the U.S. press coverage of the peace movement meeting with Gorbachev was negative or ignored important aspects of the meeting (Hertsgaard 1989). Many of the press reports were critical of Jesse Jackson for supposedly upstaging and embarrassing President Reagan. However, local news reporting in the United States was more favorable because a major grassroots component had been built into the NWFC's summit program from the outset. Local freeze groups all across the country sponsored events to support the citizens' delegation in Geneva. Many of the groups that had collected signatures for the "Appeal to World Leaders" participated in these events. During the first night of the summit on 19 November 1985, hundreds of local freeze groups gathered for peace vigils and demonstrations in their communities. The theme of the local actions was "Watching in Hope," and they were designed, as was the entire campaign, to raise public expectations for progress at the summit and to generate pressure on Reagan and Gorbachev for an end to the arms race. The grassroots structure of the NWFC was critical for generating what positive press coverage the meeting in Geneva received; the event is a good example of the effectiveness of peace groups acting locally *and* globally.

Contact with the Soviet Peace Committee

The growing threat of nuclear war and the dramatic growth of the peace movement in the West provided the context for the emergence of dissident and peace groups in East Central Europe and the Soviet Union. Though most of these groups were rather small, Western peace groups had to decide if they would try to establish relations with them and, if so, what forms of cooperation would be most appropriate. The opportunity for contact with these groups varied from country to country in the Soviet bloc and was especially limited in the case of the Soviet Union itself. In the early and mid-1980s several small, loosely organized groups of scientists, students, religious activists, and other dissidents were formed in the Soviet Union, including Friendship and Dialogue, Democracy and Humanism, and the Group to Establish Trust Between East and West. The latter was the most significant group in the Russian independent peace movement (see U.S. Helsinki Watch Committee 1987). The Trust Group was formed in June 1982 by eleven scientists and other dissident intellectuals in Moscow and, though it remained small, it grew in size and spread to other locales. Members met and discussed issues in their apartments and staged occasional demonstrations and petition campaigns. The Trust Group provided a place for Westerners and Russians to meet. Hundreds of Russians from all over the country eventually participated in Trust Group discussion meetings and took its peace literature, buttons, and ideas back home with them. The Trust Group, as well as many of the other small peace groups that sprung up, has

> tended to refrain from comment about disarmament proposals made by the Soviet Union and the United States. Rather, in promoting the guarantees of the Helsinki Accords for the free flow of information and people, the independent peace movement sees itself as creating a space where an exchange of views can take place between ordinary citizens of the Soviet Union and the West outside their respective political systems. The activists see the fostering of widespread grass-roots contacts and an increase in the openness of Soviet society as a fundamental requirement for peace, without which disarmament negotiations are doomed to fail. (U.S. Helsinki Watch Committee 1987: 110–111)

One of the reasons these groups did not comment on arms control proposals was that they would have been seriously repressed if they criticized Soviet policies; thus they were constrained from making even balanced criticisms of the United States and the USSR. In spite of their silence, members of these groups were often harassed and sometimes arrested or sent to psychiatric hospitals.

In the Soviet Union, independent peace initiatives from citizens were viewed as potentially threatening to the Communist Party's rule. The Soviet government had an official peace organization that it considered the only truly legitimate one—the Soviet Committee for the Defense of Peace, commonly called the Soviet Peace Committee. Western peace groups had to decide what relations, if any, they would have with the official committee and the unofficial groups. In the early to mid-1980s many of the West European groups opted to have contact with both the official and unofficial peace committees in the Soviet Union and the Soviet bloc countries. Contact with the independent groups was seen as part of the process of "détente from below" that would help to transcend the logic of the blocs and build the ties necessary for peace.[4] Many of these West European groups worked through two transnational movement organizations, European Nuclear Disarmament (END) and the European Network for East-West Dialogue (ENEWD). From the early to mid-1980s, hundreds of Western peace activists regularly visited the Trust Group.

The NWFC National Committee and Executive Committee had lengthy debates over whether to work with the Soviet Peace Committee or the independent Russian groups of both. Some peace activists feared that contact with unofficial groups might undermine chances for a nuclear freeze, whereas others argued that contact solely with the Soviet Peace Committee might hurt the independent peace movement. The NWFC was finally forced to make a decision when the Trust Group sent a message through the AFSC that it wanted to establish contact with NWFC leaders. After long discussion the NWFC was unable to agree on how to respond and decided that it would not formally have contact with either the Soviet Peace Committee or unofficial organizations like the Trust Group (Solo 1988: 113). The narrow, bilateral focus of the NWFC constrained it from overcoming the Cold War logic of the blocs and made it "a captive of the politics we were trying to overcome" (Solo 1993).

The Central America Solidarity Movement

The escalating nuclear arms race was a major concern of peace activists and the American public in the 1980s. However, increasing U.S. intervention on the side of brutally repressive regimes in Central America also became an important issue during the decade. The movement against U.S. intervention in Central America grew dramatically in the 1980s. Although there were only a handful of groups at the beginning of the decade, by 1987 over 1,000 groups were involved in the movement (Peace 1991: 79).

Mobilizations of solidarity with the oppressed and opposition to U.S. military intervention in Third World countries have been common in the U.S. peace movement's history. In 1898, for example, the American Anti-Imperialist League was organized after President William McKinley decided to annex the Philippines. When U.S. troops were sent to put down a rebellion in the Philippines in 1899, the league mobilized opposition throughout the country. Mark Twain, vice president of the league, wrote sympathetically of those Filipinos struggling to be free of domination by any country, including the United States. In the 1960s and early 1970s, the anti–Vietnam War movement adopted many of the same themes. In turning their attention to Central America, then, peace groups were following a long U.S. tradition.

Cultural links and geographic proximity contributed to the strongly transnational character of the Central America solidarity movement of the 1980s. Missionaries, church workers, and Central American opposition leaders and refugees were all part of a transnational network that opposed U.S. policy toward the region and provided firsthand information that sometimes contradicted that given by the Reagan administration and the mainstream media. Many North Americans traveled to the region, and numerous church, human rights, and peace groups sent delegations to Central America and brought up speakers to describe U.S.-sponsored oppression in their countries (Erickson Nepsted 1995).

As the U.S.-sponsored wars in Central America intensified during the 1980s, the NWFC was drawn into the issue. A heated debate ensued over what the freeze movement should or should not do about the wars in Central America and potentially in other parts of the world. To a large extent this debate over political focus echoed earlier debates over the INF missile issue. Should the agenda be narrowly confined to nuclear issues and specifically to the freeze proposal itself, or should the movement address other questions of nuclear and military policy? Is it possible to build support for a nuclear freeze while also working to stop the wars in Central America? To gain the widest possible support for halting the arms race, some argued, the movement should concentrate on the freeze and avoid taking a stand on other issues. Opponents countered that the issues could not be separated, that the nuclear arms race and military interventionism derive from the same policies and assumptions about the use of military force.

Although the national leadership of the NWFC tended to prefer the more narrow agenda, support for the broader view was considerable at the grassroots level, where pressure for involvement in the Central America debate steadily mounted. Freeze groups in local communities worked on Central American issues even when the national office did not, particularly in smaller towns. For a growing number of activists, the questions of non-intervention and disarmament became linked. How can we be concerned about the potential threat of a nuclear war, they asked, and not care about the actual war underway in Central America? Typical of the evolution that many freeze activists experienced was that of Helen Seidman, president of the Ohio Freeze Campaign.

> In the early 1980s I was one of those who argued for a narrow agenda, but by the later years the situation changed. People began to work on other issues, and we realized we had no choice but to broaden. Initially we thought of disarmament as a separate issue, but the more we learned we saw that the issues are connected. (Seidman 1991)

A decisive influence in convincing freeze supporters to broaden their agenda was the personal contact many had with victims of the wars in Central America. During the 1980s more than 70,000 U.S. citizens traveled to Nicaragua alone (Peace 1991), and nearly all came away deeply troubled by the pain and suffering inflicted by U.S. policy. As Erickson Nepsted (1995) and others document, visiting Central America was often a transforming experience that compelled those affected to make an intensive commitment to working for peace in the region. The proximity of Central America and the strong religious and cultural bonds between North Americans and their neighbors to the south created an acute sense of awareness and concern.

Central America peace activists referred to their cause as the solidarity movement. The phrase was an apt one, for it helped to describe the motivations that inspired many North Americans to work for peace in Central America. For many activists, solidarity meant "standing with" the people of the region—providing political and material support for victims of poverty, oppression, and war. Clergy and religious people involved in the movement were particularly influenced by the teachings of liberation theology and the doctrine of the preferential "option for the poor." Papal encyclicals and other statements by religious leaders called for rooting out the structural causes of poverty and oppression in the Third World. Many North Americans believed they were doing this by opposing U.S. imperialism in Central America.

The NWFC passed resolutions at its national conferences opposing military intervention and committing it to support the Central America solidarity movement, but few resources were put into the effort. The resolutions were limited in scope and often were placed in an ill-fitting context of bilateralism or concern about nuclear war. The resolution passed at the third national conference in December 1983, for example, called for opposition to both U.S. and Soviet intervention in developing countries (Fine 1984). In one sense, this was a perfectly legitimate statement of opposition both to U.S. policy in Central America and Soviet intervention in Afghanistan. As critics pointed out, however, the statement also put the Central America issue squarely within a Cold War, East-West context, which was precisely where the Reagan administration wanted it. In so doing, the statement implied that East-West dynamics were responsible for the conflicts in Central America, while it ignored the long history of U.S. exploitation and military intervention in the region dating from before the Soviet Union even existed. By attempting to place the Central America issue in a bilateral straitjacket, the NWFC unwittingly reinforced the very interventionist politics it was attempting to challenge.

Similar contortions resulted from placing military interventions in the context of nuclear policy. Intervention is a legitimate issue, freeze leaders argued, because conventional wars of intervention could escalate to nuclear war (Fine 1984). Again, this was a legitimate argument. As Daniel Ellsberg (1981) points out, threats to use nuclear weapons had indeed been made several times in wars of intervention, in Korea, Vietnam, and the Middle East. Some activists opposed this approach, however. They found it "morally bankrupt" that freeze activists would become interested in the intervention issue only when the threat of nuclear war was involved (Solo 1993). This selectivity seemed to imply that the suffering of the victims of military intervention, all of whom were people of color in the Third World, was not in itself a sufficient motivation to become involved. The issue was important only when it threatened to involve predominantly white North Americans through the risk of nuclear war. This perception offended some members of the Third World Task Force within the NWFC and contributed to political and racial tensions within the movement.

Ultimately the freeze movement became actively involved in Central America solidarity work on its own merits, without reference to other issues. Especially at the grassroots level, freeze groups contributed significantly to lobbying campaigns against military aid for the contras. The expertise that local groups had acquired in earlier fights for the congressional freeze resolution was put to good use in pressuring legislators to vote against aid to the contras. By 1986, when the NWFC voted to merge with SANE, the issue of Central America no longer divided the two groups. Previously the NWFC had adopted a narrow focus on nuclear arms, while SANE had advocated a broader perspective that included nonintervention. Differences over the issue posed real difficulties for the unification process. As merger discussions proceeded, however, it became apparent that many freeze groups at the local level were already working on Central America and other issues. Although some in the national leadership continued to hold out for a narrow, nuclear agenda, grassroots delegates at the 1986 conference overwhelmingly adopted a merged political program that emphasized disarmament as the top priority but also included a strong commitment to nonintervention. This action brought the new organization into the Central America solidarity movement.

Conclusion

The original proponents of the nuclear freeze were correct in their belief that this simple, evenhanded proposal could have wide appeal beyond the traditional small constituency of the peace movement. By emphasizing its bilateralism, freeze advocates recruited many Americans who, after decades of Cold War socialization, had difficulties seeing the world in anything but bipolar terms. Similarly, the moderate nature of the freeze allowed it to receive support in Congress, a bastion of Cold War ideology.

As we and others have argued, however, the bilateralism of the freeze, though no doubt largely responsible for its large number of supporters in the United States, also constrained the movement in many ways. This is especially clear when one looks at the transnational activities of the NWFC.

Like many liberal-internationalist peace groups, the NWFC saw value in trying to work with intergovernmental organizations and in transnational cooperation with other peace groups. Its successful efforts at the United Nations in 1982 and its collaboration with West European peace groups in organizing for the Geneva summit in 1985 showed the NWFC's skills in the use of transnational tactics. Nevertheless, largely because of its bilateral perspective and focus on domestic politics, the NWFC did not try to build on its successes at the United Nations by increasing citizen participation in that multilateral institution and helping it develop a greater role in the disarmament process. Similarly, the NWFC's narrow focus constrained it from fully cooperating with the massive West European peace movement and developing ties with the unprecedented independent peace movement in the Soviet Union. The NWFC's orientation also prevented it from fully participating in the transnational movement, against U.S. involvement in the wars in Central America. By looking at the transnational dimension of the freeze movement we not only gain a fuller understanding of this remarkable campaign, but we also see how domestic sociopolitical environments can make transnational cooperation difficult even for citizens' groups committed to the establishment of world peace.

Notes

We would like to thank Randy Kehler and Pam Solo, formerly of the Nuclear Weapons Freeze Campaign; Helen Seidman, formerly of the Ohio Freeze Campaign; Bruce Kent of the Campaign for Nuclear Disarmament in Great Britain; and Ben Schennink of Pax Christi–Netherlands for generously taking the time for interviews with us. We also would like to thank the staff of the Swarthmore Peace Collection at Swarthmore College for their help in our archival research. Finally, we would like to thank Tom Rochon and David Meyer for their helpful comments and editing.

1. For a discussion of the efforts of peace groups at SSDI (1978), SSDII (1982), and SSDIII (1988), see David Atwood (1997).

2. The quick freeze called for a congressional effort to suspend funding for warhead testing and the testing and deployment of ballistic missiles. See Pam Solo (1988).

3. One of the authors, David Cortright, was a member of the delegation.

4. Patricia Chilton (1994) describes how these ties contributed to the democratic transformation of several countries in East Central Europe.

PART 2

The Social & Political Impact of the Freeze

6

Freeze Frame: News Coverage of the Freeze Movement

ANDREW ROJECKI

In this chapter I examine the diversity and quality of views in the media during the course of the nuclear freeze and explore the way media news shaped the movement during its public trajectory. The issue that guides this chapter is the extent to which the media remained independent of elite influence.

Model and Method

Communication scholars have described the mass media as the "site on which various social groups, institutions, and ideologies struggle over the definition and construction of reality" (Gurevitch and Levy 1985). How one defines an issue has a powerful effect on its outcome. E. E. Schattschneider (1960) calls this process the "mobilization of bias," defining an issue in such a way as to maximize support for it. In other words, this suggests selecting and highlighting those elements that make the strongest case for one's position, much as a trial lawyer and prosecutor grapple with different subsets of the same facts to make the strongest case for their sides. In this example, the jury is conscious of the struggle for its hearts and minds. It is, in other words, conscious that the issue is being framed. In other venues, framing may take place with no struggle at all.

A news frame selects, from the infinite variety of world events and causal agents, a finite set of elements that embody an implicit theory of problem identification, causal diagnosis, evaluation, and solution proposal (Entman 1993). Unlike the example of the jury, the power of a news frame partly lies in its not being recognized as one. The wizard achieves power over his subjects only to the degree that he is successful in focusing their attention on his chimeras and not on the man behind the curtain. To the degree that one party or the other in a conflict has succeeded in convincing bystanders of the merit of their position, he or she has succeeded in a fair fight. To the degree one has either excluded consideration of the opponent's position or managed to hide the position as a position, one has succeeded by presenting a contestable proposition as a fact. The news media enjoy a powerful authority for sense making of just this kind and for their role in mediating the struggle between political movements and government for public support.

Movement Frames

To successfully expand its influence, a political movement must attract potential converts to its cause. This is tricky in the realm of foreign policy because of the widespread belief that the public is too ill-informed or volatile to make sober judgments. Thus movement leaders must convince the public that (1) it has a legitimate role to play in the making of foreign policy, (2) that a concerted effort will bring about the desired change, and (perhaps most difficult) (3) that it is obliged to act in some meaningful way (Tyler and McGraw 1983). Threats to successful appeals therefore include the following.

1. The situation may be defined as hopeless.
2. News coverage elevates the importance of the problem rather than the solution, thereby blocking a connection to the political process.
3. The frame renders public action superfluous, for example, by defining the issue in terms so technical that only experts seem qualified to tackle it. A variant of this is domination by experts on only one side of an argument. Citizens depend on elected representatives and experts for clarification of issues and cues on them. To the extent that citizens are uncritical of media content, such domination is possible if citizens are induced to hold opinions they would not hold if they were aware of the best available information and analysis, supported by ample coverage of a range of expert viewpoints (Zaller 1992: 313–314).
4. The frame fails to resonate with common belief systems, by marginalizing movement values or associating its agenda with one that is marginal (Snow et al. 1986). For example, peace movements often include small minorities that advocate utopian ideas for wholesale reform of human society and perhaps of human nature itself. Undue emphasis on these groups draws attention away from issues that unify the entirety of the movement.
5. Participants in movements may be subject to disparaging judgments regarding their rationality, expertise, and extremism. This may dampen public support for their cause (Entman and Rojecki 1993).

Administration Frames

A highly interested party to the debate is the government itself, which seeks to mobilize and manage public opinion for support of its policies. Although foreign policy may call for subtle judgment, historical erudition, and precise understanding of the complexities of policy and events, limited cognitive capacity and the need for quick summary judgments leads national leaders to construct simplified "cognitive maps" of the international scene. Philip Tetlock (1983) analyzed these coping strategies and discerned two principal images used to process Cold War relations between the United States and the Soviet Union (see also Russett 1990: 52–54).

The *deterrence* frame cast the Soviet Union as a remorseless aggressor and as an exploiter of opportunities that tested the resolve of the Free World. Profound incompatibility between the two political systems prevented realistic rapprochement. Supporters of this view often argued that offers to negotiate might lead the Soviet Union to underestimate the resolve of the Free World. Thus a responsible government would match increases in Soviet arms with its own increase or, better, a new generation of weapons. Munich and the appeasement of Hitler provided the telling historical object lesson for this point of view.

In contrast, the *conflict* frame portrayed both powers as victims of an anarchic state of international relations. Arms caches and alliances were the unfortunate response to this unstable condition, resulting in an excessive buildup of arms. Every scheme used to gauge the effectiveness of arms included a fair amount of uncertainty, justifying the development and accumulation of even more weapons. All of this risked a sequence of miscalculations and misperceptions that might lead to accidental war. The solution was to be found in an atmosphere of mutual trust developed by making conciliatory gestures coupled to announcements of peaceful intentions. The spiral of miscalculations that led to World War I illustrates this perspective.[1]

These frames parallel distinctions made between hawks and doves, conservatives and liberals, realists and idealists. Regardless of name, they embody a perhaps necessary but nevertheless false delimitation of options and thus achieve their power by excluding other paths of action from consideration. As the administration seeks to promote its foreign policy goal, the image of the international scene changes to comply with it: an aggressive enemy to be mistrusted and deterred becomes the fellow victim of a dangerous arms race. The Cuban missile crisis of 1962 was one example of such a transformation.

Detecting Media Frames

Addressing the primary research question of this chapter—whether the media provide a durable space for oppositional politics—involves two steps. First I examine the historical record to trace the development of official policy and to assess the degree of support within the executive branch for the policy in effect. On the latter point, Daniel Hallin (1986) finds that the U.S. news media established the legitimacy of a policy position—opposition to the Vietnam War—on the range of support for it by elites. Similarly, Lance Bennett (1990) finds that the media covered an issue mainly when Congress or the executive debated it; he termed this phenomenon "indexing" and found it in his analysis of *New York Times* coverage of the Nicaragua issue.

Then I consider the news coverage itself. How do the media characterize movement activities, positions, and participants? The difficulty with interpretation of news frames lies with journalistic notions of objectivity, which in their preference for the language of empirical science typically present bare-bones "just the facts" treatments (who, why, what, where, when, and how). Consequently, I find it sometimes necessary to infer a news frame from the presence of certain themes and catchphrases, emphasis on certain categories of facts, characterizations of the participants, and appeals to principle: in short, an unspoken set of assumptions and guideposts that indicate how to think about the issue (Gamson and Modigliani 1989).

Table 6.1 provides some examples of news frames, positive and negative, for movement messages. The basic points of view contested in these frames are whether citizen involvement in arms control policy is feasible, effective, and appropriate. The typical perspectives in support of and in opposition to citizen involvement are listed in Table 6.1. The important point to note is that these perspectives seep into coverage of collective action such as the freeze movement. They are not part of the factual "who, why, what, and where" coverage, though such facts may be highlighted in support of these news frames.

These ways of framing a movement have their counterparts in perspectives about movement participants. Table 6.2 displays a variety of news frames that depict movement participants in ways that indirectly support or undermine the integrity of the movement message. The central themes here are whether movement participants are serious, knowledgeable, high-minded, and representative, or whether they are instead emotional, ignorant, partisan, and extremist.

Framing operates through the selection of images and themes that are emphasized about a movement and its participants. The news media do not need to resort to name calling in order to convey a particular image of the

Table 6.1 Frame Indicators: Movement Messages

Positive	Negative
Citizens and government can work together to prevent war (causal role)	Policy is best left in the hands of experts or diplomats
	USSR is not pressured by its citizens; action by U.S. citizens is futile
There is potential for doing some good (effectiveness)	Peace is a utopian ideal; a lost cause
	U.S. policy is hostage to the actions of the USSR
There is a moral obligation to get involved	Involvement is unpatriotic

Table 6.2 Frame Indicators: Movement Participants

Positive	Negative
Participants are serious, rational	Participants are emotional, flighty
Participants are knowledgeable, mature	Participants are ignorant of complexities of foreign policy; well meaning but simpleminded; utopians
Participants motivated by justice, morality, other high-minded purpose	Motivation is whimsical, selfish, partisan, or unwittingly seditious
Participants are unified	Participants are wrought by division, infighting, incompatible goals
Participants are mainstream, average Americans	Participants are extremist in appearance or belief; otherwise set apart from the mainstream
Public opinion is in favor	Movement is not supported by public; or public opinion is irrelevant to proper policymaking
Participants are likely to be successful	Participants are unlikely to influence policy; their action is merely symbolic

movement and thus to affect public support for the movement. By framing, the media have a powerful impact on the seriousness with which the movement's ideas are examined.

The News Media and the Freeze

I selected two sources for the study, the *New York Times* (hereafter *NYT*) and the *CBS Evening News*. The *NYT* is the self-styled (and influential) newspaper of record, and the *CBS Evening News* enjoyed during the early 1980s the highest ratings of the early evening television news programs. For the *NYT* I selected only the most prominent stories—national news items that appeared in the first section of the paper. During twenty-seven months' coverage, the *NYT* published fifty-seven stories on the freeze, including the debate in the House and Ronald Reagan's various speeches and comments on the merit of the issue. During roughly the same period, CBS broadcast forty-one stories on the freeze, the first in March 1982, the last in February 1984. Figure 6.1 shows the visibility of the issue in both sources[2] and indicates how internal dissension and the absence of a unified arms control policy provided the movement with its greatest visibility in early spring 1982. Note also the drop in coverage after the announcement of Strategic Arms Reduction Talks (START), despite the New York City demonstration in June 1982. Once again, visibility increased as the Geneva talks began to stall. But after the issuance of the President's Commission on Strategic Forces (the Scowcroft Commission) report, the House vote on the freeze, and the Korean Air Lines 007 shootdown, movement visibility dropped off again. On the surface, patterns of coverage suggest more media sensitivity to administration initiatives and dissent than to movement activities.

A comparison of the two sources shows much similarity, with a few expected and unexpected differences. As expected, the *NYT* led television coverage temporally, in the first instance by seven months. The *NYT* continued to lead until the House debate in May 1983. Also, the *NYT* paid more sustained attention to the issue than CBS.

The comparison shows as well that although the *NYT* was first on the scene, it was also the first to leave after elites had disposed of the issue. Television provided the movement with more follow-up coverage after the House debate. This may be because of the television news policy of assigning a single correspondent to the issue, in contrast to the *NYT* assignment of a variety of beat reporters who were less likely to develop a sustained relationship with movement organizers. The television correspondent was assigned more or less permanently to the story, but *NYT* reporters covered the movement only as it intersected with their prescribed beats in the White House, Congress, or the specialized areas of arms control and national politics. Thus the *NYT* reporter was more likely to view the movement in terms of reactions to it by politicians. When elites perceived that the movement had achieved its goals of stimulating debate and development of an arms control proposal, they were less likely to continue to respond to the movement. I hypothesize that this structural difference accounts for the difference in perspective on the movement by the two news sources.

The analysis that follows conforms to the three periods of arms policy formation in the Reagan administration and focuses on four groups in the controversy: (1) the movement itself, including its leadership; (2) potential movement supporters (the public); (3) government officials, including members of the Senate and House, members of the Reagan administration,

Figure 6.1 Movement Visibility: Coverage by *CBS Evening News* and the *New York Times*

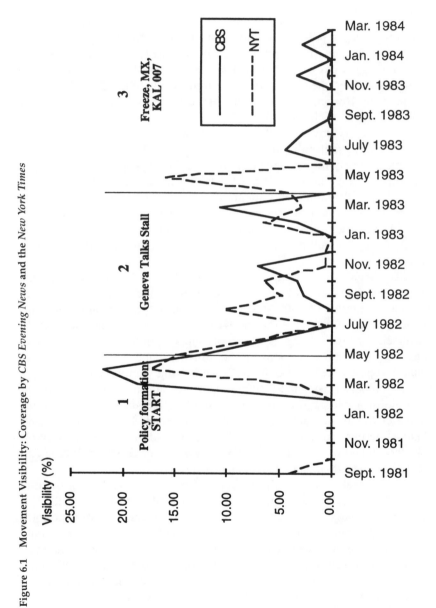

and the arms control community; and (4) sympathetic allies, such as the moderate arms controllers and the Catholic bishops.

Confusion and Dissent (January 1981–April 1982)

The freeze movement made its greatest gains during the first year and a half of the Reagan presidency, during which the administration found itself deeply divided on arms control. Hard-liners had revived the notion of a war-winning strategy that alarmed many citizens (Meyer 1990; Russett 1990). As a result, the period preceding formulation of the START proposal provided the freeze movement with its best opportunity for influencing public opinion.

In this early coverage, the news media did not distinguish between general public sentiment and the movement itself, suggesting that the movement merely rode a wave of public sentiment. The *NYT* for example, began its coverage in September 1981 with a front-page story on Catholic Bishop Leroy T. Matthiesen's attempt to close down a Texas nuclear bomb factory. The story granted legitimacy to the movement by noting that it had crossed over traditional pacifist (that is, extremist) boundaries: "Some members of the movement are pacifists but many are not" (*NYT*, 8 September 1981: 1).

CBS began its coverage seven months later, when it reported on a series of Vermont town meetings, the result of local American Friends Service Committee (AFSC) staff efforts to put the freeze on the meeting agenda (Solo 1988: 55). Like the *NYT*, television news legitimated the movement by highlighting its grassroots support. In the story, earnest citizens went on record as opposing the arms race and persuaded the town council to pass a freeze resolution. Bruce Morton (who became the principal CBS reporter assigned to the movement) said that this was but one example of a wider movement that included five state legislatures and twelve city councils, including "middle of the road" Fort Wayne, Indiana. Contrasting this movement to that of the 1960s, Morton said that Vermont was "no hotbed of radicalism" (*CBS Evening News,* 3 March 1982). This would become a dominant theme in the coverage.

A few weeks later, a Bill Moyers commentary noted the growth of opposition to nuclear weapons in the United States and Europe. Refuting the Reagan charge of Soviet influence on the movement, Moyers noted widespread support in public opinion. He mentioned that recently published essays by Jonathan Schell (*Fate of the Earth*) "open the public mind to dimly perceived truths" and concluded that "citizens seem to be determined to close the gap between policies of the government and desires of the heart that species survive" (*CBS Evening News,* 22 March 1982). The

Moyers commentary endowed "the people" with the moral authority to require government responsiveness on an issue traditionally left to its discretion. Movement strategy for enlarging the scope of political debate and democratizing the issue—moving it beyond the control of a small elite— had succeeded, even with the editorial board of the *NYT:*

> The problem is not nuclear but political. The freeze movement members are not lobbyists pressing for a specific piece of legislation. They are people, ordinary citizens, pressing for something much less intricate. They want to put nuclear restraint back on the track, to give diplomacy, and peace, a chance. The wonder is that the Reagan Administration seems so determined to take the other side. (*NYT,* 16 March 1982: A22)

By the end of March 1982, the *NYT* considered the movement significant enough to warrant two front-page analyses by its political reporter Hedrick Smith. In a news conference on 31 March 1982, Reagan announced that the Soviets had achieved a margin of offensive superiority over the United States. Using these remarks as background for his analysis, Smith attributed the freeze movement's success to the absence of an administration consensus on arms control. Smith also noted that 70 percent of the public favored smaller increases than those proposed by Reagan. This was, in fact, nearly the same number who favored the freeze: "Now, with its ambitious military buildup, assertive talk of confrontation with Moscow and public comments about limited nuclear war, the Reagan Administration seems to have touched a sensitive public nerve and fed the climate of controversy" (*NYT,* 9 April 1982: 1). Significantly, Smith's analysis included a reference to public opinion polls that indicated an anomaly; notwithstanding acceptance of Reagan's assessment that the Soviet Union now had "a definite margin of superiority," Smith asserted that Americans wanted both to move ahead with arms control negotiations and to moderate the military buildup.

Feeling growing pressure from public opinion and needing to bolster its case for increases in the military budget, the administration launched a counterattack. In an April 1 broadcast, CBS Capitol Hill correspondent Phil Jones began his report with this announcement: "CBS has learned that [Senator] Howard Baker has agreed to hold an unusual super secret briefing on the Soviet threat." At pains to refrain from revealing the secret details, Jones said that Baker was in possession of a confirmed statement from a Soviet general that "Russia is now on a war footing."[3] Already having gotten the briefing, Senator David Boren (D, Oklahoma) said that the Soviets had every year tried to achieve superiority in every area, and asked, "What are we to do about it?" The assessment was much worse than Americans thought. Jones mentioned that some Republicans feared the "controversy" might make them politically vulnerable but once again provided no specific information that would either confirm or refute the alarming "findings," which supported the argument that a freeze on arms development would amount to a permanent de facto Soviet strategic advantage (*CBS Evening News,* 1 April 1982).

No movement spokesperson was on hand to comment in this (or any other) story on the balance of nuclear power. This was perhaps in part due to the decision to locate movement headquarters in St. Louis to reinforce its nonradical image. Putting it beyond the reach of national media centers also restricted the movement's control of its message, a limitation that became increasingly apparent later that spring with the ascent to media attention of Ground Zero.

Ground Zero and the Arms Controllers

Led by Roger Molander, a former National Security Council (NSC) staffer and arms control adviser, Ground Zero was a campaign designed to enhance public awareness of the dangers of nuclear war. Although Molander sympathized with the freeze movement's general purpose of raising public awareness of the nuclear issue, he opposed the proposal itself as simplistic and unverifiable. Molander's opposition to the freeze proposal reflected a general reluctance within the arms control community to ally itself with the freeze, a severe blow to overall movement strategy because the merit of the proposal rested heavily upon its technical credibility (Meyer 1993b: 164).

Because Ground Zero marked the first round of public activities since the Vermont town meetings, the media covered it extensively but obscured its central political message by conflating it with the freeze movement and by featuring sideshow activities rather than its central political message. Much of a *NYT* front-page article on Ground Zero catalogued the whimsical events that made up the week's events, including a "run-for-your-life" race in which participants established that people could not outrun the blast wave of an exploding nuclear weapon, and a "swim for peace" by a seal to demonstrate that animals were no better equipped to survive a nuclear war. The scrupulous "nonpartisan" quality of Molander's position had made it attractive even to administration officials. The media reported that Eugene Rostow (head of the Arms Control and Disarmament Agency [ACDA]) and even Ronald Reagan favored this educational campaign.

The presence of such high-placed allies in this nonpartisan venue would not contribute to the movement's democratizing strategy, however. The article noted that although many freeze advocates favored direct political action, others "acknowledged the possibility that entering the political process as a lobbying group might fragment the movement, which has been growing rapidly" (*NYT,* 18 April 1982: 1). Here and in later instances the media contrasted the movement's laudable efforts to educate the public on the dangers of nuclear explosions with the dangers to movement coherence and unity when it entered the political process. Molander's campaign to restore traditional arms control policies to the Reagan administration undermined the freeze by offering a middle ground that would divert attention from its goal of changing fundamental thinking on the arms race.

Television coverage did not differ markedly. CBS noted the weekend kickoff of Ground Zero week with scenes of children and balloons, the visual theme that would come to dominate Bruce Morton's reporting of movement activities. There was little in the way of substance in the report: a soundbite from Roger Molander proclaimed that people needed to be educated on the dangers of nuclear war. This was followed by footage from several cities showing rallies of varying sizes, with such things as toy bombs in evidence. The theme of nationwide support for a serious political issue ran counter to the festive images of balloons and children that dominated the coverage (*CBS Evening News,* 18 April 1982).

The images of movement festivity coupled to high purpose suggested an ambivalent attitude toward a phenomenon television news could not quite catch up with, in part the result of the absence of a convenient location for reporters to get messages that cogently articulated the case for the movement. With disciplined communication absent, the colorful images served as distractions that transformed the movement's message to stop the arms race to a more general concern with the risks of nuclear war.

As evidence of the movement's loss of control of its issue, the *NYT* traced the freeze movement to the Carter and Reagan military buildups and the absence of an arms control initiative. The article presented the case for and against the freeze, but the case against was bolstered by "many arms control specialists" who argued that it would benefit the Russians, who stood to gain "many of the limits on American forces they have been seeking" (*NYT,* 24 April 1982: 8). Moreover, "negotiating an agreement that increases stability requires expertise, a more than passing acquaintance with military issues, and considerable patience. When, for example, does modernization become a new weapons system? How does one go about verifying production of cruise missiles? The freeze, specialists assert, is misleading in its purported simplicity."

The experts also worried that the issue was becoming too partisan, a political weapon wielded against the administration. As such, it represented "all things to all people." One reason for this lack of clarity was the freeze movement's loss of issue definition to opponents and even to Congressional supporters. *NYT* analysis further muddied the waters by failing to distinguish between the two freeze resolutions proposed in Congress. The Kennedy-Hatfield resolution, the experts said, was difficult to distinguish from the Jackson-Warner: both called for negotiations now, not an immediate moratorium. In fact, there was a significant difference between the two proposals. The Kennedy-Hatfield proposal—a nonbinding resolution—called on the president to "decide when and how to achieve a mutual verifiable freeze on the testing, production, and further deployment of nuclear warheads, missiles, and other delivery systems" (quoted in Meyer 1990: 225). The Jackson-Warner proposal called for a freeze *after* both the Americans and Soviets had achieved a sizable reduction in their stores of nuclear weapons. This was, in fact, a ploy (assumed by Washington pundits to have been designed by Richard Perle) to co-opt the language of the movement while supporting Reagan's goal of avoiding arms control (Garthoff 1985: 1023; Meyer 1990: 226). In the end, the analysis continued, the fate of the freeze itself was not all that significant. Rather, "the force of the freeze is . . . likely to be affected by the extent to which the position put forth by the Reagan Administration is viewed as a 'serious' negotiating posture by arms control specialists here and overseas" (*NYT,* 24 April 1982: 8). In short, the *NYT* had set as the test for movement success the good faith offering by the administration of an arms control proposal, not the adoption of the freeze proposal itself. The *NYT* saw the center of debate as resting with the expert judgment of the arms control community, whose self-interest depended on a return to proposals of the past rather than on the radical departures represented by the Reagan military buildup and by Randall Forsberg's call to end the arms race.

To summarize, in this first phase the national media seemed to be caught off-balance by the movement. Both media sources failed to distinguish the movement from a general mood of antinuclear sentiment, and both legitimated it on the basis of mainstream participation in it. But this early coverage also included signs of thematic framing that seemed driven more by the necessity for symbolic coherence than for a nuanced rendering of the facts. Moreover, the festivals of Ground Zero week, with their themes of children and balloons, already seemed overmatched by the oxymoronic "super secret" meetings in congressional chambers to which television news responded uncritically. Meanwhile the window of vulnerability, the administration's case against the freeze, shifted the rhetorical balance in favor of technical expertise. The movement here was conspicuous by its absence, unable (or unwilling) to comment and unable to delineate the technical merits of its position. This rendered the freeze politically vulnerable to those with institutional links to the media.

START (May 1982–March 1983)

Ronald Reagan announced his administration's first arms control proposal at Eureka College in May 1982. Seriously flawed, START nevertheless altered the news media's views of the movement. After the announcement, the news began to distinguish between the movement and the general public, despite continued high levels of support shown in opinion polls. Added to the movement's woes was its continued inability to prevent the arms control community from moving the issue entirely onto technical grounds, where ordinary citizens and even presumably sophisticated journalists could not discern the hidden political implications of ostensibly technical arguments.

The *NYT* headlined its story on START, "Reagan Asks U.S.-Soviet Cut of 1 in 3 Nuclear Warheads as Step to an 'Equal Ceiling'" (*NYT*, 10 May 1982: 1). Although the report noted that the Eureka proposal would be more costly for the Soviet Union because of its greater dependence on land-based missiles, the thrust of an accompanying analysis characterized Reagan's remarks as firm but conciliatory and the proposal as "sharply reducing each side's strategic arsenals." In fact, START would have applied unequal cuts to the disadvantage of the Soviet Union, which would have been required to cut about half of its intercontinental ballistic missile (ICBM) warheads and two-thirds of its SS-18 and SS-19 warheads even as it permitted a U.S. increase in ICBM warheads and left off the table its plans for deploying 200 MX missiles and modernizing all other U.S. strategic forces. Raymond Garthoff, Soviet scholar and a member of the diplomatic team that negotiated the Strategic Arms Limitation Talks I treaty (SALT I), summarized the net effect of the Eureka proposal for the Soviets:

> Overall, while the proposal would have alleviated the vulnerability of American land-based intercontinental missiles, it would have greatly *increased* the vulnerability of Soviet land-based missiles. As a Soviet general remarked to me in 1983, "You [the United States] want to solve your vulnerability problem by making our forces vulnerable." And he was right. (Garthoff 1985: 1025–1026)

Quoted as "disappointed," Senator Edward Kennedy accused President Reagan of hiding his intent to build a new generation of weapons. Because neither the reporter nor someone from the arms control community offered supporting evidence (which presumably would have exposed the one-sidedness of the proposal), Kennedy's rebuttal, though correct, appeared as partisan and thereby suspect.

The next day a more sobering front-page analysis by Leslie Gelb asserted that the Eureka proposal would be very hard to negotiate. The problem was that the Soviets would be asked to trade their current advantage in land-based missiles for an American concession later (not building the MX and Trident II). Gelb's analysis traced the outlines of the difficult position for the Soviets, who would have been expected to eliminate twice as many missiles as the Americans. A second phase would deal with the issue of equalizing throw-weight, a concession intended to "mollify" Secretary of Defense Caspar Weinberger. Other problems centered on the cruise missiles (how to verify which were nuclear), ways of counting them (how many warheads they carried as against what the Central Intelligence Agency [CIA] believed they could), and the overall issue of inspection. Gelb gave the last word to Robert McFarlane, who said, "everything is on the table and Moscow's leaders have to make some tough choices and so do we" (*NYT*, 11 May 1982: 1). The impression one got from these two analyses is that although the START proposal seemed tough, it was a proposal nonetheless and welcome for that reason. Gelb's analysis came closest to discerning the nonstarter nature of START but stopped somewhat short of that conclusion.

In fact, hardly anyone on the *NYT* editorial staff seemed capable of making sense of the varieties of weapons on both sides and their varying offsetting qualities to discern the hidden implications of the proposal. An editorial following the speech praised Reagan's rhetoric in favor of restraining the arms race while chiding Senator Edmund Muskie for "missing the mark" with his accusations that the proposal was a secret agenda for sidetracking disarmament (*NYT*, 11 May 1982: A18).[4] Anthony Lewis similarly praised Reagan's change in rhetoric and his "realism" in forgoing arms control until a military buildup was in place (*NYT*, 13 May 1982: A27). Flora Lewis commended Reagan for his change of heart and credited the debate in the House and the nation for producing it, though she recommended the debate avoid the "details," leaving these to the negotiators (*NYT*, 13 May 1982: A27). Tom Wicker saw the proposal as the "death knell" for the MX, assuming it was to be used as a bargaining chip to induce the Russians to dismantle their land-based missiles (*NYT*, 14 May 1982: A31). William Safire was the only one on staff who detected the win-win position of the White House—the proposal reduced the immediate political pressure while administration hard-liners hoped for a Soviet rejection so that they might achieve their aim of strengthening the U.S. position before returning to the negotiating table (*NYT*, 14 May 1982: A31).

Unlike the *NYT*'s labored and opaque analysis of the Eureka proposal, television analysis of the speech came to a comparatively sharp focus. CBS reported that Reagan's Eureka proposal to give up on SALT and begin START was a phased reduction plan to reduce ballistic warheads to equal levels. "Officials" acknowledged that the Soviet Union was being asked to give up more of its present strength than the United States but that there was something in it for both sides, "and if it seems tough, remember that it is a negotiating position." The Democrats responded through Edmund Muskie, who pointed out that the president had proposed reduction of a class of weapons on which the Soviets were most dependent, that the United States was being asked to give up less from its balanced triad, and that the proposal was a secret agenda for sidetracking disarmament while the United States got on with rearmament in a "hopeless" quest for superiority (*CBS Evening News*, 9 May 1982).

This first clear statement of the hidden purpose of the Reagan proposal (albeit delivered by a partisan critic) contrasted sharply with the Leslie Gelb piece in which only the most carefully trained or highly motivated could discern the political intent of the START proposal. Doing so required making sense of the varieties of warheads and delivery vehicles on each side, the different counting systems used to make the estimates, and of the significance of the land-based missile system to the Soviet Union. The superficial thrust of Gelb's analysis was that negotiations would be "difficult"; the deeper message was that only experts could make sense of it. In the CBS report, the message needed to be simple because the structure of television news limits the time to develop a story. In this case, simplicity provided a clearer statement of the truth.

Despite the difference in reporting styles, the administration's START proposal marked a change in both media sources' coverage of the movement. The first sign of this was their reinterpretation of public support for it.

Public Opinion and Expert Support

Indications that the START proposal had altered the *NYT*'s coverage of the movement came on 16 May 1982. A front-page analysis of increasing citizen activism (in reaction to Reagan cutbacks in social programs) included this passing comment on the significance of the freeze: "Political analysts generally agree that President Reagan's recent decision to negotiate on arms reductions with the Soviet Union without preconditions resulted in large part from the political strength exhibited by the antinuclear movement" (*NYT*, 16 May 1982: 1). The movement had, in other words, already passed the test set out a month earlier by the arms controllers, rendering its proposal an impediment to responsible arms control.

As evidence of this, an important poll appeared in a front-page story two weeks later in which public opinion showed overwhelming but now *qualified* support for the freeze. Headlined "72% in Poll Back Nuclear Halt If Soviet Union Doesn't Gain," the front-page story reported that the success of the freeze movement would depend on whose version of Soviet strength the public believed. Based on this, a White House official said that "this issue is very much up for grabs" (*NYT*, 30 May 1982: 1). Yet comparative Soviet strength was not a material issue for the freeze campaign, nor for public opinion reported a month earlier. Then, before the administration had proposed START, Hedrick Smith interpreted public opinion as favoring arms control *despite* the ostensible arms lead by the Soviets. Now the *NYT* interpreted public opinion as favoring the freeze *only* if the Soviets did not gain by it, an oblique reference to the window of vulnerability and an indication of the success enjoyed by the Reagan strategy of importing its dubious assumptions into public discourse.

Ten days before reporting the same poll, CBS broadcast an unusual analysis of the Reagan administration's case against the freeze. Unusual for its use of a news anchor—Dan Rather—the analysis was supported by selected facts and figures and expertise offered by Herman Kahn, senior fellow at the Hudson Institute, a conservative think tank.[5] Rather began by explaining the theory of the window of vulnerability that underlay the Reagan case for a large increase in the military budget. An animated scenario showed missiles arcing from their launch pads in the Soviet Union into U.S. missile silos, a "nuclear age Pearl Harbor."

RATHER: Many experts believe the Soviets have built up enough advantages to pull off such a crippling first strike.
KAHN: They have significant kinds of advantages, not enough to make me lose sleep at night, but if one is president, it would be totally irresponsible to depend on Soviet caution and prudence.

The answer to the threat was to counter with a massive military buildup: MX, B-1 bomber, Trident II, cruise, Pershing II.

Rather asked Kahn whether the United States really needed to build the weapons or whether the threat to build them could be used as a bargaining chip.

KAHN: I think that's a weak argument. Russians won't let you trade programs for dismantling.
RATHER: That means that we have to put muscle behind our words, the total estimated price tag—more than seventy-five billion dollars. Can we afford them?
KAHN: If we feel that our lives are being threatened sufficiently, we can rearrange our expenses.
RATHER: If we freeze now, there is no way to catch up, no way to ease the nightmare of a Russian first strike. If we keep nuclear weapons at the present level, there is no incentive for either side to negotiate reductions. (*CBS Evening News*, 20 May 1982)

This was the best possible case against the freeze, a case complete with the smuggled assumptions of the fallacious window of vulnerability, unopposed by other experts and made by the most credible news sources, a television commentator and an expert (see Page, Shapiro, and Dempsey 1987).

Less than two weeks later, CBS ran a story on the same poll reported in the *NYT* (*CBS Evening News,* 29 May 1982). Just a few months earlier, CBS commentators had reported a groundswell of support for the freeze, but now Bruce Morton revealed that a poll showed "very wide but very shallow" support for the freeze. Although 72 percent approved the measure, the numbers changed as soon as qualifications were added. For example, if the freeze gave the Russians greater strength, support for the freeze dropped to 30 percent. Similarly, support dropped to 17 percent if either the United States or the Soviets could cheat on it. On the question of whether a buildup or freeze was more dangerous, 49 percent thought a buildup more dangerous. Morton concluded that "the public doesn't seem to know much about the issue." Only 30 percent knew Reagan's position, and 59 percent believed it too complicated for ordinary citizens to understand.

This confusing analysis of public opinion embodied a number of contradictions and indications that the Reagan plan to obfuscate the administration's true arms control strategy appeared to be working. The first point—that support dropped if the Russians had an advantage—depended on assumptions that the media had not subjected to scrutiny. On this point, Muskie and Kennedy had been the only ones to clarify the significance of the START proposal as cutting into the muscle of the Soviet strategic forces and thus its role as a smokescreen for obstructing arms control. Their assertions, however, could have been construed as partisan, for they represented conventional political opposition rather than disinterested expertise. A month earlier the briefing detailing the Russian war footing had prepared the ground for these poll results by raising the salience of Soviet gains. The Rather/Kahn report provided presumably disinterested expert support for the window of vulnerability. That support for the freeze remained shallow was in large part due to an absence of information and to highly partisan viewpoints argued under the guise of "expert analysis." Thus it was not at all unreasonable for the public to feel the issue was too complex to understand; in point of fact the public had insufficient information to develop an informed opinion for or against the measure. Indeed, even the highly informed editorial staff at *NYT* could scarcely understand the implications of an arms control proposal characterized by the secretary of defense as "a nonnegotiable package . . . a two-faced proposal which was clearly going to fall of its own weight and did" (cited in Garthoff 1985: 1025). Only a handful of administration figures and the arms control community understood its implications. Despite all this, the public still supported negotiations over an arms buildup, notwithstanding the administration public relations campaign. The movement's expertise was absent in this critical period, leaving the field open to administration spin doctors and arms control experts. With expert analysis absent from its foundation of support for what was largely a technical issue, the movement became politically vulnerable. Evidence for this comes from news coverage of the New York City freeze demonstration, the largest political gathering in U.S. history.

The New York City Demonstration

On the surface *NYT* coverage of the New York City demonstration in June 1982 seems impressive (nearly four times the coverage of a major story). But only a small fraction of this coverage, about 15 percent, focused on the central political message voiced by the speakers at the rally. The remainder, including the front-page story, described the logistics of moving a crowd that size and compared the participants to those at comparable rallies in the 1960s. The focus on logistics and portrayal of the participants separated the demonstration from its political purpose, illustrating an antipolitical framing judgment and paralleling Gitlin's (1980) findings on media portrayal of the movement against the war in Vietnam.

A short, boxed story that summarized the results of the poll reported two weeks earlier accompanied the spread of pictures and articles. This reasserted the finding that although the public favored the freeze, its support hinged upon the Soviets not gaining by it: "The survey found the public greatly concerned about giving the Soviet Union a military advantage and easily swayed in favor of or against a freeze depending on the conditions surrounding it" (*NYT*, 13 June 1982: 43). Since there was little in the way of a rebuttal to the smuggled assumptions in the START proposal, the public remained ill-equipped factually to judge which side was ahead.

CBS covered the New York City demonstration in much the same way: "The largest anti-nuclear protest in U.S. history included famous rock stars, politicians, and hundreds of thousands of lesser lights." Bruce Morton's report began on a familiar note: "Children led them, puppets followed," and described the crowd as mostly Americans, mostly in their twenties and thirties, mostly white, and including many veterans of the antiwar movement of the 1960s. The piece used a familiar formula, focusing on the release of balloons (symbols of the weapons "they want to get rid of") and a sunny, placid mood.

After proclaiming the rally a big success, Morton said the question was where they were to go from here. Two nonsubstantive soundbites from a speech by Randall Forsberg followed: "Until the arms race ends, until we have real peace with real justice, we will not go home and be quiet; we will go home and organize. Stop the arms race, Reagan; if you don't we will remember in November." Morton noted that the president did not support the freeze, "so the question is, will the freeze which has grown quickly be able to move from rallies to the tough politics necessary to change his mind." His report ended with a song from the stage.

By now the media had shifted their view of the movement from a spontaneous impulse by the American public as a whole to a now-directionless organization populated largely by veterans of the 1960s. Denied the opportunity to defend the merits of its proposal and thus to strengthen the basis of its support in public opinion, the movement lay open to the vagaries of political opportunism in Congress.

Congress

Media coverage of the congressional debate and the midterm election provide further evidence of the movement's enfeeblement. In early August 1982 the House rejected the Kennedy-Hatfield resolution by a two-vote margin. Once again, the *NYT* indicated that the line of division paralleled the question of current strategic arms advantages; whether one supported the freeze depended on whose version of the truth one believed. In an accompanying news analysis, both sides laid claim to victory. Freeze supporters said that Reagan had to spend valuable political capital defending his position and the movement—now bent on direct political action—had developed a "hit list" of the 204 representatives who had voted against the measure and were vulnerable to strong opponents. The last word in the unresolved "meaning" of the vote went to a State Department official who commented that a vote for the measure was equivalent to a vote for apple pie and motherhood: "All of these guys are up for re-election in November, and they could have considered a vote for a nuclear freeze a safe political bet" (*NYT*, 7 August 1982: 2).[6] To convert the freeze movement into a mushy preference for peace stripped the public (and the movement) of its influence.

Two months later an article on the significance of the issue for Senate and House races revealed that few would be determined by the incumbent's position on the freeze (*NYT*, 19 October 1982: 18). Because the movement permitted opponents to focus attention on the technical issue of military balance, public opinion continued its susceptibility to differing interpretations (the article repeated the May poll results). Straining to maintain a nonpartisan image, the movement had made another strategic error by failing to endorse Democratic candidates. This, coupled to Republican support of movement offshoots such as Ground Zero, had so thoroughly clouded the issue that movement leaders had no power to discern supporters from opponents.

Media coverage dropped off following the New York demonstration, despite the movement's success at the polls in state-sponsored freeze referenda. Although the measures won majority support in all but one state where they were on the ballot and in numerous cities, a front-page *NYT* analysis by Adam Clymer on the "lessons" of the election characterized the freeze victories as indicating a "widespread concern on the arms control issue that stands a reasonable chance of becoming an important part of the 1984 Presidential campaign. With only a couple of exceptions, however, neither this nor any other issue of foreign or military policy mattered in electing candidates in 1982" (*NYT*, 4 November 1982: 1).

Television news traced the freeze referenda through statewide fall elections. In mid-September a story appeared on the Wisconsin primary, the first such referendum on the nuclear freeze. Once again, children played a prominent role in the coverage. Over an image of several boys swinging languidly from a tree, a reporter asked, "To freeze or not to freeze," to which a boy of about ten responded, "Nobody wins if you drop a bomb on one side, they're just going to come back and drop one on your side." The increasing prominence of children in these reports as movement spokespersons suggested a linkage with naiveté and symbolic politics. Its principal ideas overtaken and claimed by others, the movement had devolved into a child's innocence, its principal motivation fear.

Although television had earlier established the November elections as an important test of the freeze, coverage of its successes was modest. The anchor took twenty seconds in the middle of a newscast to mention that the freeze movement had made a successful transition from the streets to the polls: it had scored a "near clean sweep" in eight of nine states, with only Arizona turning it down (*CBS Evening News,* 2–3 November 1982). The brief mention indicated television news no longer considered the movement a noteworthy political force, despite its having achieved the criterion of success set out for it earlier.

In summary, the freeze movement achieved its greatest prominence just as the Reagan administration offered its START proposal. Despite the proposal's one-sidedness and its intent to derail the freeze movement, the *NYT* found much to like about it.[7] START signaled that the movement had done its job of stimulating an arms control proposal. Less than three months elapsed between media characterizations of the movement as earnest, serious, and high-minded and descriptions of the freeze as enfeebled and politically irrelevant.

Television coverage of the freeze changed character as well, exaggerating the shift found in the *NYT* coverage. CBS provided some criticism of START by airing Muskie's remarks on START as a way of sidetracking disarmament, but the report also highlighted the partisan quality of his analysis. Much more significant was the one-sided, cartoonish depiction of the Soviet threat delivered by a narrowly partisan expert source, a longtime proponent of the war-fighting view of arms control who was not identified as such and thus enjoyed the prestige of nonpartisan expertise. Significantly, the news anchor himself presented the administration's case for the "window of vulnerability" as if it were established fact and not a contested theory. Two weeks later the media interpreted the results of the *CBS/NYT* poll through the assumptive framework of the window of vulnerability. Coverage of the New York demonstration extended the frame established early on, of the festivities surrounding the events and not the central message of the movement. Meanwhile the images of the participants as "mainstream and white" converted an apparent asset (large numbers) into a liability (skewed demographics).

The Freeze and the MX (January 1983–September 1983)

During this period the movement's loss of control over its political message proved fatal as a faltering economy and, perhaps more serious, a loss of moral authority undermined its influence. Had its leadership been more politically astute, the movement might have been in a better position to take advantage of the situation presented in late winter of 1983. By then the Geneva talks had stalled, and public support for the arms buildup began to decline.

For example, in February 1983 the *NYT* reported a poll on defense spending that showed a growing number of Americans no longer feared that the United States lagged behind the Soviet Union in military prowess. Only 11 percent said that more money should be spent on new weapons; a quarter said spending levels were about right, and half believed the United States spent too much. Despite the failure of the Congress to approve the MX or other new weapons systems, the public believed the military standing of the United States had improved vis-à-vis the Soviet Union. While one year earlier 44 percent believed the United States trailed the Soviet Union, now less than a third believed U.S. forces to be inferior. The *NYT* did not attribute this to the efforts of the freeze movement but to the recessionary state of the economy, dragged down by federal deficits and high unemployment (*NYT,* 6 February 1983: 1).

Both the administration and the freeze needed a public relations boost. In fact, the day following the poll results, a story in the *NYT* described the leaders of the freeze movement plotting a "more political approach." The movement's waning influence could be discerned by the positioning of the story on an interior page and by the opinion of "many political analysts" that the movement had peaked despite its success in the November referenda.

Now defending itself from charges by opposing groups that the campaign favored a unilateral approach, the movement divided on competing objectives and faced a "deep dilemma" about the deployment of the new Pershing II and cruise missiles in Europe—whether to offer bilateral proposals or simply to stop deployment of the U.S. missiles (*NYT,* 7 February

1983: 6). Here the *NYT* characterized discussion among freeze organizers as internal division and weakness and provided indirect corroboration of the unilateralism charged by its opponents. Yet the administration itself continued to be deeply divided on its approach to arms control negotiation. The *NYT* characterized the essentially obstructionist proposal of START, itself the result of the deep division, as conciliatory while deriding the freeze as a simplistic slogan.

Meanwhile, CBS coverage highlighted the freeze coalition's weakening political influence. For example, Bruce Morton began a report on a movement conference with a visual of a folksinger strumming on a guitar and the comment that "on the surface the movement had lots to sing about"; yet, as Forsberg admitted, there had been no slackening in the production of nuclear weapons. There followed another balanced account of familiar arguments for and against the freeze. Now, however, Morton identified another weakness—the movement was made up of largely white, middle-class people, the result of its failing to reach out to Hispanics or blacks. Moreover, it had little labor support (Morton did not mention that Lane Kirkland, president of the AFL-CIO, had been a member of the Committee on the Present Danger). Morton characterized the November referenda as "beauty contests" that had little effect in congressional elections (*CBS Evening News,* 7 February 1983).

Such was the weakened position of the movement that the *NYT* described House passage of the freeze resolution in May 1983 not as a movement success but as a symbol. Both supporters and opponents claimed victory, and the amended version of the resolution had captured the essence of the Reagan position—reductions of weapons first before imposition of a ceiling. Republican House majority leader Robert Michel, for example, termed adoption of the amendment "a victory unthinkable only weeks ago." Tip O'Neill also claimed victory, saying the freeze nevertheless remained a first priority. Regardless, the freeze faced an uncertain future. Republicans dominated the Senate and held the White House: "'If it ever gets to the President's desk, it's going to be vetoed,' said Representative William Carney, Republican of Suffolk, L.I." (*NYT,* 5 May 1983: 1). With its political power diminished by the media's shifting criteria of success, the movement's moral efficacy came under attack next.

Moral Authority and Self-Interest

In May 1983 the Catholic bishops issued a pastoral letter that denounced the use of nuclear weapons and endorsed the freeze.[8] Its political significance rested on the fact that the language of the letter closely paralleled the text of the freeze resolution before Congress and that the bishops disseminated the missive in every parish in the country. Although the letter did not have the moral authority of church doctrine, it had the potential nevertheless to influence the views of roughly a quarter of the nation's population. Contemplating potential erosion in support of a military buildup, various administration officials lobbied the bishops to moderate the language of the letter, for example, by changing the language of one sentence from "halting" the development of weapons to "curbing" development. The bishops declared they were not politicians but pastors and retained the original language. The *NYT* provided prominent and essentially friendly coverage of the bishops' letter on two front-page stories. The *NYT* quoted large portions of the declaration, accompanying it with this comment:

> The bishops take a forceful and historic position in their letter, breaking some new ground in church thinking and assuming a leadership role in the effort for disarmament. Many of the 50 million Catholics in the United States consider the bishops' action to be the boldest and most decisive step on social issues in the history of the American hierarchy. It caused the White House great concern and efforts were made to modify drafts. (*NYT*, 4 May 1983: 1)

A week later a front-page article charted the reactions of Catholics to the bishops' letter (*NYT*, 9 May 1983: 1). Far from a random sampling of Catholics from across the country, the *NYT* reporter had gone to talk with a dozen members of a single parish in Preston, Connecticut, home to Electric Boat's facility for manufacturing nuclear submarines. Some of these parishioners worked in the boatyard and were understandably divided on the issue. An engineer raised the issue of Soviet atheism: "I don't think they care what God's words are. They've got to listen to something that's meaningful to them—our deterrent force." Another said that the stigma of working for the movement had been removed. On the larger point of whether it was a mortal sin to work on the Trident, the local bishop said that the pastoral letter didn't say that. It was a matter of conscience.

Questioning the moral force of the freeze in this context was somewhat like testing the moral force of a church prohibition against theft by asking a group of starving people whether they would steal bread to feed their hungry children. The *NYT* had not applied such a test to House members who had first voted for the freeze and then the MX and had not judged the quality of elected officials' work based on the consistency of their actions.

The *NYT* took a similar tack a week later in a more secular setting. An article detailing the "wooing" of the nuclear fleet into northeastern ports— in which there was considerable blue-collar unemployment—pointed out that several House members who had voted for the freeze resolution were now lobbying the Defense Department for the fleet, even though it would be carrying nuclear-tipped cruise missiles, the most destabilizing element in the U.S. strategic forces. The story highlighted the opportunism and duplicity of local officials:

> Alan Sagner, chairman of the Port Authority, is also general chairman of the New Jersey Campaign for a Nuclear Weapons Freeze; last November, a nuclear freeze referendum in New Jersey carried the state by 66 percent. "I don't see any inconsistency as chairman of the Port Authority in doing everything we possibly can to get the fleet home-ported here and our efforts for a nuclear freeze. If there's a nuclear exchange, they're not going to go for three or four battleships in New York or Boston. Anything that we can do to reverse the trend, to start building the port back up, is very important from an economic point of view and from a symbolic point of view. It feeds on itself." (*NYT*, 14 May 1983: 1)

Television news questioned the moral integrity of the Catholic bishops from the start of their campaign. In a story aired on 8 April 1982—at the height of movement influence—Bruce Morton led with the question, "Are priests becoming too political?" He contrasted Cold War support offered by Cardinal Fulton Sheen a generation earlier ("nuclear war may be justified") with several contemporary bishops who recommended against working in nuclear factories and in favor of withholding tax payments. About a fifth of the nation's bishops were said to support some form of the freeze. Morton then asked, "Is the church being radicalized?" The report went on to quote a reporter for a Catholic newspaper who mentioned that the church had taken on a much broader range of social issues, including civil rights and right-wing rule in El Salvador. But Morton detected confusion among Catholics perplexed by the ideological inconsistency of the church's rigidity on celibacy and the role of women. Morton ended the report with the statement that 50 million Catholics united would be a powerful force. But how many would follow? (*CBS Evening News*, 8 April 1983). Like the *NYT*, television news held nonpoliticians to a higher standard of ideological consistency.

A subtle but perhaps more serious undermining of moral authority threaded through television coverage of the movement's apparent success in Congress. In March 1983, CBS reported a House committee vote in support of the freeze, in spite of lobbying efforts by the administration. The report began with a visual of a group of cheering freeze supporters standing on the Capitol steps and then followed a lobbying effort on an undecided representative from Connecticut. Once again a child figured prominently in the coverage, with a young girl urging a Republican representative to vote for the resolution. The theme of feckless naiveté carried through the report as Morton noted that even if the House passed the measure, it wouldn't matter because Reagan opposed it. "But this is really just a game. The freeze is a symbol. The genuine issue will come in votes on individual weapons. And the opposition there is not a rally. It is the defense lobbyists who last year gave six and a half million dollars to Congressional candidates, a tactic the freeze movement did not employ."

Replacing success at the polls as a criterion of strength was the amount of money one could spend. To illustrate his point, Morton presented a chart showing that over $1.1 million in political action committee (PAC) money had been provided by defense contractors to members of the House Armed Services Committee and Defense Appropriations Subcommittee. Gordon Adams, a (leftist) specialist and author on congressional defense politics, said the movement was out of its league in what he called the "iron triangle" of defense companies, key members of Congress, and Defense Department offices. The report then cut to the freeze rally with guitar-strumming singers on the Capitol steps. Morton observed that the movement against the Vietnam War showed that civilian amateurs could make a difference: "Of course, it also showed that it can take a long time as well" (*CBS Evening News,* 8 March 1983).

Television news reflected the change in the rules of the game. Once it considered the referenda important; now the movement needed to buy influence. But there was an interesting complication in that the news provided a view of the powerful defense PAC network that (apparently) bought the votes of key House and Senate committee members. Moreover, use of the right-wing expert Herman Kahn (presented as a disinterested expert) was now balanced by the use of Gordon Adams, whose unidentified politics came from the other direction. Television had illuminated the corners of political life, but in a way it normalized them by failing to react with any surprise, let alone outrage.

The Movement Fades

The movement suffered a major loss of public support for arms control on 1 September 1983, when a Soviet fighter shot down Korean Air Lines flight 007. A Gallup Poll conducted in mid-September showed that half the public thought that Reagan was "not tough enough" in his dealings with the Soviet Union, a rise of 16 percent from a poll conducted only a month earlier. Moreover, the percentage feeling that too much was being spent on defense fell from 42 to 37, while those feeling too little was being spent increased from 14 to 21 percent. Finally, the negative reaction to the Soviet Union—heavily promoted by Reagan (Sherry 1995)—lowered Americans' estimation of the country to a point not seen since the 1950s (Gallup 1984: 219, 224, 227).

The Reagan administration made the most of this change in political atmosphere as it successfully lobbied for a House vote to end a fifteen-year moratorium on the production of chemical weapons and for approval of the largest military budget ever passed. Attempts by the Democrats to delete $2 billion in production funds for the MX were unsuccessful. As the window of opportunity closed for the freeze, it opened for an arms buildup.

That December CBS covered a conference at the headquarters of the national freeze campaign. Bruce Morton reported on plans for a new campaign and opened with the lead that the delegates had some things to "shout about," such as the Vermont town meetings and state referenda, the big rally in New York, and the House vote for the freeze. But on the negative side, the House had approved the MX, and freeze constituents continued to be overwhelmingly white and white collar. In a brief soundbite, Randy Kehler indicated he wanted to broaden the campaign and to focus on PAC money. But, Morton reminded the audience, the 1984 Congress would be the same one that voted in the MX. Moreover, freeze supporters would be outspent. In 1984 four profreeze PACs gave candidates $140,000, whereas a single defense contractor gave $200,000. To compensate, the freeze would mobilize people: they wanted a million volunteers for the coming election campaign. So far they had been amateurs; could they now be effective pros? The report ended with an image of a mother and child, the visual cue that once again emphasized innocence and naiveté (*CBS Evening News,* 3 December 1983).

In its last phase of movement coverage, television news returned to a familiar theme, the contest that this time pitted the movement against Congress. Accordingly, stories described the underfinanced and underorganized movement going up against rich and powerful defense industry PACs. Although this could have plausibly provided the raw material needed for constructing a sympathetic account of the "little guy" against established interests, the stories focused instead on the movement's artlessness and lack of means. The moral resources for the movement already having been preempted by implicit questioning of the Catholic bishops' right to endorse the freeze, the movement was now left to its meager political and financial resources. These were caricatured by stories that spent an inordinate amount of time on images of children. Although sympathetic, they nevertheless called attention to the ingenuousness and powerlessness of the movement rather than to the substance of its proposal and to its implications for arms control.

The following year, Ronald Reagan's landslide reelection applied the coup de grâce to the movement. Forsberg had targeted Reagan's campaign as a test of the movement's political leverage. His victory so disappointed and discouraged movement volunteers that they lost the drive to carry on (Hogan 1994: 185).

Conclusion

The media window of opportunity for the movement opened to its widest point during the first several months of the campaign in spring 1982, during the height of bureaucratic infighting within the Reagan administration (see Jeffrey W. Knopf, Chapter 7, this volume). Both media sources analyzed in this chapter transmitted movement messages without qualification on either technical or political grounds during this period. The absence of an arms control position by the administration provided the movement with an opportunity it never fully grasped, either to articulate the substance of the administration's proposal or to challenge its claim for the "window of vulnerability." The movement also failed to capitalize on the Scowcroft Commission's report, whose recommendations on means of basing the MX missiles undermined the original rationale for building the weapons. By that time, Reagan had revealed his plan for a missile shield—the Strategic Defense Initiative (SDI), or "Star Wars"—that undercut the movement's sole remaining potential support, the moral ground (Bjork 1989).

Coverage in the *NYT* and on *CBS Evening News* showed some interesting similarities and unusual differences. Television and newspaper alike noted "citizen concern," rather than the freeze organization itself, as driving the movement. Because the movement lacked prominent leadership, the *NYT* reduced the freeze to a slogan that permitted both Democrats and Republicans to support it as an apple pie issue that risked no disapproval from voters or (apparently) the defense industry PACs. The absence of such leadership also permitted the *NYT* to convert the freeze into a generalized desire for arms control. Thus the arms control community became a sounding board for judging the freeze's value, and even the flawed START proposal was seen as responsive to concerns articulated in the freeze movement (*NYT*, 24 April 1982: 8). Far from having a nonpartisan position, this community viewed the freeze as leverage on an administration that had replaced moderate arms controllers with members of the Committee on the Present Danger. The arms controllers' fears of the freeze being too partisan may have been a veiled fear of its being effective enough to threaten their self-interest. Some support for this interpretation comes from Albert Carnesale, then dean of the Kennedy School of Government at Harvard and former SALT I negotiator:

> The arms controllers who have been working on all of this complicated stuff were afraid that they might ultimately lose support for arms control rather than gain it. Now, there isn't a lot of support for arms control—it's never had a huge consistency—and the freeze movement was at first viewed as a godsend. But then there grew this fear that it might pass right by, and suddenly [there was] this big political movement for this

unachievable nirvana. And when it's not achieved nobody will want to bother with this boring complicated stuff. Their motives were understandable; they were trying to build political support to get something done, and the more complicated you make things the more people fall off the edges. . . . [But] the arms controllers felt that the freeze people were overselling the proposal, that if you put all those words together you can't get from here to there—or it's going to take a long, long time, and it's still not going to be comprehensive. (quoted in Leavitt 1983: 7)

A year after these comments, Carnesale and a group called the Harvard Nuclear Study Group published a report titled "Living with Nuclear Weapons," in which they characterized both the freeze and Reagan's calls for a military buildup as "atomic escapism." They recommended the familiar incrementalism of traditional arms control as the most reasonable alternative. The report recommended specifically that the United States work harder in certain areas of arms control while also developing the Stealth, air-launched cruise missiles, and the single-warhead Midgetman to replace the larger Minuteman. The group could not come to agreement on the desirability of MX (see *Time*, 30 May 1983: 16). Their claim to the "middle ground" of the debate was their raison d'être, which the *NYT* defined as expert and thus beyond the pale of political discourse. It was, of course, no less a political position than any other.

The *NYT* and CBS were similar in their portrayal of movement-related activities with apolitical themes of festivals and whimsy. Both sources focused on the color of movement events rather than their underlying political themes and the significance of the numbers at the New York City demonstration. Because images so dominate television coverage, portraits of the freeze supporters defined the scope of the movement's influence. As we saw, these reports focused predominantly on children and what children do. Taking this theme to its logical extreme led Bruce Morton and his camera crew to record the protestations of a girl to a nonplussed Republican House member undecided on the merits of the freeze resolution. Although the "child bites adult" story may have been appealing for its novelty, it was a measure of television's absence of interest in the substance of the issue. Morton finally defined the freeze as "only a symbol."

On this issue, CBS and *NYT* coverage also agreed, but for different reasons. The *NYT* relied on the arms controllers as its reference group for judging the merits and meaning of the freeze. Television coverage focused more on the legislative process where (perhaps inadvertently) it limned the influence of the defense industry. Where the *NYT* delegitimized the movement on the grounds of expertise, television news judged it deficient in its ability to raise sufficiently large amounts of money to compete with PACs. The reporting lacked moral bite, however, because the coverage accepted the system of PAC influence as a simple fact rather than judging it as a cancer on the practice of democracy. To be fair, the reporter gave no indication of countenancing the system. In fact, the reports made plain the connection between PAC money and the election of representatives favorably disposed to voting for weapons systems developed by their benefactors. The reporter left it to the viewer to judge whether this was ethically sound and an appropriate way to elect representatives. In any case, the movement failed to take advantage of the moral high ground implicitly offered by the reporting, perhaps because the freeze proposal beat with a mechanical, technical heart.

Where the *NYT* used the expertise of its columnists (Hedrick Smith, Leslie Gelb) and the arms controllers to gauge the influence of the movement, the credibility of the administration's position on Soviet arms strength, and the merits of START to render an ambiguous judgment, CBS used partisan experts. In one instance, Herman Kahn and the anchor bolstered the administration's case against the movement, with both presenting the argument as fact rather than as a contested theory. No such case was presented for the freeze, nor was Randall Forsberg consulted to offer a counterargument.

Balancing the narrowly partisan case for the administration was the revealing analysis of the influence of the "iron triangle" offered by a partisan expert from the left. The failure to identify him as such provided the report with greater credibility than it might otherwise have had. In this respect, the seemingly blind reliance on expert judgment without regard to underlying political preferences was fair to the extent that it was truly random. By contrast, the *NYT* used public opinion to support its framings. Because public opinion was sufficiently ambiguous on the issue of movement support, especially with reference to the "window of vulnerability," the statistics served both sides of the argument. CBS made a single reference to public opinion and no further references to these statistics in any of its subsequent reporting.

As mentioned earlier, the different structures of the organizations seemed to have an effect on the quality of their reporting. In the case of the *NYT,* its seasoned reporters and columnists were superbly positioned in executive departments to get firsthand information and interpretation from the highest sources in government. Their reporting demonstrated the strengths and weaknesses of this access; they covered the movement as an instinctive reaction to a process gone awry rather than as a substantive issue in its own right.

By contrast, the itinerant Bruce Morton followed the movement as it interacted with "ordinary citizens." His sympathy, however, was with the people and not with the issue, the substance of which he failed to explore fully except in the context of the single poll that reported shallow public support. Consequently he treated the movement as a fun activity, as a way for the 1960s generation to relive an earlier dream, this time with their children. Children, in fact, came to symbolize the humanity of the issue. Morton could not help but see the issue as a symbol because he never addressed its substance, and his knowledge of the inside politics of Washington put him in the role of a wise old uncle patiently advising the movement on the extreme difficulty of its task in negotiating the back halls of Washington power politics. Although creditable, his attitude was also patronizing and morally debilitating—especially when one considers journalism's self-proclaimed role for rejuvenating democracy that has been subverted by narrow interests.

Notes

1. Popular culture offers its own compelling examples as well: *Fail-Safe* and its satirical cousin *Dr. Strangelove* were among the most popular movies during the tensest periods of the Cold War.

2. For press coverage, the index of visibility is derived by multiplying the reciprocal of the story's page number by the number of words and summing the story values for that month. For television coverage, the index is the number of minutes of coverage in a given month. For both sources, the final figure is expressed as a percentage of total coverage.

3. In fact, it was the Russians who thought the United States was on a war footing, taking seriously Reagan's remarks that it was possible to win a nuclear war (Talbott 1984).

4. A follow-up on 16 May praised Reagan for his "conversion," especially his decision to forgo "linkage," conditioning negotiations on Russian restraint in Afghanistan and Poland. The editorial presumed the Russians would "crow" about the effect of the freeze movement, but "few knowledgeable Americans actually favor a freeze or think it can work." It concluded that "Mr. Reagan's new approach is neither extreme nor only defensive. It deserves a solid reply" (16 May 1982: IV, 22).

5. In the 1950s and 1960s Kahn had argued for a nuclear war–winning strategy. (See *Time*, 3 January 1961: 16).

6. On the political benefits of avoiding a definitive stand on an issue, see Benjamin Page (1978: 178–179).

7. The *NYT* opposed the freeze referenda in an editorial, calling the idea a "simplistic, sloganeering response to a complex issue" (*NYT*, 24 October 1982: IV, 20).

8. The bishops continued, however, to affirm their support of the just war doctrine and supported Reagan's call for deep cuts in both nations' nuclear arsenals (Hogan 1994: 188).

7

The Nuclear Freeze Movement's Effect on Policy

JEFFREY W. KNOPF

In this chapter I examine the influence of the freeze movement on U.S. nuclear arms control policy during its peak in the first half of the 1980s. I begin by developing a framework for ascertaining the influence of citizen activism. I then use that framework to show that the freeze (1) led the Reagan administration to enter strategic arms talks and make serious efforts to achieve progress earlier than it had intended to; and (2) encouraged the administration to give greater declaratory emphasis to avoiding nuclear war and reducing nuclear weapons as goals of strategic policy.

Theoretical Framework for Assessing Influence

Existing social movement theory mostly seeks to explain the rise and nature of movements rather than their impact on policy (Rochon 1990: 300). The few studies that do focus on political impact narrowly define movement success or failure (Gamson 1975), which is inappropriate in this case. The freeze did not succeed in achieving its stated policy objectives, but this does not necessarily mean it failed to exert any influence at all. When it comes to determining whether movements like the freeze achieved some limited influence on policy, though, the social movement literature offers little guidance (Huberts 1989).

To get a clearer picture of how influence might be exerted, I turn to more general theories of American politics that deal with the actors that are the most similar to social movements. I adapt models of influence developed in studies of how public opinion and interest groups can affect policy. I have identified three processes that could provide pathways for a movement impact on arms policy: (1) mobilizing public opinion to exert electoral pressure, (2) working with sympathetic political elites to alter the amount of support for the president's policy in Congress, and (3) generating ideas that have utility for certain agencies within the executive.

I distinguish these influence mechanisms in terms of three attributes. First, I identify for each a necessary "precondition" or set of circumstances that must exist before that mechanism could be activated.[1] Second, each causal pathway involves an interaction between a citizens' campaign and some other actor and can therefore be distinguished by the other actor involved. Finally, for each pathway I specify a particular kind of policy effect that will be produced. These potential effects are defined to involve change from a policy baseline established by the incumbent presidential administration before the activist campaign took off.

If any of the three defining features of a mechanism do not arise, I conclude no influence was exerted through that pathway. If the prior conditions necessary to activate a mechanism exist, the interaction specified in that mechanism occurs, and the expected policy change develops, I take this as one piece of evidence that popular protest may have made a difference. Before concluding that the freeze movement could have exerted influence through that pathway, though, I require corroborating evidence from more traditional historical sources. The primary source is interviews I conducted with former Reagan administration officials who were involved in formulating arms policy.[2] I supplement this with evidence from decisionmakers' memoirs and contemporary media coverage. Finally, I also consider other variables that might have caused the policy change in question and evaluate whether these alternative explanations can better account for any policy changes that appear to result from advocacy group efforts.

Two Types of Policy Effect

Before describing the potential influence mechanisms, I consider the types of policy changes they might produce. Arms control policy reflects several different kinds of choices. The most obvious involve questions such as whether to accept an opponent's offer or to modify an offer of one's own. However, before these sorts of matters even come up for decision, there must first be decisions about whether to enter negotiations at all and, if so, what topics these talks should cover.

It proves most useful to divide these aspects of arms control policy into two levels, which I label the general and the specific. The general level concerns national priorities. In particular, it involves the question of whether the United States should attach greater importance to arms control or should instead deemphasize it while pursuing a buildup of nuclear arms or focusing on other policy areas altogether. The general level also includes the scope of U.S. objectives, such as whether to seek far-reaching reductions or only modest limitations on nuclear arms. In short, the general level consists of the priority arms restraint enjoys as a policy objective.

Once arms control is accepted as a goal or an inevitability, more specific questions arise. What types of weapons or activities are most important to regulate or eliminate? What should be the content of U.S. proposals that address these goals? These questions make up the specific level of policy. The general level of policy involves the place of arms control on the national agenda and the scope of the goals that are set for it. The specific level is the arms control agenda itself, in the form of the types of proposals that receive top priority and the details of those proposals.

Three Influence Mechanisms

Having distinguished two types of policy that could be influenced by activism, I now describe three possible mechanisms for exerting influence and specify which level of arms control policy each would affect. The three mechanisms reflect three more general techniques for influencing others: applying pressure by manipulating their incentives, altering their capabilities to act, and changing their minds.

Mechanism 1: Mass Electoral Pressure

One obvious potential route to influence is electoral pressure. To specify conditions under which electoral incentives could affect arms control policy, I draw on findings derived from the spatial modeling of elections. This approach represents candidates' positions and voters' preferences as points on a graph in order to investigate when and how such voter concerns will constrain party platforms. It turns out that a citizens' campaign could meet the criteria to apply electoral pressure, but only at the general level of arms control policy, not the specific level.

The key finding is the "median voter theorem." It predicts that two parties in electoral competition will converge on the position of the median voter when majority rule determines the outcome, provided that policy preferences are distributed along a single dimension (like left versus right). However, once voters' choices reflect multiple dimensions (for example, economics and civil rights), the center can be defeated by other positions. Early models even suggested it would be possible for outcomes to cycle over the entire policy space, making prediction nearly impossible (Downs 1957: 115–118; Ordeshook 1986: 160–175; Mueller 1989: chaps. 5 and 10).

The median voter and cycling results have been softened somewhat by recent research based on more realistic initial assumptions (Chappell and

Keech 1986; Ordeshook 1986: 183–187; Mueller 1989: 185–189; and relevant essays in Enelow and Hinich 1990; and Grofman 1993). However, though these findings suggest that complete convergence on the median voter may not occur, there will still be pressure to move toward the center in unidimensional situations, provided voters care about party differences. In the multidimensional case, recent studies imply that cycling will be limited to a subset of the Pareto-optimal outcomes. This means, for example, that the president could not gain electorally by moving to a position more extreme than that of any of the major actors in the system. As long as his proposals stayed within the parameters of the existing debate, there is no reason to expect that public pressure on one dimension would necessarily bring about movement on that dimension.

This can be illustrated through a concrete example. Even a cursory review of arms control debates in the United States reveals that the specific level of policy contains multiple dimensions. There were debates about the necessary level of verifiability, about whether or not numerical limits had to be strictly equal, and about whether arms control should give more emphasis to quantitative or qualitative restrictions, to name just a few.

To give an example suggested by the freeze, take a case in which there was popular concern that the president was not doing enough to slow modernization of nuclear weapons. The president could respond on that dimension, deciding to seek stricter limits on the qualitative arms race, could respond by raising verification concerns, using fear of Soviet cheating to limit his proposal to more easily monitored quantitative ceilings, or could make the issue one of equality, arguing that preventing modernization would lock in a Soviet advantage. By invoking either of these other two dimensions, the president could avoid having to alter the policy on qualitative restrictions. There are thus many different packages of trade-offs at the specific level that could achieve majority support rather than just a single median point. Presidents are therefore able to avoid being forced to move toward the specific-level proposals of their opponents.

In short, the party in office can experience pressure to move toward voters' preferred position, but only if the issue can be reduced to one dimension. The specific level of arms control policy was multidimensional in the period covered by this study, thus enabling the president to resist influence. In contrast, the general level of policy, which concerns the priority given to arms control overall, was characterized by a single dimension. During the Cold War, opinion research repeatedly found that public preferences on nuclear arms reflected a mix of two opposing core values, which analysts labeled somewhat imprecisely as peace and strength (W. Schneider 1984).[3] The two opposed poles arose because arms control policy was buffeted by two different fears, fear of the Soviet Union and fear of nuclear war (see Thomas R. Rochon and Stephen P. Wood, Chapter 2, this book). As Michael Nacht (1985: 53) puts it, "Some see nuclear weapons as protecting the United States from the Soviet threat, while others see their possession as the principal threat." These two concerns pulled in opposite directions, since one could not simultaneously build to meet the Soviet threat and disarm to address the nuclear threat. Since one could map preferences at the general level onto a line between the two extremes of pure buildup and pure restraint, opinion at this level did fall along a single dimension.

In examining the dynamics of opinion during the Cold War, Miroslav Nincic (1988: 458) finds that, "desiring both, the public will tend to reward behavior enhancing that value (either peace or strength) which appears currently most slighted in U.S. foreign policy." This characteristic of public opinion created an opening for activism to take advantage of the median voter theorem. At times, a president may not have set the balance between the goals of strength and restraint where most of the public preferred. I call this situation, when presidential policy diverges from the median public position, an "opinion disjunction."

Under these circumstances, there were likely to be advocacy groups arguing that the United States should adopt a "tougher" or a "softer" stance (depending on which way the president was out of line). As a result, many citizens may have decided to voice their concerns by giving support to the organizations that advocated this change of course. If the resulting growth of activism suggested that arms control might be an important enough issue to make a difference in electoral outcomes, the requirements of electoral competition could have forced an incumbent administration to shift its policies toward the center. The White House would have worried that the opposition party would pick up the votes of those dissatisfied with existing arms policy in the next congressional or presidential election, or that the president's approval rating would go down, lessening his or her legislative influence (Rivers and Rose 1985).

I call this situation "mechanism 1," or the "electoral pathway." The precondition for this mechanism is the emergence of a disjunction between the priority the administration gives to arms control and the median position among an electorally relevant body of public opinion. Subsequently, citizen activism must mobilize a portion of the dissatisfied public. If the intensity of resulting activism serves as a signal telling administration officials that they are out of line with middle America about how hard-line to be toward Russia and that this could matter electorally, they will have an incentive to change policy. Specifically, when a citizens' campaign activates mechanism 1, I expect that administration policy at the general level will move toward the position supported by the citizens' movement, thereby increasing or decreasing the priority given to making progress in arms control. But for the reasons described earlier, mechanism 1 will not necessarily force any particular change at the specific level.

Of course, electoral pressure does not operate only on the president. Because members of Congress have to run for office in geographic districts, even when a movement lacks the national strength to threaten a president's electoral chances it may be enough of a force in many localities to make Capitol Hill sit up and take notice. Mechanism 1 could thereby influence an administration's approach to arms control by affecting the assertiveness and policy preferences of Congress on nuclear arms issues. If, in response to public pressure, Congress threatens to (or does) vote against administration defense or arms control programs, the president would likely take steps to meet public concerns and take the pressure off Congress. When Congress is responding solely to public concerns and not disputes of its own with the president, the general-level shifts in administration policy entailed by mechanism 1 should be adequate to bring Congress back into the fold. The essence of the electoral pathway, in short, is that the president sees broad public concerns as the source of his or her problems and can, by addressing them, remove the opposition to certain policies.

Mechanism 2: Shifting Elite Coalitions

Of course, members of Congress and other political elites do not necessarily have to perceive electoral incentives before they would challenge a president's arms control policies. They might also be motivated by intellectual or ideological differences. Under these circumstances, organizations seeking a change in U.S. arms policy can play a different role than in the electoral pathway. By pooling their resources and coordinating their activities with elites who share some of their policy goals, citizens' groups can stimulate action by and enhance the capabilities of like-minded political elites.[4] Rather than exerting pressure through the manipulation of electoral incentives, advocacy groups in this second pathway become part of the dynamics of elite coalition formation.

Leverage is possible through this process because the president needs the support of a majority of Congress for certain elements of programs related to arms control policy, such as weapons' appropriations and appointments of negotiators; and of course two-thirds of the Senate must ratify a treaty. Because of this, the president will normally also be concerned about the stance of other elites who might affect congressional opinion, such as nuclear scientists. Because presidents need a winning coalition in Congress and value an elite consensus behind their policies, there is a route for activist influence even when arms control is not a major concern with most voters. Here, citizens' groups must work with political elites whose positions they prefer to the likely alternative. This process gains effectiveness if it alters the degree of support for the administration's policies in Congress or among others, such as recognized national security experts, whose support an administration regards as vital. I call this process "mechanism 2," or the "elite coalition-shift pathway." I discuss mechanism 2 as a process that works against the president, but in principle coalition building by activists could also help an administration facing Senate opposition to a treaty that both activists and the president support.

Whereas mechanism 1 is based mostly on a single finding, the median voter theorem, mechanism 2 draws on several recent developments in studies of interest groups and agenda setting. The traditional understanding of interest groups assumed a pressure logic similar to that behind mechanism 1. However, the rise of public interest groups, which lack the money to gain influence through campaign contributions, prompted a search for an alternative basis of influence. A number of studies have now coalesced around explanations that involve information and ideas (Tierney 1992: 216). These studies imply that a key function of citizens' groups may be to provide assistance to elites who are favorably disposed to their objectives, rather than pressure elected officials who are averse to or neutral toward a group's policy goals.

The body of research from which I draw the elite coalition-shift pathway is built on a path-breaking analysis by E. E. Schattschneider (1960). Schattschneider argued that a losing coalition can sometimes reverse a decision against them by broadening the scope of conflict. In a larger arena, the previous losers may now have majority support. Thus, a movement's activities might be able to alter the degree of support behind the president's policies by, for example, getting an issue moved from a committee that is unsympathetic to their concerns to the floor of Congress or by involving new actors, like churches, who do not normally comment on arms policy but carry a certain moral authority.

At times, activist organizations will actually be responsible for getting sympathetic elites to act in the first place.[5] No member of Congress can possibly be fully informed about all of the issues and policy options that the legislature might consider. Advocacy groups can therefore point out alternative interpretations of a given issue or policy that persuade members, especially those of an entrepreneurial bent, that it would be desirable to take action (R. Smith 1984; Gais, Peterson, and Walker 1984: 178; Salisbury 1990: 211; Mansbridge 1992: 32). In a recent study of agenda setting, Frank Baumgartner and Bryan Jones (1993) even argue that this process of redefining an issue is the main way Schattschneider's notion of the expansion of conflict is brought about.

Once congressional action has been triggered (regardless of whether activism is responsible), citizens' groups can also contribute to the shifting of elite coalitions by supplementing officeholders' own staff resources. Activists can provide their legislative allies with intelligence about other members of Congress and arguments they can use in congressional debate and can also serve as go-betweens to forge an alliance among elite actors who would not otherwise have worked together. In extreme cases, the fact of activism may itself be a key factor. If part of the movement involves more unruly forms of protest, this can boost the bargaining position of more moderate elements in the movement and their elite allies by enabling them to point to the danger of growing radicalism unless the administration agrees to change policy (McAdam, McCarthy, and Zald 1988: 718–719; Huberts 1989: 418).

Recent studies of relations between interest groups and Congress have found legislators thirsting for the information and assistance that interest groups can provide. Thus, by strengthening their congressional allies' ability to strategize on behalf of an arms policy initiative, advocacy groups also increase their chances of doing so successfully (Ornstein and Elder 1978: and 84–85; Schlozman and Tierney 1986: 263 ff.; Petracca 1992: 25; Baumgartner and Jones 1993: 104–109, 195). Through any of the specific steps discussed in this section, advocacy groups can increase the capabilities of legislators to pursue goals that activists support, thereby creating a possibility of altering the winning coalition on arms policy.

The necessary precondition for this coalition-shift pathway is a division among the elite. For activism to change policy, such divisions must be followed by interaction between the movement and like-minded elites. The elite-level debate involved in this process could concern either the balance between the competing goals of strength and restraint or the specific details of how to proceed in arms talks. Thus, in contrast to mechanism 1, which operates only at the general level of policy, mechanism 2 can affect either the general or the specific level. Which level of policy is affected by mechanism 2 will follow directly from which level forms the focus of debate among elites, so that it will still be possible in any given instance to anticipate where policy adjustment should occur.

Mechanism 3: Bureaucratic Use of Movement Ideas

Research on policy networks and the role of ideas suggests that movements might also gain influence, not by pressuring or changing the capabilities of political actors but by influencing their ways of thinking. This research can be adapted to the case of disarmament activism by combining it with the bureaucratic politics approach to explaining foreign policy. The latter approach is relevant in the case of arms control because a number of different bureaucratic agencies are typically involved in policy formulation.

Studies of bureaucratic politics have revealed that government agencies tend to assess policy options in terms of how they might affect the agency's ability to carry out those missions most vital to the agency's identity and future well-being (Allison 1971; Halperin 1974). Because there are differences in what the agencies involved in arms control regard as vital, there will often be differences of opinion within the executive regarding what new proposals to make or what details of existing proposals should be changed. Thus, as Steven Miller (1984a: 82) observes, "arms control proposals are usually the result of internal bargaining."

There are conditions under which domestic activism could impinge on bureaucratic politics. For example, agency officials are recruited from outside and, once in government, may retain ties to the "policy community" (Walker 1981) or "issue network" (Heclo 1978) to which they previously belonged. Thus, there may be outsiders affiliated with citizens' groups whose views and recommendations officials would still listen to even after they are inside the government.

Even if advocacy groups lack direct connections of this sort, the "garbage can model" of administrative behavior suggests there are other ways in which the perspective they develop may attract the interest of an executive branch actor. In the garbage can approach, organizations are seen as "collections of choices looking for problems," so that problems and solutions constitute separate streams of ideas that can be joined together in many different ways.[6] Part of what activist campaigns usually seek to do is make others perceive some condition as a major problem requiring government action. The garbage can approach suggests that movement success in this endeavor can open a window of opportunity for a particular agency to promote a policy it has already been working on as a solution to the newly identified problem (Kingdon 1984: 155; O'Heffernan 1991: 45 ff.). Alternatively, the proposals that movements or specialist groups advocate might serve to meet problems that already occupy policymakers or provide an ideal vehicle to advance an agency's own mission.

Whether activism points to a possible problem or a possible solution, the key step is that arguments arising from movement activism are used by officials inside the policymaking system to gain an advantage in debates with other executive actors. I call this situation "mechanism 3," or the "bureaucratic utilization pathway." The precondition necessary for mechanism 3 to operate is divisions on arms control within the administration. A movement gains influence here only when the arguments it raises then interact with the course of the bureaucratic debate. Because the solutions or problems arising from activism will be tied to agency efforts to promote particular proposals, the bureaucratic utilization pathway will affect the specific level of policy. It will cause certain objectives to move up on the administration's arms control agenda or boost one idea for how to achieve an existing goal over the alternatives.

Table 7.1 provides a summary of these three potential mechanisms for movement activism to result in policy influence. We now turn to an examination of these mechanisms in the case of the nuclear freeze.

Table 7.1   The Three Potential Influence Mechanisms

Mechanism	Necessary Precondition	What Activism Must Interact With	Source of Leverage	Level Policy Affected
Mechanism 1: Mass electoral pathway	Disjunction between administration approach to USSR and median public opinion	Expressions of mass or attentive public opinion	Electoral pressure	General
Mechanism 2: Elite coalition-shift pathway	Policy debate at elite level or absence of elite consensus	Actions of Congress or foreign policy elites	Changing the relative strength of elite coalitions	General or specific (whichever is focus of elite debate)
Mechanism 3: Bureaucratic utilization pathway	Divisions within executive branch	Goals or interests of an agency or adviser	Utilization of movement ideas by executive branch officials	Specific

How the Freeze Influenced Policy

Applying the theoretical framework just outlined reveals that the nuclear freeze movement had a significant impact at the general level, where the importance of nuclear issues on the national agenda and the balance between the goals of strength and restraint are set. This result obtained because this citizens' campaign engaged mechanism 1, a mobilization of public opinion that alters the electoral incentives of government officials. The freeze movement also activated mechanism 2, a shifting of elite coalition patterns, in a way that reinforced the influence of mechanism 1 at the general level. These pressures led the Reagan administration to respond as expected, formulating a strategic arms control plan earlier than it otherwise would have and increasing the emphasis it gave to making progress toward strategic arms reductions.

The freeze movement had only a limited impact with regard to the specific details of arms control policy. This is a result of the nature of the pathways activated by the movement. Despite some potential for its operation, mechanism 3—the bureaucratic pathway—came into play hardly at all, whereas the pressures arising through mechanism 2 were directed mostly at the general level. Lacking leverage at the specific level, the freeze never got its proposal adopted as an official objective of arms control policy. The anti–nuclear weapons movement did have some unintended effects on the specifics of the arms control agenda, however, as a by-product of the pressures exerted through the electoral and elite pathways. To show how the freeze changed policy, I begin by establishing a policy baseline for the Reagan administration.

Reagan Policy Baseline

When Ronald Reagan took office, arms control enjoyed very low priority at the general level; at the specific level the chief objectives were to force cuts in Soviet land-based warheads while allowing U.S. modernization programs to proceed. To start with the general level, the administration saw no urgency in getting arms talks underway. For one thing, the president and his advisers felt it was a mistake to try to focus on too many issues at once. They gave top priority to domestic economic issues and a major defense buildup, and according to David Gergen, White House communications director until early 1984, "deliberately deemphasized" everything else (interview by author; see also Anderson 1990: 57, 283–284; Meese 1992: 73).

With respect to arms control, this meant that a military buildup took precedence over talks. Reagan and his aides argued that the Strategic Arms Limitation Talks (SALT) negotiations of the 1970s had allowed the Soviets to gain an advantage in land-based missiles with multiple warheads. Because of the counterforce potential of such weapons, Reagan administration officials claimed that the United States was facing a "window of vulnerability" to threats of a Soviet first strike. They felt the United States would have to reverse this situation before entering new talks. In the words of Robert Linhard, senior director of arms control policy on the National Security Council (NSC), the administration "had a serious concept of negotiating from strength, which meant we had to pursue the military buildup first" (interview by author).

Moreover, according to a source familiar with Pentagon deliberations, Defense Department officials believed the United States "could outspend and out-tech" the Russians on defense and thereby force internal reform on them (interview by author). This strategy for dealing with the Soviet Union would require delaying arms talks so as not to alleviate the pressure on Moscow and was apparently shared by the president (Meese 1992: 166–167). At the extreme, therefore, some officials like Defense Secretary Caspar Weinberger suggested it might take eight years before the United States was ready to get serious about arms talks (Cortright 1993: 8). Even if not all officials shared this timeline, given the administration's top two priorities, "no one in the new administration was too keen to get [arms negotiations] under way, at least before the Reagan economic program and military buildup were begun," observed Kenneth Adelman (1989: 260), who was an assistant to Jeane Kirkpatrick at the UN at the time.

At the specific level of policy, administration objectives followed from the proposition that the United States had to remove an imbalance in counterforce capabilities favoring the Soviet Union. Administration defense planners thus felt strategic arms control should emphasize ballistic missiles, requiring greater cuts from the Soviet Union than from the United States. At the same time, they sought to avoid any restraints on such U.S. strategic modernization programs as the MX and Trident II, which would give the United States a more substantial counterforce capability of its own.

Developing an actual plan to achieve these objectives took a long time. Beyond the fact that the administration placed a military buildup ahead of arms negotiations, formulation of an arms control position also proceeded slowly because officials disagreed sharply about how to translate Reagan's specific-level objectives into an actual U.S. offer. Reflecting the low priority given to arms talks, the administration initially placed responsibility for arms control policy at a relatively low level, in interagency groups chaired by officials at the assistant secretary level or below. Since no one department was given final authority over the interagency process, splits at these lower levels prevented progress in formulating an arms control plan. The main split was between relatively moderate officials in the State Department, led by Richard Burt, and conservatives in the office of the secretary of defense, who had Richard Perle as their chief spokesperson. The conservatives wanted the U.S. proposal to cover only ballistic missile warheads initially, whereas the moderates argued it would have to include areas where the United States had an advantage if the administration's proposals were to have a realistic chance of interesting the Soviets (Talbott 1984).

Because of disagreements at the Burt-Perle level and below, the administration could not decide what it would propose in a strategic arms control plan. Nor did the president intervene to force his system to move forward more quickly. According to Robert Dean, an aide to Burt at the State Department, "If Ronald Reagan had asked for an arms control proposal, he would have gotten it. But there was no leadership from the White House on [strategic] arms control" (interview by author). Reagan did not even get his first briefing on the various options being considered by his bureaucracy until late April 1982, fifteen months after he took office (Talbott 1984: 248).

Evidence of Opinion Disjunction

Besides assigning a low initial priority to arms restraint, administration officials also made a number of casual pronouncements about nuclear war during Reagan's first year in office.[7] This combination proved quite troubling to much of the American public. Evidence soon emerged of a divergence between majority public preferences and the administration's approach to nuclear arms. The difference was wide enough to create the potential for activism and to generate electoral incentives for a change in policy through mechanism 1.

The most direct evidence for this opinion disjunction comes from public opinion polls. For example, in five questions in 1982 and 1983 about whether the administration's arms limitation effort was adequate, either a plurality or an outright majority always said no (Leavitt 1983: 4). This indication of divergence between public preferences and the administration's approach shows that the precondition for activating the electoral pathway was present.

To engage mechanism 1, however, it is also necessary for activism to interact with this broader current in public opinion. One significant indication of such interaction is a focus in opinion polls on the freeze itself. Between 1981 and 1984, all the major polling operations asked about public support for a nuclear freeze. Before the formation of the Nuclear Weapons Freeze Campaign (NWFC), in contrast, survey organizations had never queried the public about whether they would support such a step (Kramer, Kalick, and Milburn 1983: 14). Since the freeze was not a proposal made by the U.S. government or some other world leader, pollsters' sudden interest can only be due to a rapid growth of public interest in the citizen initiative on behalf of a freeze.

Moreover, surveys consistently showed large majorities in favor of the freeze proposal. After fall 1983, in fact, the polls rarely found less than 80 percent approval for a bilateral nuclear freeze (Milburn, Watanabe, and Kramer 1986: 664). Even when asked to compare the freeze directly with the administration's basic approach, a sizable majority preferred a freeze. In a *New York Times*/CBS poll in April 1983, the public in fact preferred seeking an immediate freeze by a 64-to-25 margin over building up U.S. forces in order to stimulate reductions.[8] This pattern of survey data indicates that activist efforts were interacting with concern in the wider public, as required to engage the electoral pathway.

Support for the freeze, however, did prove sensitive to changes in question wording. Approval of the freeze fell dramatically if the question specified that a freeze would leave the Soviet Union ahead, that it would be a unilateral U.S. action, or that Soviet cheating could not be detected.[9] This suggests the high public approval in other formats was less a product of attraction to the nuclear freeze as a specific proposal than of unease at the general level about the nuclear arms race and how the Reagan administration was handling it. Indeed, in a survey that asked respondents about their reasons for favoring or opposing a freeze, by far the majority of freeze supporters cited fear of nuclear war or concern for the future of their children or grandchildren (Milburn, Watanabe, and Kramer 1986: 670). They were, in other words, generally worried about nuclear war rather than attracted specifically to the freeze proposal. The extent of concern at the general level is indicated by a 1984 Gallup survey in which 25 percent named nuclear weapons and the arms race the most important problem facing the country, more than any other issue selected. This contrasted sharply with the period from 1973 to 1979, when defense and foreign policy issues as a whole were rarely cited by more than 10 percent of the public (Aldrich, Sullivan, and Borgida 1989: 129–131).

Beyond survey data, the speed with which anti–nuclear weapons protest grew and spread is itself further evidence of the two requirements for engaging mechanism 1: opinion disjunction and interaction between activism and public opinion. Besides the freeze, a number of other public interest groups decided for the first time to address nuclear weapons issues, and many other new organizations were also created for this purpose (Wirls 1992: 72–74). In addition, already established arms control groups saw their memberships increase as much as tenfold.[10] The fact that activism grew so much across the board in the early 1980s again suggests the movement took off more because it was tapping into concern about Reagan's views on the appropriate balance between buildup and restraint than because of the technical merits of the freeze idea itself.

Worries at the general level are also what official Washington perceived as being behind popular support for the freeze. Congressional staffer Bob Sherman, who was active in maneuvering the freeze through the House, argues that support for the freeze in public opinion polls "was really for nuclear restraint, a black box with a label 'nuclear restraint' but no specific content" (interview by author). Administration officials had a similar reading. Thomas Graham, who handled public affairs for the Arms Control and Disarmament Agency (ACDA) in the early 1980s, reported that in ACDA's analysis the freeze movement "represented peoples' fear, not desire for that proposal per se" (interview by author). In short, to politicians, the freeze movement served to dramatize a feeling among much of the American public that pursuit of arms control should have a higher place

on the national agenda than it was being accorded by the Reagan administration.

How Elite Concerns Reinforce General-level Pressures

Many of the general-level issues motivating public support for the freeze
were also a concern to members of the liberal foreign policy establishment
and their allies in Congress, who came to see the citizens' campaign as a
potential ally in altering Reagan administration policy. To many
Democratic politicians, moreover, the freeze appeared to be one of their
best hopes for defeating President Reagan or other members of his party at
the polls, as well as reversing the arms policies being pursued by the
administration. As a result, the whole left-liberal "new politics" coalition
rallied around the freeze as the most promising vehicle available by which
they might rebuild themselves into a force that could wrest power from
Reagan's conservative coalition (Wirls 1992). When popular activism and
the efforts of political elites began interacting, this engaged mechanism 2,
the elite coalition-shift pathway. Because most elites were motivated by a
desire to reverse Reagan's apparent dismissal of arms control as an objective rather than by strong support for the freeze proposal itself, the elite
pathway came into operation at the general level, reinforcing the pressures
generated by the electoral pathway.

The single most important step in this process was the response of
Congress. In March 1982, Senators Edward Kennedy (D, Massachusetts)
and Mark Hatfield (R, Oregon) introduced a bill calling for superpower
negotiations to establish a freeze, with House sponsorship by Edward
Markey (D, Massachusetts), Jonathan Bingham (D, New York), and Silvio
Conte (R, Massachusetts). From the outset, the actions of Congress reflected a mix of both mechanisms 1 and 2. For example, mechanism 1, the electoral pathway, created the promise of significant benefits to those politicians who could first get themselves identified with the freeze. This helped
trigger the initial decisions by Kennedy and Markey to sponsor a freeze bill
(Wirls 1992: 102–103; Waller 1987: 47, 110).

Because many other members of Congress also shared the public's
concerns about the general direction of Reagan arms policy, however, the
electoral pathway was not the only mechanism that operated in the congressional debate. Many members became interested in using the legislative
process to pull U.S. policy back to a more centrist position on the arms
buildup to arms restraint spectrum. They began to see working with public
advocacy groups to promote freeze legislation as the best way to pressure
the administration to make this policy change, bringing mechanism 2, the
elite coalition-shift pathway, into action as well.

Using the freeze to pressure Reagan. Most legislators did not share the specific-level objectives of the freeze campaign, however, so not all of those desiring to act on arms control immediately rallied around the freeze. Many members introduced their own personal arms control resolutions instead. By the end of 1982, over thirty arms control resolutions had been introduced in Congress (Waller 1987: 86–89; Feighan 1983: 33).

All of the other resolutions introduced suffered from one important flaw. They did not have the same grassroots backing as the freeze. As a result, many foreign policy elites who objected to Reagan's arms policies came to see working with groups supporting the freeze as the best way to get the administration to restore the emphasis given to arms control by its predecessors. Thus, many former government officials and other prominent national figures endorsed the Kennedy-Hatfield freeze resolution. In terms of ability to legitimate the freeze for moderates and conservatives, former Central Intelligence Agency (CIA) Director William Colby was probably the most important of these "defectors" to the freeze cause.

As the freeze movement continued to gain grassroots momentum and elite endorsements, more and more members of Congress decided to rally around the freeze, bringing mechanism 2 into play. In mid-1982, for example, House Foreign Affairs Committee Chairman Clem Zablocki (D, Wisconsin) and other prominent Democratic representatives, including Les Aspin (D, Wisconsin) and Al Gore (D, Tennessee), decided to stop promoting other alternatives they had initially favored. They all signed on as cosponsors of the freeze instead (Waller 1987: 123–124, 130–135). As all the other proposals that had been made dropped out of sight, *Congressional Digest* labeled the freeze the "current vehicle for debate over nuclear weapons policy" (quoted in Meyer 1990: 227).

The interest of members of Congress in working with the freeze brought about operation of mechanism 2 at the general level of policy rather than the specific. Instead of seeking to impose an immediate, across-the-board halt on all nuclear weapons testing and production, many congressional sponsors wanted to use the freeze as a tool to prod Reagan into doing more about controlling the arms race. Thus, in urging his colleagues to vote for the freeze during floor debate in August 1982, Aspin argued, "If we had a President who was genuinely interested in arms control, perhaps [the freeze resolution] would not be necessary. If we had a President . . . who would negotiate in good faith, . . . we would need no resolution at all" (cited in Waller 1987: 153). Even some of the freeze's strongest supporters saw the resolution as chiefly symbolic. Senator Hatfield said that he felt "the geo-politics of U.S.-Soviet relations called for some kind of . . . a pause, a breather [in the arms race]. . . . We needed to cool the environment . . . and let the diplomats come up with a plan." To do this, he noted, "we had to have a rallying point, a vehicle for public feelings" (interview by author).

The fact that both influence mechanisms operating in the congressional debate involved pressure to change the general direction of policy rather than to impose a specific ordering on the arms control agenda affected the form that the freeze resolution took. The Kennedy-Hatfield bill, as it went through a series of modifications, never took a form that could legally compel the president to offer a freeze to Moscow. It was instead largely symbolic.[11]

Passage despite countermobilization. Its symbolic nature notwithstanding, top administration officials took a combative stance toward the freeze resolution. In doing so, they suggested the nonbinding measure would be taken as a vote of confidence in the administration's existing course on arms issues. This also meant the proposal would not be allowed to sail through Congress without opposition. Starting on the very day Kennedy and Hatfield introduced their resolution, administration officials repeatedly made two arguments against a freeze. First, they argued it would, as a July 1982 letter from President Reagan to every member of Congress put it, leave "dangerous asymmetries in the nuclear balance." Second, they asserted that passage of the resolution would remove any incentive for Moscow to agree to the arms cuts sought by the administration (Waller 1987: 76, 139; Feighan 1983: 36).

On the first point, freeze advocates contended that existing numerical imbalances were not sufficient to take the superpowers' arsenals out of a condition of rough parity, so that it would actually be more dangerous to allow continued development and deployment of highly accurate new weapons. As for the second argument, according to Markey aide Douglas Waller (1987: 140), "because the [initial] Reagan plan was so lopsidedly stacked against the Soviets many congressmen privately felt there were no negotiations to undercut."

Neither side expected the freeze to win the first time the House voted on it. However, constituent pressure was sufficiently high that many members of the president's party wanted to vote for the resolution as long as their vote would not affect the outcome. As a result, Republicans had to convince two of their number to switch their votes at the last second to prevent their substitute measure, which endorsed the president's approach, from losing to the freeze. The final vote, on August 5, 1982, sustained the president's position by just 204 to 202 (Waller 1987: 157–158; Feighan 1983: 39).

Passage the following year seemed assured when the Democrats picked up twenty-six seats in the House in the November election. But countermobilization by freeze opponents made progress for the freeze resolution difficult in 1983. Prodefense interest groups of the New Right had gotten onto the issue late, but they now started putting pressure of their own on Congress and the White House.[12] The administration likewise "went all out to defeat the freeze in the House" (White House official, interview by author). President Reagan invited several groups of undecided legislators to the White House for what presidential spokesman Larry Speakes referred to as "arm twisting" sessions (*New York Times* [hereafter *NYT*], 16 March 1983: 23; 13 April 1983: 21; *Washington Post,* 13 April 1983: 3). One State Department official says he even overheard the president threaten some members of his own party that if they voted for the freeze he would not support them in their next reelection campaign (interview by author).

However, the most troublesome opposition for the freeze came from the measure's opponents in Congress itself, who offered amendment after amendment to the freeze resolution. Freeze sponsors accepted those they thought were harmless and successfully neutralized or defeated all but one of those they opposed, an amendment proposed by Elliot Levitas (D, Georgia). The Levitas amendment said that a freeze should be followed by reductions "within a reasonable, specified period of time," implying the United States could call off a freeze if reductions did not soon follow (for more details, see Waller 1987: chaps. 7–8).

Organized support for the freeze still proved stronger than the organized opposition, however, and the House passed the final freeze resolution on 4 May 1983 by 278 to 149. Though the bill was much amended, according to Reuben McCornack, the Washington lobbyist for the NWFC, "the nut of the freeze was preserved" (interview by author; for a contrasting view, see Meyer 1990: 230–231). Most important, the resolution preserved the sequence that held a freeze should be the first priority in arms talks and a prelude to reductions, rather than allowing Reagan the option of pursuing his existing reductions plan first. The final bill also called for a comprehensive freeze, with no nuclear weapons systems exempted. The Reagan administration still criticized the amended freeze resolution, indicating that it saw the final bill as a vote against administration policy (Waller 1987: 286).

The sizable margin of victory, which included sixty Republicans, thus reflects the amount of constituent pressure the freeze movement brought to bear. McCornack reports, "The Campaign could get 200 calls to a member of Congress in 24 hours. This made the difference in a lot of cases" (interview by author). Administration officials also acknowledge that constituent pressure mobilized through mechanism 1 was the main reason many members of Congress voted for the freeze. An administration official who lobbied against the freeze said a leading House sponsor told him the bill would pass because "there aren't 535 profiles in courage in Congress." This aide added, "I had probably 50 conversations with members of Congress. They'd . . . say they had to vote for it or get creamed on Main Street" (interview by author). Despite the opposition's efforts, a combination of public pressure and coalition building between activists and elites, that is, activation of mechanisms 1 and 2, had prompted the House to signal to the administration its support for the freeze movement's interest in seeing more done to end the arms race.

Although the freeze won the House debate in terms of the final vote, it was still a mixed outcome for the movement as a whole. Since the bill would not itself actually halt the arms race, the fact the battle in the House went on much longer than had been expected drained a lot of the movement's momentum. Many activists were further demoralized when, only a few weeks later, the House voted to approve funding for the MX missile. Finally, the NWFC and other arms control groups that worked on the resolution had never agreed on a strategy for where to go after the House vote, meaning their efforts diffused considerably once the resolution passed. For all these reasons, the freeze movement achieved no more victories in Congress over the next couple of years.

Policy Impact of the Freeze

For activists, though, moving legislation through Congress was not a goal in itself. It was a means to an end—changing U.S. policy. And, in response to the general-level pressures generated through the electoral and elite coalition-shift pathways, the Reagan administration made changes in arms control policy of exactly the sort the theory outlined above would lead one to predict.

Pressures Felt by the Administration

As mechanism 1 requires, interaction between the freeze movement and public opinion made arms control and U.S.-Soviet relations into significant enough issues that key officials felt the administration could potentially be hurt by them electorally. Building on the success of freeze referenda in western Massachusetts in 1980, the freeze emerged as a major issue by the 1982 congressional midterm election. Representative Edward Feighan (D, Ohio) observes, "On every talk show, and in every forum in which candidates sought to get their message across, they [found they] had to have a position on the nuclear weapons freeze" (1983: 29). Fifty-six percent of the voters in a Harris poll that year even said they would vote against any congressional candidate who did not support a freeze (Meyer 1990: 88).

The freeze remained important into the next electoral campaign. In spring 1984, pollster Peter Hart concluded the freeze was the one issue that might induce Reagan supporters to split their ticket and vote for a Democratic congressional candidate that fall, because he found most voters still felt the president had not done enough on arms control (Garfinkle 1984: 219; Cortright 1993: 82). Democratic presidential hopefuls that year also embraced the freeze. In fact, the freeze movement succeeded in making support for arms control a prerequisite for success in the 1984 Democratic primary race and in making support for the freeze itself the litmus test of such support. Seven of the eight Democrats running for their party's presidential nomination thus endorsed a nuclear freeze, including the two front-runners, Walter Mondale and Gary Hart (Waller 1987: 295; Wirls 1992: 122).

The Reagan White House watched these developments closely. According to Public Affairs Director Michael Baroody, "There was growing awareness in the White House of the nuclear issue, particularly the nuclear freeze question" (interview cited in Cortright 1993: 90). As a result, during Reagan's first few years in office, David Gergen says, White House staff asked Reagan's pollster, Richard Wirthlin, for "lots and lots" of surveys on domestic opinion on arms control (interview by author).

The political operatives, moreover, were not the only ones who worried about the freeze. NSC deputy Robert McFarlane helped engineer a change in mid-1983 in the administration's arms control policymaking system in an effort to accelerate progress on the issue. He says he did so because he was convinced "the one issue on which the President [was] most vulnerable . . . was arms control" (interview by author). The president himself felt concern. According to Strobe Talbott (1984: 267), Reagan frequently commented to his aides during the freeze movement's rise that he could not afford to subject himself to the charge "we aren't serious about wanting an agreement." Going into the 1984 campaign, Reagan's closest political adviser, Michael Deaver, felt the nuclear issue was a "big negative" and Reagan was "vulnerable on war and peace issues" (interview cited in Cortright 1993: 82).[13]

In the end, though, the freeze failed to bring about any national swing in congressional outcomes or the defeat of President Reagan.[14] But this does not reflect an inability to arouse public opinion. Rather, by signaling the possibility of electoral consequences, the freeze got forward-looking administration officials to press for action on arms control before matters could get sufficiently out of hand to put Reagan's reelection in doubt. The administration began this adjustment process not only because of a loss of support in the polls due to arms control but also because of the response of Congress to the freeze.

The greatest pressures on the administration to respond to anti–nuclear weapons activism were generated when Congress took up the freeze. If

Congress passed a freeze resolution, many officials felt, it might create an impression that Congress could vote against Reagan's defense programs with impunity or lessen administration leverage in arms talks with Russia. Thus, Thomas Graham reports "there was a lot of consternation in ACDA over . . . the danger of the wrong resolution from Congress" (interview by author). A State Department official says he and his colleagues worried in particular about whether the freeze would have spillover effects on "congressional funding of the strategic modernization program" (interview by author). David Gergen sums up these concerns, declaring "there was a widespread view in the administration that the freeze was a dagger pointed at the heart of the administration's defense program" (interview by author).

In short, both electoral incentives and coalition dynamics triggered by the freeze created pressure on the administration to make changes at the general level of policy. As one would expect, therefore, the Reagan administration began trying to move forward more quickly in arms control and changed its public description of its goals to give greater emphasis to disarmament.

Shifts in Policy

As one reaction to activism, the administration increased the priority attached to achieving progress on arms control. The administration had no desire to propose a freeze, but by early 1982 administration officials realized they had to be seen doing something on arms control. First and foremost, this required developing a proposal of their own and getting talks underway.

In its first year in office the administration did all it could to delay talks as long as possible. In their first two meetings with Reagan's first secretary of state, Alexander Haig, Soviet diplomats asked the United States to resume arms talks. These requests were turned down (Haig 1984: 104–108). Thus, at the end of its first year in office, the only decision the administration had made was on a name for the effort, START, for Strategic Arms Reductions Talks.[15] On substance, though, there was still no agreement on what the administration should propose, let alone when its opening START proposal should be offered.

Moreover, there was little push within the administration to resolve the remaining bureaucratic disagreements and get a final proposal on the table. The freeze provided that push. Robert McFarlane, as a deputy on the NSC, decided in early 1982 it was necessary to "blast apart the log-jam in the bureaucracy." McFarlane and national security adviser William Clark thus engineered an NSC directive at the end of February that gave the rest of the executive branch two months to complete work on a START proposal (Talbott 1984: 247). McFarlane explains, "I felt the President was vulnerable to Allied pressures to take a bad position, or Congress would impose one, if the administration did not develop a position of its own." Domestic pressure arising from the freeze gave him a handle on the problem of taming centrifugal forces in the bureaucracy, he says (interview by author).

Another highly placed official agrees that the freeze movement brought "some pressure on the administration to get back into a dialogue with the Soviet Union. It might have taken longer otherwise" (interview by author). Further confirmation that the anti–nuclear weapons movement gave urgency to the formulation of an arms control policy appeared shortly before Reagan announced his START proposal in a May 1982 speech at Eureka College. At that time, the *NYT* reported that "the administration's main concern, according to the officials [present at an NSC meeting to discuss START], is to go on record quickly with a simple and comprehensible plan to show that the Reagan team is for peace, thus taking some of the steam out of the nuclear freeze movements in Europe and the United States."[16] Defense Secretary Weinberger has also since acknowledged pressures generated by the freeze had at least "something" to do with the timing of the decision to open START talks (interview cited in Cortright 1993: 104–105).

Beyond getting the administration to enter strategic arms control negotiations more quickly than it otherwise would have, the freeze movement also made it necessary for the administration to keep moving forward. Assessing the impact of the freeze overall, McFarlane believes "it accelerated the pace" of government arms control policymaking (interview by author). David Gergen gives a similar assessment, saying, "The peace movement accelerated the move towards an agreement, [and] prodded the administration to act more swiftly. . . . I know all of us felt we had to move [on arms control]" (interview by author). This momentum continued after the 1984 election. In a meeting shortly after the election, which White House staff intended to signal the direction Reagan would take, Secretary of State George Shultz told the president he would have to overrule the opponents of arms control because the public and Congress would not support his weapons plans "without meaningful negotiations" (Shultz 1993: 496–497).

Changes in declaratory policy.   Another aspect of policy at the general level affected by the freeze was how officials described their concerns and objectives in public statements. Administration rhetoric about nuclear arms had helped stimulate the freeze movement. The administration recognized this, leading to an end to the earlier loose talk about the winnability of nuclear war. Lumping this together with other effects already discussed, one official who played an important role in administration public affairs efforts says the main effects of the freeze were "with respect to speed, urgency, tone, how things [were] packaged" (interview by author; see also the interviews cited in Cortright 1993: 94, 104).

Because public statements about nuclear arms constitute a form of policy—that is, declaratory policy—administration pronouncements on the issue came to entail another shift at the general level. In the areas of tone and packaging, in fact, the administration did more than just clamp down on its war-fighting rhetoric. The president, in his own statements, began to indicate doubts about the utility of nuclear weapons. This may even have reflected the president's personal feelings. Most former administration officials I interviewed contend Reagan wanted sharp reductions in nuclear weapons from day one. Reagan similarly claims in his memoirs that soon after he took office, as he learned the number of fatalities that a nuclear war would cause, "My dream, then, became a world free of nuclear weapons" (1990: 550; see also Anderson 1990: xxxii, xxxvi; Shultz 1993: 360, 376; and Adelman 1989: 20). However, no sign of the president's feelings in this regard escaped into the public realm in his first year or more in office. Instead, Reagan regularly denounced Soviet behavior; argued that the United States needed to modernize all three legs of the strategic nuclear triad; and at one point even told reporters, "I could see where you could have [a nuclear war limited to] exchange of tactical weapons against troops in the field" (quoted in Solo 1988: 70).

The president began to express more antinuclear views, however, in spring 1982. The decision to speak out at that point in time, when Reagan still primarily wanted to build up U.S. strength and focus on issues other than arms control, was due entirely to pressures arising from the freeze movement. One source familiar with discussions of the administration's private polls reported that their data at that time indicated Reagan was being hurt by the nuclear arms control issue. This source said the poll results made the administration decide to give more attention to the nuclear issue in its public statements (interview by author).

The president made one statement around this time, which he later repeated many times, whose connotations were especially significant. According to one source (interview by author), the president first made this comment at the suggestion of an NSC aide, including it in a telegram he sent to a meeting of the International Physicians for the Prevention of Nuclear War. In it, Reagan said he believed that "a nuclear war cannot be won, and must never be fought." The president also used this line in his weekly radio address on 17 April 1982 as a way to reassure "those who protest against nuclear war . . . [that] I'm with you" (transcript of Reagan address in *NYT,* 18 April 1982: 35). While claiming these statements reflected the president's true opinions, the aide (cited previously) acknowledged that advisers urged the president to express these views publicly because of the criticisms of administration policy coming from the freeze movement. In response to the criticisms of freeze advocates, the president in effect publicly disowned an important premise of his administration's nuclear strategy, that the United States could plan to prevail in a nuclear conflict.

Reagan's change in rhetoric did not imply acceptance of the freeze proposal itself. Because the administration maintained a stance of unswerving opposition to the movement's specific demands, the administration had to convince the public its own arms control program could achieve the goals motivating support for the freeze proposal. As a result, the administration changed not only its rhetoric concerning nuclear war but also its descriptions of its objectives in arms control. Rather than linger on the need to establish equality in the U.S. and Soviet arsenals or close the window of vulnerability, the administration now began to emphasize the goal of reductions per se. This enabled it to argue against the freeze by saying, in essence, "we can do better than a freeze."[17]

The first opportunity for the administration to highlight a desire for arms reductions came with Reagan's Eureka College address in May 1982. A year before, George Kennan had caused a stir by calling for 50 percent cuts in nuclear arsenals. James Goodby, designated to be the State Department representative at the START talks, drafted the section of the Eureka speech outlining the numbers in Reagan's opening proposal. He recalls his goals in writing the draft (interview by author):

> I was very conscious of Kennan's calls for 50 percent reductions. So I calculated what the reductions would be under our START proposal. They turned out to be about 35 percent [if ballistic missile warheads were taken as the unit of account]. I wrote it in Kennanesque language so it would have the same public appeal. I wanted it to look like the president was paying attention to public concern.

Reflecting on the administration's attempts to address public concerns, another official with arms control duties contends the freeze "increased support for bold steps, like the zero option and deep reductions. . . . The public debate drove people in the administration to adopt a more disarmament type focus rather than [return to more] traditional arms control" (interview by author). Once Reagan began to speak out on his desire for arms reductions, his political aides found that such a stance increased his public standing.[18] As ACDA official Thomas Graham puts it, the freeze movement demonstrated that "arms control was good politics. The White House operatives did not appreciate that at first" (interview by author).

Once they learned that lesson, however, his aides sought to ensure that all Reagan's subsequent pronouncements on U.S.-Soviet relations also included some propeace rhetoric. Before Reagan's 1983 State of the Union address, for example, the administration released a statement in his name that declared, "We have no higher priority" than arms control (*NYT,* 22 January 1983: 4). This was a remarkable shift from Reagan's initial policy baseline. White House officials admitted to reporters in spring 1983 that "voter sentiment" was "a factor in persuading Mr. Reagan to couple every appeal for military preparedness with an equally fervent appeal for peace" (*NYT,* 6 April 1983: B8).

By making all these policy shifts, the administration forestalled any possibility that the arms issue might cost Reagan the 1984 election or that the public would pressure Congress to impose a freeze. Because the opinion disjunction that opened up in the early 1980s primarily reflected concerns at the general level rather than a widespread conviction that all new nuclear weapons programs must immediately be stopped, the administration did not necessarily have to propose a freeze to lessen public concerns. It merely had to adjust its policy at the general level in a way that indicated a commitment to continue negotiating with the Soviet Union for arms control. Thus, in response to the signals conveyed by the freeze, the administration stopped claiming publicly that the United States should seek the ability to prevail in the event deterrence failed and proclaimed the goal of reducing nuclear weapons as a national priority instead. And the administration moved forward earlier and more quickly on arms control than it had intended.

These steps apparently convinced many Americans that Ronald Reagan would seriously seek arms control. A September 1984 poll found 60 percent of the public believed Reagan would "make a real effort" to negotiate an arms control deal with Moscow if he were reelected, a figure that increased to 69 percent right after the election (*NYT,* 19 September 1984: B9; 19 November 1984: 1). Richard Wirthlin says his polls for the administration likewise found the public, in a turnaround from their earlier discomfort, "at ease with Reagan's positions" on nuclear arms as the election approached (interview by author).

Achieving a centrist compromise. Although the pressures arising from the freeze movement were mostly felt at the general level of policy, this does not mean the specific level remained unaffected. As a by-product of its general-level effects, the freeze movement also helped stimulate efforts by the administration to amend the START offer to make it more negotiable. The most significant changes were not a direct consequence of the freeze, but were made possible indirectly by operation of the elite coalition-shift pathway.

Though the freeze movement was unable to place an immediate cessation to the building of nuclear weapons at the top of the arms control agenda, the larger process of coalition formation it brought about helped a different coalition to alter Reagan's policy at the specific level. This occurred

because arms control and disarmament groups in the early 1980s maintained a second major campaign alongside the freeze effort, one directed at
stopping the MX missile. The rise of the freeze movement helped boost the
anti-MX campaign. Combined with the Reagan administration's inability to
come up with a convincing basing scheme, this effort put continued funding of the MX in serious doubt (Cortright 1993: 144–148).

The administration responded by creating the bipartisan President's
Commission on Strategic Forces, chaired by Brent Scowcroft, to propose a
basing scheme for the MX. A small group of legislators from both chambers of Congress then worked behind the scenes with the Scowcroft
Commission to get certain other commitments from the president included
in Scowcroft's recommendations. The senators, led by William Cohen (R,
Maine) and Sam Nunn (D, Georgia), were interested in promoting a nuclear
"build-down" proposal, which would require that new weapons deployed
by either side be matched by the retirement of a greater number of older
weapons.[19] They were joined by representatives, including Aspin and Gore,
who wanted to promote rapid transition to a force of single-warhead, intercontinental ballistic missiles (ICBMs), dubbed the "Midgetman" (Gray
1984: 86–94; Talbott 1984: 300–307).

By helping create an opposition to the MX that held nearly a majority
in Congress, the anti–nuclear weapons movement enabled these moderate
members to threaten to vote with the opposition if the administration did
not make concessions to their more limited concerns. By playing this bargaining chip over the course of several close MX votes in 1983, the centrist
coalition extracted commitments from the administration to proceed with
Midgetman development, offer a build-down proposal, and—most significant from the perspective of the freeze movement—make its START proposal more realistic (Gray 1984: 95–104). The centrists acknowledge that
citizen activism, by placing the fate of the MX in the balance, made potent
their threat to vote against the MX. Aspin told David Cortright, "The citizens and grassroots organizations did come up very big time against the
MX. That clearly had an impact on forcing the administration to deal with
the moderates in the House" (interview cited in Cortright 1993: 145). And
Al Gore (1983: 11) wrote at the time:

> Because Congress proposed to choose between . . . [Reagan's] conduct of
> arms control and the audacious freeze, it was imperative for him to make
> his conduct in arms control and arms planning more persuasive. That led
> him to expand the charter of the Scowcroft Commission to encompass
> arms control, and to embrace its recommendations, even though they are
> in many ways contrary to his original goals.

Though the build-down idea itself went nowhere in the end,[20] administration negotiations with the congressional build-down coalition brought about another change in the U.S. START position that was more consequential. The administration initially sought a two-phase approach in START, asking for sharp reductions to equal levels in ballistic missiles as a prior step to any other nuclear arms limitations. Freeze and build-down supporters both saw this focus on ICBMs as unrealistically one-sided. They pointed out that while the United States had its nuclear weapons fairly evenly distributed across the three legs of the triad (land-, air-, and sea-based), the great majority of Soviet weapons, and those they regarded as most reliable, were exactly the land-based missiles targeted by the Reagan plan.

When he approved the initial START offer, however, the president was unaware of this difference between U.S. and Soviet deployment patterns (Talbott 1984: 263). This changed only when Reagan and Secretary of State Shultz were forced, by the precarious situation of the MX, to meet personally with the congressional centrist coalition to work out a deal. In these meetings, months after his May 1982 Eureka speech, the president finally had to acknowledge that his proposal to impose deep cuts in Soviet land-based missiles without compensating cuts in areas of U.S. advantage was bound to appear one-sided. Brent Scowcroft convinced Shultz of the corollary, that asymmetries in the two arsenals meant the United States could trade its bombers and cruise missiles for Soviet ballistic missiles. Shultz in turn convinced Reagan to give up the idea of treating ballistic missiles separately from other systems. The White House promised that it would seek to "negotiate trade-offs" between each side's areas of relative advantage (Talbott 1984: 337–339; Gray 1984: 102–104).

This decision marked the end of the two-phase approach in START. From the perspective of making arms control a real possibility, it was the most important first-term adjustment the administration made in its START proposal. It thus reinforced the general-level increase in the priority given to achieving arms restraint.

Asked later how he could have been ignorant of this important difference in the U.S. and Soviet arsenals, Reagan replied, "I never heard any one of our negotiators or any of our military people or anyone else bring up that particular point" (quoted in Talbott 1984: 263, fn.). This suggests that, if the freeze movement had not created a situation that forced the president to discuss arms control with figures outside his administration, it would have been much later, if at all, before he gained the insight that enabled him to make the U.S. approach more realistic. Of course, Reagan's compromise with the build-down coalition still left policy at the specific level far from what the freeze movement sought. It is therefore important also to recognize the limitations on freeze movement influence.

Limitations on Influence

I have shown that the freeze had a major impact with respect to arms control's place on the national agenda. However, the movement did not succeed in altering the arms control agenda itself in the way its organizers had hoped. This is in part a function of the influence pathways engaged by the freeze. By its nature, any electoral pressure generated by a citizens' campaign is felt on the broad dimension involving the balance between buildup and restraint. To get the government to pursue a freeze itself, advocates would have had to engage one of the other influence mechanisms in a way that altered policy at the specific level.

As indicated above, though, foreign policy elites who worked with the freeze movement, activating mechanism 2, generally did not share the specific-level objectives of the freeze campaign. Influence through the coalition-shift pathway was therefore also exerted mainly at the general level or else used by congressional centrists for purposes not fully consonant with freeze objectives. The only remaining mechanism by which the citizens' campaign could have brought the arms control agenda more into conformity with its preferences is the bureaucratic pathway, but mechanism 3 was never activated by the freeze in a way that could advance the movement's proposals.

Barriers to engaging the bureaucratic pathway.   Earlier sections have shown that a bureaucratic division, which is the precondition for mechanism 3, clearly existed. For mechanism 3 to take effect, however, there must be some interaction between the bureaucratic debate and ideas associated with the outside citizens' movement. Such interaction never occurred. Despite the deep divisions on arms control within the administration, both factions in the internal debate rejected the nuclear freeze proposal, believing it would leave the Soviets with a meaningful lead in ICBMs. Hence, neither side saw in the proposals of the U.S. anti–nuclear weapons movement anything that could serve as a solution to the problems with which they were concerned.

Though they rejected the freeze proposal, both factions in the internal debate did try to make the political problem posed by rise of the citizens' movement itself an argument in favor of their own proposals. However, as Robert Dean, an assistant of Burt's, observes, "the arguments cut either way. They didn't necessarily favor one position over another" (interview by author). Thus, the State Department argued its more traditional options could more plausibly be seen as containing the basis for an agreement and would, as one official who supported those options puts it, convince "the public . . . the administration [was] serious on arms control" (interview by author). Richard Perle and his allies had a rejoinder, however; they argued that the Pentagon's more radical proposals would have greater public appeal because they were simpler and more in tune with sentiment for disarmament (Talbott 1984: 156). Neither side proved able to win this debate, meaning that there was no interaction between the freeze and internal struggles over arms control that could boost the specific proposals of any side.

Influence of Soviet Diplomacy on the Freeze

The three influence pathways I have identified draw heavily on models developed in the study of U.S. domestic politics. Since arms control is not solely a domestic issue, however, the operation of these mechanisms can be affected—either positively or negatively—by developments outside U.S. borders. In this case, the most important international actor, the Soviet Union, ended up hindering freeze efforts through its negotiating behavior.

The Soviets walked out of the Intermediate-Range Nuclear Force (INF) and START talks when deliveries of the U.S. cruise and Pershing II missiles to North Atlantic Treaty Organization (NATO) countries began in late 1983. This action reduced the freeze movement's ability to apply leverage through the electoral pathway. According to Kenneth Adelman, director of ACDA at the time, "their walkout helped a lot to prevent the administration from being hurt on arms control in the election" (interview by author). As one State Department official pointed out, President Reagan could then say he was still willing to negotiate and blame the Soviets for quitting the talks (interview by author).[21]

Though activists could not get their preferred proposals adopted, this research nonetheless suggests that Reagan's arms control policy would not have developed the same way without the freeze. To make this case satisfactorily, though, requires considering possible alternative explanations for the policy developments I have attributed to the freeze.

The Impact of Other Factors

Two broad types of alternative explanation might account for Reagan administration policy. Given the president's preferences, one could argue that the administration would have eventually taken the same steps even without outside pressures. Or one could argue that other sources of outside pressure would have induced the shifts described earlier even without the existence of the freeze movement.

The first alternative line of argument suggests that policy ultimately reflected what the president wanted, so that Reagan's own preferences explain that policy. Long-time Reagan adviser Martin Anderson advances this claim, reporting that Reagan told him "I came in with a plan" for dealing with the Soviet Union and arms control and simply followed that plan all along (Anderson 1990: xxxi). Reduced to its essence, this plan involved setting out and sticking to an ambitious set of arms control objectives, then using a massive military buildup to lever the Soviets into accepting the sharp cuts in their forces called for in the opening U.S. proposal (Anderson 1990: 72–78; Meese 1992: 164–171; Pipes 1995).

The problem with this explanation is that Reagan made achievement of an arms reduction pact a high priority before the United States was in a position to implement his plan. Sources indicate that by early 1984 at the latest, the president had become seriously interested in reaching an arms control deal. Despite the fact the Soviets had walked out of arms talks less than two months earlier, Reagan decided in January 1984 to make a major speech expressing his readiness to compromise to reach a pact on arms control. Because there were obvious election year motivations, the U.S. media did not give much weight to the speech at the time. Yet a number of sources have indicated that the administration also intended the speech and various follow-up actions as a serious signal of willingness to cooperate so as to achieve arms control (David Gergen, interview by author; Newhouse 1990: 369; *NYT,* 24 February 1984: 14; Shultz 1993: 465–467; Cortright 1993: 97).

By any objective measure of the strategic balance, however, the United States had not by 1984 improved much on its position of 1980. The United States did not yet have the kind of additional leverage the administration had initially said it needed. On the contrary, two Defense Department officials noted in 1984 that the Soviets had opened up a big lead in ICBM reentry vehicles. They concluded, "The effects of the Reagan defense program are only beginning to be reflected in . . . improved readiness and . . . it will be several years before . . . [efforts] to modernize are translated into [equipment ready for use]" (Korb and Brady 1984–1985: 18). A report for the Congressional Research Service, comparing the strategic balance in 1985 with that in 1980, concluded similarly that the "Soviet posture nevertheless continues to improve in relative terms" (Collins 1985: 60).

Other administration officials pointed out that the new weapons called for in strategic modernization plans—the MX, B-1 bomber, and Trident II—had won funding, and that Reagan's Strategic Defense Initiative clearly worried the Soviets. But none of the new offensive systems had yet begun to be deployed in 1984, and any prospects for deployment of defensive systems were decades in the future at best. Given how often administration officials had argued the Soviets would never get serious in INF talks until U.S. cruise and Pershing II missiles were deployed, one would have expected them to apply the same logic to START. When one also recalls their earlier pessimistic assessments of Soviet intentions and the military balance, as well as skeptical comments about arms control, it is clear one would normally have expected the administration to wait for more concrete forms of progress in the U.S. military buildup before beginning serious negotiations toward a strategic arms control treaty.[22]

In a different domestic climate, therefore, Reagan would probably have chosen to defer the START talks until much later in order to give the buildup time to produce results. However, the public and congressional criticisms being channeled through the freeze movement served, as one official put it, as "a useful reminder of the need for concrete achievements, the need to show something out of the policy review process, of the political reality that you have to . . . engage in arms control" (interview by author). In this way, Robert McFarlane observed, the freeze "helped counter pressure from the Right to do nothing" (interview by author). In short, the president had strong motivations by 1984 to suggest that conditions for progress on arms control had improved, motivations he would not have had in the absence of outside pressure.

But was the freeze movement necessary, or could other sources of pressure outside the administration have brought about the same effects? A push from allied governments and publics is the most credible alternative to the freeze as an outside source of policy change.[23] While the Europeans clearly exerted pressure, the administration perceived it as being driven by priorities different from those of U.S. activists. In interviews, Reagan officials mostly discussed the Europeans in connection with the INF issue, not strategic arms. As a result, the pressures the administration felt from U.S. allies were reflected primarily in the zero option proposal for theater forces (Knopf 1993). In contrast, Reagan and his aides saw strategic arms control as a dominating concern only for U.S. actors.

Moreover, the allies lacked the concrete leverage on START that they enjoyed on INF. On INF, the United States needed the continued support of European governments and publics to be able to deploy cruise and Pershing II missiles there. On START, only domestic U.S. actors could derail the administration's strategic arms plans. The fact that U.S. priorities regarding strategic arms changed as much as they did between 1981 and 1984, therefore, must be attributed more to the freeze movement than to European pressure, though peace movements across the Atlantic certainly reinforced the activism taking place in the United States.

Conclusion

The anti–nuclear weapons movement of the early 1980s activated, in a mutually reinforcing way, the first two pathways of influence I have identified. The freeze engaged mechanism 1 by interacting with broader public concerns in a way that created electoral incentives for raising the place of arms restraint on the national agenda. The freeze movement also interacted with divisions among political elites, bringing mechanism 2 into play in a way that promoted congressional efforts to get Reagan to give less emphasis to increasing U.S. strength and more to achieving mutual restraint.

Mass electoral pressure and elite coalition shifts brought about by the freeze movement together produced the expected outcome: a change in arms control policy at the general level. The administration accelerated the pace of policy formulation, moving more quickly to enter strategic arms talks and to signal willingness to compromise in the search for an accord. The president and his advisers also changed their tone, giving more emphasis to the need to avoid nuclear war and achieve arms reductions.

Citizen activism failed, however, to engage any mechanisms of influence in a way that could alter policy at the specific level in conformity with freeze wishes. This does not mean that changes at the general level lacked significance. Several recent studies (Cortright 1993; Meyer and Marullo 1992) have argued that the peace movement helped end the Cold War. As part of their case, they claim activism got the Reagan administration to signal to the Soviet Union, before Gorbachev took power, that the United States was committed to arms control and not just to a relentless nuclear buildup. This in turn created the necessary political space for Gorbachev's concessions in arms talks and attempts to pursue domestic reform. In this chapter, I have shown that the freeze movement really did have the impact on Reagan policy ascribed to it by those who credit activism with helping end the Cold War, thereby supporting one of the key contentions necessary to make that argument persuasive. In contrast, the claim of former Reagan aides that the president deserves the credit for ending the Cold War must be modified in light of the fact that the administration did not actually follow its original script of first building the U.S. nuclear arsenal and only later entering serious arms control talks. This modification in U.S. policy was brought about by the freeze.

Current social movement theory, by framing impact as a matter of success or failure in seeing one's demands adopted, encourages a conclusion that the freeze was a failure. That judgment is too harsh. This study has shown that the freeze actually had an important influence on U.S. policy. By softening the Reagan stance on arms control, the movement also contributed to the end of the Cold War.

Notes

Much of this chapter has been excerpted from the author's forthcoming book, *Domestic Society and International Cooperation: The Impact of Protest on U.S. Arms Control Policy* (Cambridge, UK: Cambridge University Press, forthcoming). This research was made possible by financial support from the Stanford Center for International Security and Arms Control, a John D. and Catherine T. MacArthur fellowship, a U.S. Arms Control and Disarmament Agency Hubert H. Humphrey fellowship, the Institute for the Study of World Politics, and the Center for International Studies at the University of Southern California. The author would like to thank Alexander George, Scott Sagan, Richard Brody, Mark Peceny, J. Scott Johnson, Alison Brysk, Lee Metcalf, Cheryl Boyer, David Meyer, and Thomas Rochon for their helpful comments and suggestions.

1. This can be viewed as a way of giving a concrete definition in this issue area to the concept of "political opportunity structure," which has become prevalent in the social movement literature (Kitschelt 1986; Tarrow 1994; for applications to U.S. peace movements, see Pagnucco and Smith 1993; and Meyer 1990).

2. In 1989 I interviewed twenty-three government officials who worked on arms control under Reagan, representing all the relevant agencies. (I also interviewed seven members of Congress and congressional staff and eleven people who worked for public interest groups that concerned themselves with the freeze, either for or against.) Some officials asked that all or part of what they told me not be attributed to them by name. In these cases, I either do not identify the source at all or else identify only the agency in which the official worked. Despite the inconsistency that results, I have attributed quotes by name when I had permission to do so in order to allow others to verify my findings.

3. Labeling the dovish preference "peace" neglects the hawkish perspective that peace comes through strength. A more accurate label for this preference is "restraint." Hence this is the term I employ.

4. To my knowledge, the interest group literature has never put the point quite this way, but a number of strands in the literature that I discuss below relate to capability enhancement. I owe the idea that this is an important influence technique to Eileen Crumm (1995).

5. Mechanisms 1 and 2 may be complementary here because electoral concerns can reinforce this process. Eileen Burgin (1993) found that one of the strongest causes of decisions by members of Congress to get involved in foreign policy issues is learning that supporters in their district reelection constituency are interested in the issue.

6. Michael Cohen, James March, and Johan Olsen (1972). For an application to public policy, see John Kingdon (1984); for a perspective that links issue networks and garbage cans, see Jack Walker (1977).

7. For a recap of the statements that most worried critics, see Douglas Waller (1987: 19) and Pam Solo (1988: 70–71).

8. *NYT,* 15 April 1983: 1. Similarly, in a 1984 Public Agenda Foundation survey, 62 percent rejected building more dangerous nuclear weapons to get the Soviets to make concessions on arms control, the approach advocated by the Reagan administration, whereas only 31 percent favored this approach (Yankelovich and Doble 1984: 44).

9. Support dropped off most sharply when the question specified that cheating could not be detected. Under these circumstances, only 18 percent still favored a freeze, whereas 71 percent now rejected the idea (*NYT,* 30 May 1982: 1, 22).

10. The Center for Defense Information's (CDI's) mailing list grew from 14,000 at the beginning of 1981 to 105,000 five years later (Eugene Carroll, deputy director, CDI, interview by author). Membership in the Council for a Livable World (CLW) similarly increased from roughly 7,500 in 1979 to between 80,000 and 100,000 at its peak (John Isaacs, legislative director, CLW, interview by author). And SANE saw its membership quadruple, to 80,000 between 1980 and 1984 (Wirls 1992: 73).

11. Specifically, freeze sponsors introduced a joint resolution, which if passed by both chambers is sent to the president's desk for his signature into law. This gave it more teeth than a concurrent resolution, which merely expresses the sense of Congress, because passage of a joint resolution could force a presidential veto. Nonetheless, the bill was purely advisory, stating that the president "should," rather than "shall," make a freeze the goal.

12. They take credit for stimulating an amendment by Representative Mark Siljander (R, Michigan) that first revealed weakness in congressional support for the freeze resolution (Don Todd, executive director, American Conservative Union, interview by author; Paul Weyrich, Chairperson of the Stanton Group, an umbrella group for conservative interest group efforts on defense, interview by author).

13. In interviews I conducted, other administration officials who also admit at least some worry that the arms control issue could have hurt Reagan in 1984 include David Gergen; Fred Ikle, the undersecretary of defense for policy; and Thomas Graham of ACDA. In contrast, a number of other administration officials denied they had any worries that the freeze might cost them the 1984 election. As the reason they lacked concern, many of them cited polls in fall 1984 that indicated the arms control issue would not cost them votes. As I will explain later, these poll results reflected adjustments the administration had already made in response to public pressure, so that a lack of worry as of fall 1984 does not mean the freeze failed to generate electoral pressure on the administration.

14. Though it did not change outcomes in the majority of districts, the freeze did help determine the outcome of some congressional races in 1982 and 1984 (for details, see Feighan 1983: 41; Waller 1987: 165 and 296–297; and Johnston 1986: 122, 131–132).

15. The name was adopted because President Reagan liked the emphasis it gave to achieving reductions rather than mere limitations, as well as the acronym's connotation that the administration's approach represented a new start. These were both ways to differentiate the effort from SALT, which the administration had condemned (Talbott 1984: 222–223).

16. In other discussions with reporters, senior administration officials "described the speech, as well as several others the President is planning to make in the next few weeks, as an effort to turn public attention away from the antinuclear movements in the United States and Western Europe" (*NYT*, 2 May 1982: 16; 8 May 1982: 7).

17. In his very first public comment on the freeze, President Reagan departed from the text of a speech on income tax cuts to say, "A freeze simply isn't good enough because it doesn't go far enough" (*NYT*, 16 March 1982: 21).

18. The *NYT* reported in July 1982 that "the President's polltaker, Richard Wirthlin, says he has found a sharp rise, since April, in the percentage of Americans who think Mr. Reagan [really] wants to reduce arms. . . . The shifts followed Mr. Wirthlin's advice to Mr. Reagan to begin speaking out on arms control" (6 July 1982: 13).

19. Freeze leaders opposed build-down because they feared it could lead to a destabilizing situation as the superpowers replaced older, less accurate weapons with newer, more accurate ones. Markey thus likened build-down to "trading in two crossbows for one artillery piece" (quoted in Waller 1987: 243).

20. For an explanation, see Talbott (1984: 341–342).

21. Other Soviet actions, like shooting down a Korean airliner in September 1983 and deciding one year later to send Foreign Minister Andrei Gromyko to a meeting at the White House right before the election, also made it harder for freeze

activists and the candidate they supported, Walter Mondale, to blame the administration for an absence of dialogue with Moscow or a lack of progress on arms control.

22. I am setting aside the INF area, where deployment had begun. Such deployments had little effect on the strategic balance. In addition, strategic arms were being negotiated separately from intermediate-range forces.

23. One might also argue that Congress would have pushed for a change in Reagan policy even in the absence of the freeze. But the previous sections have shown that congressional action would not have taken the same course, nor would it have been as effective without the freeze, so I do not find this a convincing alternative.

8

Three Faces of the Freeze: Arenas of Success & Failure

THOMAS R. ROCHON

The nuclear freeze movement, which mobilized unprecedented numbers of people to protest against the Cold War rhetoric and the seemingly casual approach toward nuclear war characteristic of the first Reagan administration, is widely thought to have been a failure. A first look at the accomplishments of the freeze movement does not readily explain why this is so. The idea of the nuclear freeze consistently garnered the support of about 70 percent of the U.S. population in the early 1980s. At the height of the movement, there were between 1,400 and 2,000 local freeze organizations throughout the country (Garfinkle 1984: 81; Katz 1986: 173). The freeze was the major force behind the largest demonstration in U.S. history, the gathering of 750,000 people in Central Park in New York on 12 June 1982. Hundreds of town meetings and city councils went on record in support of the proposal. Referenda held in 1982 demonstrated the popularity of the freeze at the ballot box in nine states representing 30 percent of the U.S. population, losing only in Arizona among states where it was placed on the ballot. The House of Representatives passed a freeze resolution in 1983 by a comfortable margin. Perhaps most important of all, the Reagan administration made arms control a higher priority beginning in 1982, and that trend continued into the president's second term (see Jeffrey W. Knopf, Chapter 7, this book).

Despite these accomplishments, the freeze movement is most often characterized as a failure (Solo 1988; McCrea and Markle 1989). Its strategy of developing mass support and then working through Congress to pass freeze legislation has been dubbed a disaster. Critics point to the fact that the 1984 elections returned President Ronald Reagan in a landslide, despite the mobilizing efforts of the freeze. The freeze resolution passed in the House of Representatives in 1983 proved to be a symbolic gesture with no direct impact on policy. The freeze proposal itself was raised briefly by Soviet negotiators at the Strategic Arms Reduction Talks (START) in 1982 but was quickly dropped and never received serious consideration. Finally, critics point to the rapid collapse of the movement after the 1984 elections. In 1987 the much-reduced national staff of the Nuclear Weapons Freeze Campaign (NWFC) merged with the longer established antinuclear organization SANE. As Jeffrey W. Knopf points out in Chapter 7 of this book, the freeze movement articulated public concerns about the hard-line approach to arms control taken by the early Reagan administration, an approach that was later modified. Yet the activities of the freeze itself had only a temporary impact on the arms control policy process and none on arms control policy. Despite the massive support gained during its moment in the sun, the freeze was a failure.

The central question of this chapter is to understand how such a massive movement, a movement that enjoyed such popularity, a movement that kept alive the idea of arms control during a bleak period in the Cold War, could be considered a failure. In broad terms, the answer that will be offered here is that standards of movement success and failure remain murky and poorly understood. The reason those standards are so ill-defined is that there is a lack of clarity about what movements do and what they can be expected to achieve. As Sam Marullo (1990) points out, movements may embrace a wide variety of models of how to change political and social systems. Which change model a movement accepts will determine its choice of tactics and of goals. In order to understand what the nuclear freeze movement accomplished and failed to accomplish, we must first understand the range of possible goals that movements may address.

The Goal of Changing Policy

The manifest goal of political movements, the goal that is most often proclaimed by movement leaders, is to influence policy. The plan of the freeze movement, adopted at the first national convention in March 1981, followed the classic sequence of movement politics. Over a three- to five-year period, freeze activists would first develop the freeze idea, then broaden its popular support, and only then take the idea to policymakers and seek adoption of the plan. Thus, the ultimate goal of the freeze movement was to achieve enactment of the freeze itself: a verifiable, bilateral halt to the development, testing, and deployment of nuclear weapons.

Movements almost never have as much policy influence as their activists would like. The very difficulties of mobilizing people into a movement demands that leaders offer exaggerated promises about the potential for movement impact on policy. In practice, the specific policy proposals championed in movements are rarely enacted into law, or the portions of the movement agenda that are adopted prove to be relatively ineffectual and cosmetic. That shortfall of policy influence is an important source of perceptions of movement failure. Such evaluations are reinforced by the ironic fact that the policy proposals of political movements (or something closely resembling them) are often enacted after the mobilization cycle of the movement has come to an end.

The nuclear freeze movement provides an example of this phenomenon. Activism within the movement peaked in 1982–1984, a period in which administration officials declared consistently that a nuclear freeze or indeed any form of agreed limitations on nuclear arms would place U.S. security in serious jeopardy. It is difficult to overstate the hostility of the early Reagan presidency to arms control. As Knopf points out in Chapter 7, the early Reagan administration had no unified arms control strategy and so for over a year let the matter sit without articulating any vision of what a feasible and desirable arms control agreement would look like. When an administration position was eventually formulated, it was based on the dubious premise of Soviet nuclear superiority and consequently on the necessity for the United States either to negotiate disproportionate Soviet reductions or to avoid arms control completely while launching an accelerated missile deployment program.

The controversy surrounding Kenneth Adelman's appointment as head of the Arms Control and Disarmament Agency (ACDA) in 1983 is typical. Adelman had once described arms control negotiations as a "political sham," and critics claimed that this perspective suited that of the administration as a whole (Cole 1983: 102). This attitude was not lost on the American public, whose increased fear of nuclear war was a major factor in public support of the nuclear freeze (Milburn, Watanabe, and Kramer 1986; Thomas R. Rochon and Stephen P. Wood, Chapter 2, this book). The actions of the Reagan administration fueled the freeze movement.

In light of these considerations, the best measure of the policy success of the freeze is the extent to which the Reagan administration reversed its early positions on the Soviet Union and arms control. Rhetorically, it is possible to see signs of an effort to defuse growing concerns about nuclear war from early in the freeze movement's history. In May 1982 the president unveiled his START proposal. A year later he proposed a solution to the deadlocked negotiations on Intermediate-Range Nuclear Forces (INF), which had been stuck for several years on a plan (the zero option) under which the Soviets would give up their existing intermediate-range nuclear missiles in exchange for the United States not deploying any. These proposals were formulated, however, in the belief that the Soviet Union was unlikely to accept them (Talbott 1984).

The failure of the freeze movement to achieve policy success during the life of the NWFC is a common pattern that unites the freeze movement with many others. The fact that activists continue to mobilize for movements whose objectives fail to be translated into policy suggests that we should look elsewhere for the immediate and direct impacts of movement activity.

Social Change Goals of the Movement

If movements had only legislative goals, they would be well advised to recast themselves as conventional interest groups. Indeed, the nuclear freeze movement came close to doing so when it moved its headquarters from St. Louis to Washington, D.C., and when it chose to focus almost exclusively on congressional lobbying and electoral campaigning. These decisions, as we shall see, were products of a mistaken idea of what the resources of the freeze movement were and of what it could expect to accomplish.

The freeze movement was from the beginning more successful in mobilizing citizen activity than it was in influencing the course of arms control negotiations. Highlights of movement mobilization include the New York demonstration of 750,000 people in June 1982, the November 1982 passage of eight statewide referenda, and the success that fall in electing a Congress more favorable to the freeze idea than the outgoing Congress had been.

This mobilization of popular interest and energy, even if it did not alter the arms control process, nonetheless altered the place of nuclear weapons, nuclear war, and arms control in American culture. The freeze movement was not only about getting U.S. and Soviet signatures on a piece of paper but also about amorphous social and political goals that could only be partially expressed in terms of legislation.

These more amorphous goals are referred to by Joseph Gusfield (1981) as the "fluid dimension" of political movements. In their fluid dimension, movements have a greater impact on society than on government. By changing social values, movements expand the range of ideas about what is possible. This ultimately has an effect on politics because it changes perceptions of what the most important political problems are. Movements find new solutions to old problems, find new problems, or bring problems from the private realm into the public realm. Movements redefine the political and social environment.

Understanding the freeze movement from the perspective of social change begins with a broadening of perspective to consider the movement as being about more than the freeze proposal itself. It was rather the convergence of a variety of critiques of the Reagan foreign policy. Some critics endorsed proposals other than the freeze, such as the "no-first use" proposal outlined by McGeorge Bundy, George Kennan, Robert McNamara, and Gerard Smith in their much-discussed article in *Foreign Affairs* (Bundy et al. 1982). The freeze became the ubiquitous label for a wide variety of peace groups, many of whom embraced more dramatic steps such as disarmament or linking military spending to social justice and Third World development. The "profreeze" label was even applied to those who supported airing the television special *The Day After,* about the effects of a nuclear attack on Lawrence, Kansas. This development led David Meyer (1990: 132) to note that the freeze "came to mean simply concern about the dangers of nuclear war."

That concern was reflected in a flowering of local activity and organization for the freeze beginning in 1981 and 1982. Meetings, forums, debates, video presentations, art displays, fasts, and vigils were organized by the thousands in local churches, in clubs, in social and service organizations, and at county fairs, city councils, and town meetings (Bentley 1984; Solo 1988: 82 ff.). Initially, the NWFC was quite conscious of the importance of local action. The strategy paper developed at its first national conference in March 1981 said, in part:

> Past efforts at serious arms control . . . failed in part because they were not preceded by active educational efforts among the general public by a sufficiently broad spectrum of organizations. For this reason, the freeze effort is aimed, in the first instance, not at Washington but at recruiting active organizational and public support. (cited in Feighan 1983)

The strategy of local action was so successful because of the breadth of popular support for the freeze. Yet that very success carried with it the danger that the freeze would join God and democracy as values that many people profess without much thought. It is true virtually by definition that any political issue that attracts wide adherence from the American public is supported by many whose beliefs are not firmly held. Yet the image of "wide but shallow" support for the freeze does not square with the Gallup finding that 45 percent favored a *unilateral* nuclear freeze even if the Soviet Union did not agree to reciprocate (Meyer 1990: 88). Indeed, the freeze had consensus support in the United States *despite* the belief of 41 percent in 1982 that the Soviet Union had a stronger nuclear arsenal[1] and the belief of 60 percent in 1981 that the Soviets were "not at all likely" to abide by a freeze agreement.[2] Most indicative of the depth of commitment to the freeze may be the Harris poll finding that 56 percent of voters said they would make support for the freeze a litmus test issue in the 1982 congressional elections.[3] As Rochon and Wood show in Chapter 2, far fewer actually took the freeze into consideration in the 1982 elections. Even so, the freeze achieved a degree of mass mobilization that had not been seen on a foreign policy issue since the Vietnam War. If we restrict our focus to times of peace, there is literally no precedent for the level of interest aroused by the freeze proposal.

Active commitment and the creation of settings in which to discuss new political ideas and values are more important means of generating social change than are large levels of passive support uncovered by opinion polls. The social change potential of the freeze lies in the fact that it generated an unusual amount of local activism and media coverage. Media attention to the freeze reached a series of peaks in the run-up to the demonstration in New York City in June 1982, during the campaign to pass freeze referenda during the November 1982 elections, and during the consideration of a freeze motion in Congress in March 1983 (see Figure 6.1). Throughout that period, most of the public were familiar with only one arms control idea, namely the freeze.

The activities surrounding the state referenda drives offered a particularly useful vehicle for social change. The referendum campaign in most states created a setting in which prominent politicians were asked to state their positions, endorsements of the freeze were collected and publicized, public relations firms were hired and did their work, and—most important—doors were knocked on by the tens of thousands to distribute literature and to collect money and signatures on petitions. In California alone, a half million signatures were gathered in three months to put the freeze on the ballot. If those half million signatures represent a million contacts made in shopping malls, schools, office buildings, and homes, then the referendum campaign might best be viewed as an institutional framework for the kind of interpersonal contacts that foster changed thinking about how to pursue stable relations with the Soviet Union.

The impact of the freeze on social values was not limited to the relatively brief period of mass mobilization and media attention. To the extent that the ideas propagated by the freeze became institutionalized, it had a more lasting impact. As a proposal that briefly united many existing peace groups and brought new ones into being, the freeze left the legacy of an enhanced network of peace organizations and activists who would continue to present alternative views on nuclear weapons and security (see the chapters in Part Three of this book). The large number of peace studies programs established in high schools and colleges in the 1980s and the renewed debate about nuclear strategy in academic circles are among the social legacies of the freeze campaign. These legacies may well have long-term ripple effects on thinking about nuclear weapons and arms control even after the Cold War.

Despite these accomplishments, though, the freeze must be judged an underachiever in the realm of social change. The emphasis given to congressional lobbying led to an impatience for immediately obtainable results. Social values did not change during the life of the freeze movement so much as the freeze itself did. Even the referendum campaigns lost much of their social change value as they became better funded and took on more of the characteristics of a media campaign than a grassroots contacting effort. Media blitzes are the best technology for generating signatures and votes but not for changing social values. Door-to-door campaigns are labor intensive and reach only one person at a time, but research on attitude formation shows that personal contacting is far more powerful than exposure to the same message through printed or electronic media (Oskamp 1991: 158, 167; Eldersveld 1956).

Substantively, too, the freeze idea suffered in the drive to appeal to the political center. In order to achieve the greatest possible support in the California referendum, for example, the wording of the freeze on the ballot stressed that the proposal was dependent on adequate verifiability, an open-ended contingency that could mean almost anything. Nor did the California proposal contain a clause, found in other statements of the freeze, calling for transfer of money from the arms race to socially useful programs. Adam Garfinkle (1984: 184) claims with some justice that "many [referenda] were phrased in 'have you stopped beating your wife' language, crafted to imply that those who dared to oppose the resolutions actually enjoyed the prospect of nuclear carnage."

In its congressional version, the freeze was watered down still further. The seemingly slight changes in wording introduced into the freeze resolution passed in the House in 1982 had turned it into something that even President Reagan could accept.[4] Although freeze supporters had better luck pushing their own language in the House in 1983, the resolution passed that year was so vague in nature that both sides claimed victory. The original resolution was 202 words long; amendments tacked on before the final vote lengthened the enacted version to 1251 words (Waller 1987: 289). "The freeze still comes first," said Speaker Tip O'Neill. "The priorities [in arms control] have not been altered," claimed Minority Leader Robert Michel.[5] Michel's interpretation of the outcome is supported by the fact that the House went on that same year to approve funding for MX and Trident missile development, funding of the first segments of the Strategic Defense Initiative (SDI, or Star Wars), and deployment of the cruise and Pershing II missiles in Europe. By the time of the 1984 presidential campaign, the meaning of the freeze was so unclear that each of the Democratic candidates endorsed both the freeze and selected plans for modernization of the strategic nuclear arsenal.

In sum, there is a clear tension between the congressional and electoral strategies of the freeze, which were designed to influence policy, and the goal of social change, which is the product of millions of conversations in schools, offices, and living rooms. When a state referendum drive becomes a direct mail and mass media campaign rather than an excuse to knock on doors, then the social change potential of the freeze is diminished even as the prospect of passing the referendum goes up. Movement scholars have pointed out that ballot initiatives ask for little sacrifice from supporters and so have distinct advantages as a means of mobilizing weak support (Ennis and Schreuer 1987). This is true, but the down side is that media campaigns for ballot initiatives do little to inculcate the altered social values associated with generating strong support for a movement.

Some peace groups that made social change their first priority followed strategies involving much more attention to local action than did the freeze. Ground Zero, an organization dedicated to grassroots action, sponsored a nationwide week of teach-ins, discussion groups, art displays, and other local events in April 1980. Ground Zero's founder, Roger Molander, believes that "it was the [freeze] movement's failure to understand the role of education in movement development, not political naiveté or a lack of sufficient political base, that was the overriding cause of its failures and decline" (Molander and Molander 1990). Pam Solo, a dissident tactician within the freeze movement, also believes that "keeping education separate from strategy was like giving the movement a lobotomy" (Meyer 1990: 191). By focusing on its congressional strategy, the freeze campaign neglected the social change potential of local action. The most eloquent testimony to this neglect of local action comes from an activist in New York, who sent a plaintive message to the St. Louis office: "Just please let's have a simple, clear task for all of us to work on. . . . The five-hour-a-week volunteers want to know how to spend that time most effectively" (Solo 1988: 139).

Policy Process Goals of the Movement

Another possible goal of political movements is to alter the process by which policy decisions are made. Movement leaders frequently find that the political establishment, put under pressure by the surge of public interest in an issue area, responds by diffusing the locus of responsibility on the issue. One typical change is that the consultation of interested groups in the society is increased in order to defuse potential movement mobilization. For example, the environmental movement, both in the United States and elsewhere, has obtained a number of concessions such as the requirement of environmental impact statements and public hearings preceding major construction projects. As a result of these procedures, developers are now in the habit of consulting citizens' groups before they even go to the formal hearing phase, in order to anticipate problems and to forestall opposition (Rochon and Mazmanian 1993). That the increased use of consultation is largely a response to movement politics is suggested by both the timing of the inauguration of consultation mechanisms (often just after a movement mobilization has derailed some project) and the fact that procedures for consultation are the most rigorous in issue areas where popular mobilizations have been the most widespread (for example, in the siting and construction of nuclear power plants).

A second institutional response to movement protest has been to set up mechanisms for review of grievances and appeal of decisions. The clearest examples of this in the United States have come in the area of civil rights, for example, in the establishment of Equal Employment Opportunity Commissions (EEOCs) at federal and state levels. Cases are brought before such commissions by organized groups seeking to defend their rights. Through the provision of such avenues of appeal, authorities are able to defuse protest by channeling it into institutionalized procedures. Such concessions are not costless, though, for they give movement organizations a means of affecting policy outcomes even if they have not altered legislation.

A third form of response to movement mobilizations through change in the policy process is the decentralization of policy authority. In the United States, which has always had a relatively decentralized governmental system, this response is not as common as it is in such highly centralized democracies as France and Japan. But some areas of policy are highly centralized even in the United States, and one response to public protest may be to bring more actors into the policy system. When the activities of intelligence agencies caused public concern, for example, a congressional committee was created that effectively decentralized policy authority from the executive acting alone to executive action with legislative oversight (Johnson 1989).

It would be foolish to idealize the significance of these forms of policy process change for the power of movements to participate in policymaking. Indeed, the motives of political leaders in changing the policy process may be to defuse protest with as little substantive change as possible. Thus, for example, the EEOC was initially established without the power to enforce its findings (Freeman 1975: 81–84). Nonetheless, substantive control over issues tends to grow in bodies originally created merely to quiet protest. The EEOC was strengthened in 1972, and access to it was liberalized. Its initial mandate to examine race discrimination was later expanded to cover sex discrimination. Complaints of discrimination are today lodged with the EEOC by a wide variety of groups defined by race, ethnicity, gender, and sexual orientation. Clearly, procedural reforms tend to expand in significance as time goes on.

The issues of nuclear strategy, arms control, and superpower relations are matters that have traditionally been dominated by the executive and in which an opening of the policy process to new participants would be strongly resisted. That resistance is clearly shown in the legislative history of the freeze. The congressional strategy on which the freeze movement pinned its hopes resulted in a resolution stating that negotiations for a mutual and verifiable freeze should be incorporated into the Strategic Arms Reduction Talks between the United States and the Soviet Union. The resolution stated that this should be done only if the United States and the Soviet Union had "essential equivalence in overall nuclear capabilities," only to the extent that such an agreement would be mutual and verifiable, only to the extent that such an agreement would be compatible with North Atlantic Treaty Organization (NATO) obligations, only to the extent that the credibility of the U.S. nuclear deterrent would be maintained, and only to the extent that such an agreement would not jeopardize the ability of the United States to preserve freedom. Section 3b of the Joint Resolution calling for a mutual and verifiable freeze on and reductions in nuclear weapons states: "Nothing in this resolution shall be construed to supersede the treatymaking powers of the President under the Constitution."

In short, the freeze resolution passed by the House offered the president a variety of reasons its mandate to negotiate a freeze agreement could be refused. Since the president had frequently gone on record to state that the U.S. nuclear arsenal was no match for the Soviets' and since he insisted that a freeze would be neither verifiable nor consistent with the maintenance of a credible deterrent, the House resolution (taken by itself) had no more practical impact than a "sense of Congress" motion urging the president to action. Before even introducing the resolution in the House, Representative Edward Markey and his staff agreed that "we should make clear that we are introducing a symbolic measure. . . . We're concerned in this resolution only with making a statement" (Waller 1987: 52). That President Reagan did not act in accordance with the urgings of the resolution can have come as a surprise to no one.

Could the freeze movement have brought about an opening of the arms control policy process had it followed a strategy less reliant on congressional passage of a freeze resolution? In 1982 and 1983, when popular mobilization for the freeze was at its height, the movement was positioned to claim that President Reagan's handling of superpower relations was inadequate to the seriousness of the threat of nuclear war. Popular support for the freeze was less an endorsement of the freeze proposal per se than it was a belief that *something* had to be done to alter the seeming drift toward military confrontation with the Soviet Union.

Under such circumstances, freeze leaders might have argued that arms control policy cannot be entrusted solely to the executive office. Indeed, the Democratic Congress took steps in precisely this direction. Douglas Waller (1987: 303) argues that never has a modern president faced so much legislative advice or so many restrictions on nuclear weapons as Mr. Reagan did after 1982. Congress finally capped deployment of the MX missile at half of what the president wanted. It temporarily halted the production of nerve gas and the testing of antisatellite weapons. It called on the president not to undercut the SALT II treaty and . . . to resume negotiations toward a comprehensive ban on the testing of nuclear warheads. It approved the establishment of a federally funded U.S. Institute for Peace. It put restrictions on U.S. military involvement in Central America. It cut sizable chunks out of the president's Star Wars budget.

Each of these actions demonstrated the readiness of a Democratic Congress to meddle in the policies of a president whose hard-line rhetoric meant that his remarkable popularity with the American people tended to stop at the water's edge of foreign and defense policy. In general, Congress kept the Reagan administration on a shorter security policy leash than any other twentieth-century president was forced to endure. However, these battles over weaponry, defense appropriations, and arms control had to be fought one at a time. Because they were never linked to a formal mechanism for Senate oversight of the president's international diplomacy, the moment was lost in which reform of the policy process might have been achieved. Allowing movement pressure to take the form of a joint congressional resolution was a mistake. Had the freeze movement demanded changes in the policy process rather than a symbolic freeze resolution, it might have had a greater long-run impact on nuclear arms control policy.

Counterfactual hypotheses, such as the question of what would have happened had the freeze movement sought a greater role for Congress in arms talks with the Soviet Union, are necessarily highly speculative. To launch such a campaign, the freeze would have had to shift all its resources to the Senate, which alone is given a constitutional role in the treaty process. The Senate was never as receptive to the freeze as was the House, so this would have been a risky strategy. Moreover, the Constitution prohibits even the Senate from ordering the president to negotiate a particular treaty.

What the Constitution does permit is an expanded "advice and consent" role in which the Senate would establish a more active dialogue with the president on desirable directions in arms control.[6] To do so would mean a return to the role of the Senate in an earlier period in U.S. history, as, for example, when President George Washington sought Senate approval of treaty negotiators as well as Senate advice on their negotiating instructions (Fisher 1990: 308). Above all, it would mean pressing home the argument that arms control policy is too vital to the national interest to be left solely in the hands of the executive branch.

It was just such arguments and concerns that led to other instances of congressional assertiveness in the realm of foreign policy, such as the 1973

War Powers Act (passed over presidential veto) and the series of acts establishing greater congressional control over intelligence operations, passed in the wake of revelations concerning covert intelligence activities abroad.

In an ironic twist, President Reagan seems to have realized better than freeze movement leaders themselves the extent to which public discontent was linked to his personal style of rhetorical confrontation with the Soviet Union. In order to reduce the high and controversial profile that superpower relations had achieved during his first years in office, the president began to revive the arms control process and to change the rhetoric emanating from his administration. This had the effect of placing arms control issues in the hands of a small group of expert negotiators chosen by the president's office (Kazin 1984: 446). The president himself changed his tone on nuclear arms and arms control, presenting his Star Wars package as a means of eliminating the risks of a breakdown in nuclear deterrence.

By removing arms control from the political arena and returning it to a setting dominated by technically oriented experts, President Reagan defused the concerns felt by many about his sincerity in reducing superpower tensions. When, on election night 1984, the president said that the top foreign policy priority of his second administration would be to revive the arms control process (Waller 1987: 5), the death knell for the freeze movement was sounded. The arms control policy process reverted to the expert arena that had been dominant prior to 1981. Members of Congress—along with many other Americans—lost further interest in the issue.

Conclusion

The movement for a nuclear freeze continued to be the focus of local organizing for some years after its peak in 1982 and 1983, but the movement had come to define itself in terms of its impact on the national political arena, and at that level the movement simply disappeared. Senator Patrick Moynihan's (D, New York) mail contained 130,000 letters about the freeze in the first five months of 1983, but only 350 letters in the last five months of 1984 (Waller 1987: 299). Efforts in 1984 and after to pass a more stringent freeze resolution (the so-called Quick Freeze) attracted few sponsors and ended up going nowhere.

The pattern of rise and decline of the movement should not be described as a failure of the freeze, for all movements go through cycles of mobilization and demobilization. Indeed, the central lesson of this chapter is that the freeze movement cannot be evaluated as a success or failure along any one dimension of activity. Rather, and in common with other social movements, there are three faces of the freeze: policy influence, social change, and impact on the political process.

Freeze leaders themselves came to place their exclusive emphasis on policy change, which movements frequently fail to achieve. To pass a freeze resolution in Congress was an enormous undertaking, one that demanded of movement leaders a narrowness of purpose and vision that was alien to most of them. Success of the congressional effort required that the freeze movement not take any positions that would be controversial. Thus, for example, congressional staffers argued at the national freeze conference in 1983 that the movement could not take a position against cruise and Pershing II missile deployment without hurting the freeze resolution in the House that year (Waller 1987: 173–178). People like Randy Kehler were forced to turn their backs on a long history of grassroots organizing in order to concentrate on the search for support among congressional moderates.

Passage of the freeze resolution was an all-consuming task and one that was doomed to achieve less than the movement organizers hoped. The effort to write freeze legislation was very much like an attempt to script your side of a conversation when you do not yet know how the other person is going to react to your opening words. In his detailed account of the battles in the House of Representatives to pass freeze legislation, Waller shows that debates on the freeze were quickly caught up in the impossible task of legislating outcomes for hypothetical negotiations. The freeze idea is simple in principle, but to put it into practice requires that a host of decisions be made concerning which weapons are to be included or excluded, whether testing and replacement of existing weapons is to be allowed, how to draw the line between improvement of existing weapons systems and the creation of new ones, and how to dovetail timing of the freeze with other arms control proposals.

Because of these difficulties, the freeze resolution could never have been anything other than symbolic. But the symbol was not worth its cost: neglect of the grassroots movement and the narrowing of focus by the critical arms control community to a single proposal. Everything that the freeze movement stood for had become hostage to the wording of a congressional resolution, to the votes on a long series of amendments, and to the media interpretation of whether the convoluted language that was eventually adopted represented vindication or defeat for the Reagan administration's foreign policy.

The grassroots strength of the freeze movement suggests that change in social values might have been a more appropriate goal of the movement. To place change in social values high on the freeze movement agenda would have required a shift in emphasis away from congressional and media campaigns in favor of the local activism that animated the movement in its earliest stages. It is difficult to say no to individuals and organizations that offer to bankroll a statewide referendum campaign and even more difficult to say no to a Senator Kennedy who wants to introduce freeze legislation in the Senate. In fact, even if there were a will to say no, there may not have been the option to do so. The choice was available, however, for the movement to continue the grassroots educational effort while others championed its cause on the floor of the House.

The most significant lost opportunity of the freeze movement may lie in its failure to press for reform of the arms control policy process, liberating it from the exclusive control of the executive office. With the overtly negative attitude toward arms control displayed during the first years of his presidency, Ronald Reagan created an unease among the American public and in Congress that superpower relations were not being handled well. In analogous situations in the recent past, Congress has reacted by restricting the president's freedom to maneuver. In this instance, it was up to the freeze movement to make the case that the arms control policy process must be opened to a greater degree of public accountability and control, presumably through expansion of the "advice and consent" role of the Senate.

An upsurge of public interest and activism such as that displayed on behalf of the nuclear freeze between 1981 and 1984 can be a powerful tool in the hands of a movement. The freeze movement chose to use its mobilization capacity to organize referenda and to work on election campaigns. These efforts led to impressive results in the 1982 elections and were instrumental in the passage of a freeze resolution in the House of Representatives in 1983. But, by November 1984 the possibilities of electoral action were exhausted. The focus of the movement narrowed to the halls of Congress, and the grassroots of the movement were reduced to a fund-raising mechanism.

At the height of the freeze movement mobilization, George Kennan (1982: 201) wrote, "The public discussion of the problems presented by nuclear weaponry which is now taking place in this country is going to go down in history . . . as the most significant that any democratic society has ever engaged in." By failing to see this surge in public discussion as the truly significant aspect of the freeze movement, strategists of the movement allowed Kennan's vision to remain unfulfilled.

Notes

1. A 41 percent belief in Soviet superiority is nearly six times as many as the 7 percent who believed that the United States had nuclear superiority. Cited in Frances McCrea and Gerald Markle (1989: 97).

2. This is from a Gallup Poll in May 1981, cited in L. Marvin Overby and Sarah Ritchie (1990).

3. This self-reported role for the freeze surely exaggerates its importance in

the 1982 congressional elections but does nonetheless signal the importance of the issue to many voters. The Harris poll result is cited in David Meyer (1990: 88).

4. The original wording advocating a "mutual and verifiable freeze followed by reductions in nuclear weapons" was changed to "an equitable and verifiable agreement which freezes strategic nuclear forces at equal and substantially reduced levels." This modified language, close to the spirit of the Reagan arms control proposals, was widely assumed to be unacceptable to the Soviet Union and therefore a "safe" position for opponents of an arms control agreement.

5. Both are cited in Overby and Ritchie (1990).

6. Article 2, section 2, paragraph 2 of the Constitution says in part that "[The president] shall have Power, by and with the Advice and Consent of the Senate, to make Treaties, provided two-thirds of the Senators present concur; and he shall nominate, and by and with the Advice and Consent of the Senate, shall appoint Ambassadors, other public Ministers and Consuls, Judges of the Supreme Court, and all other Officers of the United States."

PART 3

Demobilization and
Movement Transition

9

Persevering for Peace: Organizational Survival & Transformation of the U.S. Peace Movement, 1988–1992

SAM MARULLO & BOB EDWARDS

During its long and rich history the U.S. peace movement has cycled through numerous periods of mobilization, decline, and abeyance (Wittner 1984; Chatfield with Kleidman 1992). Since the late 1800s such cycles of peace action have been punctuated by heightened mobilization to prevent or oppose U.S. involvement in wars. Following each of those conflicts, the shape and character of the peace movement has been transformed. The organizations and strategies preeminent in the movement as the country went to war have typically been eclipsed by newer groups advocating goals and strategies more attuned to the postwar sociopolitical context (Pagnucco 1992).

The period between 1988 and 1992 is particularly interesting from the standpoint of social movement theory because by 1988 the peace movement's resurgence around the Nuclear Weapons Freeze Campaign had clearly crested and was in decline. Although there has been a great deal written recently about "cycles of protest" (Tarrow 1989a and 1989b) and the cyclical aspects of specific movements (Buechler 1990; Meyer 1993a; Kleidman 1993), most analysts have focused on movements' emergence and growth (Lofland 1993; McAdam, McCarthy and Zald 1988). The peace movement's resurgence in the early 1980s is no exception, and already more than a dozen books about the nuclear freeze campaign and the broader U.S. peace movement of the 1980s focus on its dramatic growth from an idea to a national political campaign. The movement's decline has received relatively cursory coverage by comparison. In this chapter we examine the U.S. peace movement during just such a period of transformation (1988–

1992) as it adjusted to the end of the Cold War and opposed U.S. involvement in the Gulf War.

Recent trends in social movement theory offer political, cultural, and organizational approaches to understand the actions, agendas, and evolution of social movements (McAdam, McCarthy, and Zald 1988; Morris and Mueller 1992). More politically oriented analysts frequently track media coverage of collective action events to chronicle patterns of movement activity, often linking them to fluctuations in political opportunity (McAdam 1982; Tilly 1993–1994; Meyer 1993b). Those stressing cultural factors have examined movement framing processes (Snow and Benford 1988; Benford 1993) or collective identity (Whittier 1995; Cohen 1985; Taylor and Whittier 1992) in relation to changes in the political or cultural climate. More organizationally minded analysts, inspired by recent trends in organizational theory (Hannan and Carroll 1992; Powell and DiMaggio 1991), have examined patterns of founding (McCarthy, Britt, and Wolfson 1991; Walker 1991) or demise (Weed 1991; Minkoff 1993; Edwards and Marullo 1995) among social movement organizations.

In this chapter we use an organizational approach to analyze changes in the U.S. peace movement between 1988 and 1992. We assume that social movement transformations occur, in part, as existing groups disband and are replaced by newly founded ones whose forms, strategies, or repertoires are more effective or innovative by comparison. A systematic understanding of which groups disband during periods of decline and which persist to struggle another day is a crucial yet little examined component of the transformation of social movements over time. Consequently, we consider the relevance for social movement research of findings from a comprehensive analysis of survival among U.S. peace movement groups between 1988 and 1992, a period of movement decline and of profound fluctuation in political context.

In the next section we discuss three reasons why demographic aspects of social movement organizations (SMOs), such as patterns of founding and demise, must be considered in analyses of social movement evolution. We then introduce the concept of SMO "domains" and describe how we categorize peace groups into small, large, and national peace movement organization (PMO) domains. This is followed by an examination of how size, structure, operating strategy, and peacemaking activities relate to organization persistence or demise during a period of movement decline and how these relationships vary across the three PMO domains. We conclude the chapter with a discussion of the patterns of perseverance among PMOs and their meaning for the kinds of groups that will be on hand to shape the next surge of peace movement mobilization.

Mobilization Cycles and
the Evolution of Movement "Industries"

Much of the theoretical attention to the emergence of movements focuses on the dramatic wave of protest specific to the 1960s. To help explain the timing and pattern of coincident mobilizations of multiple movements during this period, Sidney Tarrow (1989a) conceptualized a "cycle of protest" and linked its emergence to a variety of macrostructural factors common throughout the West. However, the 1970s found the civil rights and peace movements in abeyance, while other movements such as feminism, environmentalism, and gay pride/rights were surging. By the early 1980s the peace movement had resurged with the advent of the nuclear freeze campaign. Yet, the Washington-based environmental movement was on the defensive against the Reagan administration's push for deregulation, and the grassroots environmental mobilizations prominent in the late 1980s were still forthcoming (Scarce 1990; Bullard 1995; Edwards 1995b; Jasper and Nelkin 1992). Similarly, the women's movement was in abeyance or repression (Rupp and Taylor 1987; Faludi 1991) with professionalized abortion rights SMOs (Staggenborg 1991) and lesbian, feminist cultural institutions predominating (Whittier 1995).

Unlike the "cycle of protest" in the 1960s, during which multiple movements arose simultaneously, these post-1960s variations are better conceptualized as mobilization surges (Lofland and Marullo 1993). This movement-specific concept enables a more differentiated assessment of how cyclical aspects of particular movements are affected by fluctuations in political and cultural opportunity and resource availability. Accounting for the kinds of groups that disband or persist during periods of demobilization and decline helps us understand the subsequent evolution of social movements.

First, social movement emergence has been a central theoretical concern, with relatively little analytical attention paid to subsequent periods of demobilization and decline. And yet, the importance accorded to preexisting organizational infrastructures (McAdam 1982; McCarthy 1987; Morris 1984; Tilly 1975) and the availability of external and internal resources (McCarthy and Zald 1977; Freeman 1979; Gamson 1975) in the many accounts of movement emergence indirectly point out the significance of SMO survival through prior periods of demobilization and decline.

Second, the ideological, tactical, and organizational innovations of newly founded groups are often framed in contrast, even overt opposition, to those represented by the core constituencies and long-standing SMOs of their own movement (see Robert Kleidman and Thomas R. Rochon, Chapter 3, this book). Organizational survivors of prior campaigns often serve as the foils for groups founded during subsequent mobilization surges.

Third, resurgent movements like the U.S. peace movement in the early 1980s are neither new nor merely repeats of prior mobilization campaigns (Kleidman 1993). Groups that survive prior periods of movement decline often exert a disproportionate influence over issue framing and tactical choice early in subsequent movement campaigns, even if newly founded SMOs eventually eclipse them in later phases of the mobilization surge. Such key organizations (Taylor 1989; Edwards and McCarthy 1992) and long-enduring core peace constituencies like the historic peace churches and world federalists have been instrumental in initiating resurgent peace protest (Wittner 1984; Boulding 1990). As a surging movement wanes into decline, a substantial remnant of groups founded during the surge will survive to initiate, shape, and be co-opted by subsequent mobilization campaigns.

Data and Methods

Our analysis here both parallels previous research emphases and distinguishes variations in the dynamics of survival across the spectrum of small, large, and national SMOs. It is made possible by a unique data set based on a survey of a nationally representative sample of peace movement groups active in 1988, which was replicated in 1992. These rich organizational data enable us to consider how differences in key PMO characteristics in 1988 are associated with survival to 1992. In contrast to most research on social movement organizations, we are able to analyze PMOs active in 1988 across the entire spectrum of this diverse social movement "industry." By using the group's 1992 status (disbanded or still active) as the dependent variable in a series of multivariate logistic regression analyses, we examined a broad range of group attributes in 1988 to construct "survival profiles" for the population as a whole and separately for each of three distinct PMO domains.[1]

The data used in the analysis discussed here come from a 1988 survey of peace movement organizations, conceived and undertaken by Mary Anna Colwell (1988 and 1989), which was constructed from a nationally representative, stratified sample of PMOs drawn from the 1987 edition of the *Grassroots Peace Directory* (*GPD*) (Topsfield 1987). The *GPD* was a comprehensive listing of organizations working for peace compiled by the Topsfield Foundation and updated bimonthly until it ceased publication in 1989. As a major foundation funder of peacemaking activities, Topsfield developed the directory as a means of promoting cooperation and networking among groups working for peace. Using its extensive contacts throughout the country, the foundation included over 7,700 peace groups in the 1987 edition of the *GPD*.

Organizations listed covered a broad spectrum of local, state, and national peace groups. They ranged from informal groups of friends working together locally to large national organizations with local affiliates and extensive memberships. The PMOs in this population pursued a variety of peace goals, including promotion of arms control and disarmament, opposition to U.S. policies in Central America, and promotion of alternative methods of conflict resolution at the local level.

For sampling purposes, the population of organizations was divided by budget size into large and small categories. All 491 large PMOs (budgets greater than $30,000) were included in the sample. These large-budget organizations make up roughly 7 percent of the PMO population. From the remaining 7,160 groups listed, a 5 percent random sample was drawn, yielding 346 PMOs that had not reported a 1986 budget of over $30,000. Response rates are as follows: 56 percent (n = 272) for the large-budget groups and 43 percent (n = 139) for the small-budget groups.[2]

The PMO survey instrument was a twenty-page questionnaire completed by one of the group's leaders. The questions covered a broad range of organizational attributes, strategies, activities, values, and goals. In 1992 these organizations were surveyed again with an updated questionnaire (Colwell, Bond et al. 1992). Based on this replication, we found that ninety-one of the 411 peace groups in our stratified sample (22 percent) had ceased operations between 1988 and 1992 (Colwell and Bond 1994).[3]

SMO Survival, Size, and Domains

The internal dynamics and environmental challenges confronting SMOs as organizations vary substantially as a function of their size and geographic scope of operations (Martin 1990; Edwards 1995a). With respect to survival, large groups in competitive environments typically operate at an advantage over smaller ones. This "liability of smallness" has been demonstrated in a variety of organizational populations, including nonprofit organizations and firms (Singh and Lumsden 1990). Analyses of national SMOs have come to similar conclusions, finding that larger groups were more likely to win new advantages and acceptance than smaller groups (Gamson 1975) and be more likely to survive (Minkoff 1993). However, "minimalist organizations" are said to possess survival advantages of their own (Halliday, Powell, and Granfors 1987). Minimalist organizations, like most SMOs, have relatively low overhead and start-up costs and are said to be rather resilient because they can weather hard times by relying on core members or patrons.[4] Furthermore, they are thought to be highly adaptive, capable of quickly redefining their mission or issue focus to fit changing situations.[5]

In our analysis of mortality among PMOs, we found that there was a liability of smallness (Edwards and Marullo 1995). We examined several commonly used indicators of size, such as total expenditures, number of paid staff, and number of members. Smallness of membership base, having less than 100 members, was the only indicator related significantly to mortality among the entire population. Small PMOs were more likely to disband than large-budget PMOs or national PMOs. However, *within* each of these three PMO categories, group size (measured by members, budget, or staff) was not related to survival. We also found that the dynamics of mortality varied significantly across the three categories of PMOs. The profile of surviving groups among small-budget PMOs is different from that of nonnational large-budget PMOs. National organizations also have a distinct mortality profile.

Table 9.1 displays the three categories we use to represent organizational domains. Small nonnational peace movement organizations (small PMOs) operate primarily at the local level, and their annual budgets are less than $30,000. Large nonnational peace movement organizations (large PMOs) have budgets larger than $30,000 and operate over a local, regional, or statewide area. National peace movement organizations (national PMOs) operate at the nationwide level and have budgets that are generally (but not always) larger than $30,000.

An SMO domain is an intermediate level of analysis between the social movement "industry" and the single organization. The derivation of domain categories used here builds on Patricia Martin's (1990) distinction between the scale (size) and scope of feminist organizations. Domain effectively controls for the broad effects of variations in SMO size and scope of operations. Using this ecological distinction enables us to examine SMO survival both across and within the separate domains of the movement.

Table 9.1 Peace Movement Organization Domains

Budget Size	Local	State/Regional	National
<$30,000	Small PMOs (N = 128)		National PMOs (N = 135)
	98	30	5
≥$30,000	Large PMOs (N = 147)		
	91	56	130

Source: Colwell and Bond (1994).

Note: N = 410; one of the 411 peace movement groups did not report its scope of operations.

Table 9.2 presents differences by domain for a variety of PMO characteristics. The attributes have been grouped into demographic, resource and
legitimacy, organizational structure, operating strategy, and tactical repertoire and playlist categories. In the next section we review pertinent aspects
of these literatures and examine the association of specific attributes with
PMO survival. In the subsequent section, we discuss the characteristics
found to be associated with survival across the entire population and separately within the small, large, and national PMO domains. Attributes listed
in Table 9.2 but not further discussed were not associated with PMO survival at any level.

PMO Attributes and Patterns of Survival

Demographic Attributes

Numerous studies of firms have demonstrated that rates of mortality
decrease with age (Carroll 1983; Singh and Lumsden 1990). However,
analyses of groups more closely resembling SMOs have not found such a
"liability of newness." Furthermore, the work of Howard Aldrich and his
collaborators has shown that even among certain business populations and
national trade associations, mortality rates peaked some years after founding and tapered off thereafter (Aldrich et al. 1990; Aldrich and Auster
1986). This pattern has been labeled a "liability of adolescence" (Fichman
and Levinthal 1988), a phenomenon that focuses analytic attention on intra-
organizational processes that might favor newly founded groups over those
whose newness has worn off.

During the period of our study, PMOs founded before 1979 and after
1984 were more likely to survive until 1992 than those founded from 1979
to 1984. As is indicated in Table 9.3, this "liability of adolescence" pattern
was true both populationwide and separately within the small PMO
domain. Among large PMOs and national PMOs there were no age effects
on survival.

By dividing the movement into domains, we have discovered a plausi-
ble explanation for the mixed results regarding organizational age and mortality cited earlier. Among SMOs, large and national groups do not gain the
same survival advantages that benefit minimalist groups in their early
years. Among minimalist organizations, the initial stages of euphoria and
empowerment provide some protection against organizational demise that
is not found in national organizations or business firms.

As the minimalist groups pass through these early years, the more
routinized grind of oppositional organizing begins to take its toll. Early
leaders often tire or burn out from devoting too much time and energy to

Table 9.2 Peace Movement Organization Attributes by Domain

PMO Attributes	All PMOs (N = 411)	Small PMOs (N = 128)	Large PMOs (N = 147)	National PMOs (N = 135)
Demographics				
Age of PMO, mean years (SD)	16.7 (26.9)	11.1 (17.1)	16.6 (18.6)	21.5 (38.3)
Median age, years	8	7	8.5	10.5 years
New (1985+)	5%	10%	2%	4%
Adolescent (1979–1984)	49%	61%	47%	38%
Established (pre-1979)	54%	29%	49%	57%
Resources and legitimacy				
1987 expenditures, mean	$366,494	$7,270	$266,922	$757,172
(SD)	(1,481,483)	(11,742)	(988,951)	(2,245,074)
Median	$65,000	$2,500	$65,000	$150,000
Paid FT&PT staff (median)	2	0	3	5
Individual members, mean	11,783	519	13,362	21,766
(SD)	(72,940)	(1,678)	(76,583)	(100,711)
Median	500	70	800	1,800
Organizational members, mean	33	10	30	58
Volunteers (min. 5 hours/month)	28	8	44	27
Positive media relations	82%	63%	93%	88%
Range of cosponsorship*	.36	.29	.44	.33
Perceived legitimacy[a]	5.0	4.0	5.5	5.2
Member empowerment[a]	5.3	4.9	5.7	5.3
Organizational structure				
Informal	8.0%	26.4%	0	0
Semiformal	35.7%	65.3%	26.7%	18%
Formal	56.4%	8.3%	73.3%	82%
Centralized financial tasks[a]	4.8	3.6	5.1	5.4
Procedural formality[a]	5.1	3.9	5.8	5.6
Organizational evaluation[a]	5.1	4.2	5.4	5.5
Operating strategy				
Professionalization				
Fully professionalized	7.1%	2.6%	7.5%	11.4%
Moderately professionalized	17.0%	0	11.3%	41.2%
Moderately voluntary	38.9%	8.5%	67.7%	36.8%
Fully voluntary	37.0%	88.9%	13.5%	10.5%
Issue focus				
Narrow peace focus	27%	28%	19%	35%
Broad peace focus	52%	51%	57%	46%
Multimovement focus	23%	22%	24%	19%
PMO has exclusively individual members	60%	77%	52%	51%
Vague goals[b]	.14	.12	.15	.13
Tactical repertoires and playlists				
National insider legislative[b]	.18	.09	.19	.25
State/local insider legislative[b]	.35	.27	.51	.26
Party electoral[b]	.25	.30	.31	.14
National outsider legislative[b]	.67	.70	.69	.62
Citizen action[b]	.74	.82	.81	.59
Grassroots electoral[b]	.21	.16	.30	.15
Nonviolence[b]	.28	.28	.36	.20
Citizen exchanges[b]	.65	.67	.67	.62

Source: Colwell and Bond (1994).

Notes: * PMOs reported whether or not they cosponsored events in 1987 with thirteen different kinds of groups. The scale ranges from 0 to 1, with 0 indicating no event cosponsorship and 1 indicating cosponsoring with all possible types of groups.

a. Scales range from 1 to 7.

b. Scale ranges from 0 to 1.

Table 9.3　Multivariate Logistic Regression for All PMOs, by Domains[a]

	All PMOs N = 411 (odds ratio)	Small PMOs N = 128 (odds ratio)	Large PMOs N = 147 (odds ratio)	National PMOs N = 135 (odds ratio)
Demographics				
Age of organization				
New	3.45*	14.3*		
Adolescent	—b	—b		
Established	2.04	7.7		
Resources and legitimacy				
Individual members				
1–99	—b			
100–999	1.89*			
1,000+	2.08*			
Perceived legitimacy	1.27*		2.0	
Positive media (Yes)		.33		
Event cosponsorship		57.1**	.49*	.39*
Member empowerment		1.32	.44*	
Organizational structure				
Informal	—b			n/a
Semiformal	2.86**			.34
Formal	4.17**			—b
Centralized finances			1.56*	
Organizational evaluation		1.69**		
Operating strategy				
Professionalization				
Fully professionalized		115		
Moderately professionalized		n/a		
Moderately voluntary		.04*		
Fully voluntary		—b		
Issue focus				
Narrow peace focus	—b	—b	—b	—b
Broad peace focus	1.91*	3.22*	.92	3.45*
Multimovement focas	1.98*	.44	6.25*	2.47*
Individual members only			.36*	
Goals type (vague)			16.7*	
Tactical repertoires and playlists				
State/local insider legislative	2.44*	9.09*	3.85*	
Party electoral	.38**		.20	
Citizen exchanges			6.24**	2.53
Summary statistics				
Base log likelihood	402.49	153.88	118.02	104.26
Model log likelihood	335.67	98.00	81.76	94.67
Improvement	66.82	55.88	36.26	9.60
Degrees of freedom	11	8	10	5
Significance	< .001	< .001	< .001	.088

Source: Colwell and Bond (1994).
Notes: * = $p < .05$ (two-tailed test).
** = $p < .01$ (two-tailed test).
　　a. Only coefficients significant at the .10 level (two-tailed) are shown in the table. A coefficient greater than 1.0 indicates the factor by which likelihood of persistence is increased by one unit change in the independent variable; a coefficient smaller than 1 shows the factor by which the likelihood of persistence is decreased.
　　b. Indicates contrast category.

organizing. They are either unwilling or unable to pass on the reins of organizational leadership. Sponsors get bored with the organization's activities or make strategic decisions to provide only start-up funds and subsequently move on to support newer activities. Outreach efforts to movement adherents have been fairly well tapped, and new venues are too costly to create or pursue, resulting in fewer new members being brought in. Some old members move on to new organizations or return to more routine daily activities. In short, the organization has to adjust from a period of growing internal resources to stable or declining resources. Large and national PMOs do not enjoy these early benefits because they depend more on fundraising to carry their overhead and face a more competitive environment from the start.

Legitimacy

Conceptually, legitimacy is an important linkage between macropolitical or cultural contexts and meso- or microlevel social movement processes. Legitimacy is also an important, yet problematic, resource for organizations (Meyer and Rowan 1977). Minkoff (1993) found that, among national women's and racial/ethnic SMOs, legitimacy conferred "survival advantages" by improving resource acquisition. The constricting opportunities facing declining movements make legitimacy both harder to come by and more crucial to survival. We consider here two types of legitimacy, internal and external, and examine their relationship to PMO mortality.

Perceptions of SMO success or effectiveness depend, in large measure, on backstage social constructions among members and the external reception of the group's frontstage impression management. Intragroup constructions of collective efficacy, interpretations of external contexts as "opportunities," and the collective resonance of their social change agenda constitute a type of internal legitimacy (Melucci 1988; Friedman and McAdam 1992). As a form of member empowerment, internal legitimacy refers to a group's perception of its own sense of solidarity, efficacy, and ability to mobilize people for action.

External legitimacy originates in how a group is perceived and judged by various publics. Legitimacy is reflected in the willingness of those publics to support the group and its agenda. PMO self-reported data do not enable us to examine directly the legitimacy accorded to particular PMOs by funding elites, polity members, the media, or the general public. However, we do examine three indirect indicators of external legitimacy. First, we consider the degree to which groups perceived themselves to be legitimate. Groups were asked to rate their success in gaining public support and recognition as a force for social change and in maintaining steady funding from diverse sources.

Media institutions are powerful arbiters of external legitimacy, and SMOs often engage in media framing contests to shape public perceptions of issues in favor of their concerns (Gamson 1992). In fact, merely getting media coverage is often a goal in itself for many groups (Ryan 1991; Greider 1992). Cultivating positive relations with members of the news media figures prominently in this regard; this is our second indirect indicator of external legitimacy. Our third measure of external legitimacy considers the range of civic, religious, nonprofit, student, professional, and other social movement groups that cosponsored events with each PMO during the preceding year. We take a wider range of cosponsorship to indicate that a broader array of other groups accorded the PMO legitimacy as an advocacy partner.

Our findings (in Table 9.3) indicate that the relationship between PMO survival and measures of legitimacy is strong but complex. External legitimacy (perceived) was associated with survival movementwide and separately among large PMOs but not among small or national PMOs. The difference by domain in our findings for media relations, broad cosponsorship, and member empowerment indicates that the dynamics of legitimacy vary within the movement, affecting small, large, and national PMOs differently.

For small PMOs, being well integrated into local and community networks as well as establishing ties with a wide range of other groups is important. Among small PMOs, broad cosponsorship may indicate a resource-enhancing strategy at the local level that brings together relatively small numbers of like-minded individuals within the community (see John MacDougall, Chapter 10, this book). At the local level there is less need for peace groups to worry about how they are perceived as agents of change in national security policy because in fact there are relatively few practical avenues of influence available to them. Similarly, because they tend to depend upon the work of members and volunteers, they can worry less about the perceptions of potential funders. Thus, building solidarity and empowerment among one's members, something that is undoubtedly enhanced by broad event cosponsorship, is more likely to increase small PMOs' chances of survival. To the extent that working with the media actually resulted in publicity for small PMOs, the negative impact suggests at least two explanations. Publicizing small PMO activities may raise the interpersonal stakes of involvement among members with crosscutting solidarities. It may also create tensions within the local movement sector that marginalize the small PMO's position within it.

Increased empowerment does nothing to improve national PMO chances of survival, but it is associated with a greater likelihood of mortality among large PMOs. Among these larger groups, undertaking such empowerment activities may be a diversion of resources from the pursuit of policy changes, or it may be perceived as such by other significant actors. This latter process may entail the withdrawal of financial backing by potential supporters or the decrement of political clout in the eyes of the other players in the system. A more empowered membership may be more likely to challenge PMO leadership over policies or goals, diverting attention from organizational maintenance. Like the negative survival impact of positive media relations among small PMOs, this finding is curious and merits further analytical attention.

At the state and national level, the significance of event cosponsorships is more political. Broader cosponsorship is likely to produce turmoil and conflict among participants as they try to articulate their goals. For example, in 1991 during the peace movement's mobilization against the U.S. military buildup in the Persian Gulf, two "warring" coalitions formed to oppose U.S. intervention, culminating in rival "national" demonstrations on successive weekends in Washington, D.C. The conflict between them played out all too publicly in the national press and exacerbated mainstream disaffection with Gulf War opposition. An organization's affiliation with either coalition brought with it an immediate set of labels from the media, potential funders, and other PMOs. At the local level, movement leaders are less aware of such controversies or more willing to ignore them in order to accumulate the necessary resources to undertake antiwar activity.

Organizational Structure

Research on organizational structure, including that on SMOs, tends to focus on larger, formal organizations. Much is known about centralization of authority, formalization of operating procedures, and organizational cultures within large organizations (Scott 1992). Researchers have found that formalized SMOs are more likely to win acceptance (Gamson 1975) and have survival advantages over informal ones. Formalized SMOs can regularize core organizational tasks and have continuity amid shifts in leadership or environmental conditions (Staggenborg 1988). However, PMOs are generally small, local groups. Only about 14 percent of them have even minimal levels of formal structure (Edwards 1995b).

Compared to groups with a semiformal or formal structure, informal groups were less likely to survive,[6] demonstrating their vulnerability. However, formally organized groups were no more robust than those with a semiformal structure, indicating the importance for survival of the lower range of formality among SMOs. As we show in Table 9.3, this was the case for the population as a whole. Among national PMOs, those with semiformal structures were more vulnerable than formally organized groups. There were no informal national groups, and the semiformal ones were primarily task forces or peace committees within larger, denominational, occupational, or political organizations. Such semiformally organized groups would have been quite vulnerable to shifting administrative priorities as the peace movement declined in the late 1980s and political opportunity shifted to other issues.

Our findings show the existence of a rather low institutional threshold that enhances SMO survival. Below rather minimal levels, such as having no characteristics of formal organization, the chances of a group disbanding are quite large. Beyond this, however, thresholds seem to vary by domain. For small PMOs, a semiformal structure in conjunction with regular organizational evaluations seems optimal for survival as long as they avoid the overhead of paid staff, which in itself entails a substantial mortality risk. Not surprisingly, among large PMOs already carrying this overhead, the centralization of financial tasks among group leaders enhances survival. The returns for acquiring such characteristics are quite high at first. Beyond that, however, increasing the annual budget, hiring additional staff, and instituting more formal operating rules all fail to enhance survivability. Thus, above domain-specific and rather low thresholds, we see evidence of a declining marginal return for more bureaucratic SMO forms.

Operating Strategy

To help explain patterns of PMO mortality, we consider variations in three PMO operating strategies: professionalization, generalist or specialist issue focus, and membership type. Professionalized SMOs, in which paid staff utilize sophisticated technologies to mobilize the resources of a dispersed "paper membership," have been contrasted to staffless groups dependent upon member involvement and jack-of-all-trade volunteer activists (Zald and McCarthy 1987; Piven and Cloward 1977; Staggenborg 1991). Classic formulations of resource mobilization theory predict that professionalized PMOs would be more likely to survive than those relying solely on volunteer labor. Because groups with organizational members incorporate many benefits of a coalition, they will likely survive more often than those with memberships composed exclusively of individuals.[7]

Conventional wisdom about organizations expects generalist groups to be more persistent than issue specialists because diversification spreads out their risks, making them less vulnerable (Singh and Lumsden 1990). From this perspective, multimovement groups would be the most likely survivors, whereas PMOs with a narrow peace focus would be the most vulnerable. To test this proposition, we categorized PMOs as having a narrow peace focus, broad peace focus, or multimovement focus.[8]

Across the board, PMOs with a narrow issue focus were less likely to survive from 1988 to 1992 than those with a broad or multimovement focus. The survival of large PMOs was enhanced by pursuing primarily vague goals and by having a membership base that included both individual and organizational members. We offer two explanations as to why groups with vague goals and a multi-issue focus might be better able to survive the decline phase of the peace movement. First, groups pursuing concrete goals must confront failure directly, but groups with vague goals find it easier to construct a variety of rationales for continued activism. Second, multi-issue groups can avoid failure altogether by altering their emphasis from one issue or movement to another. In different ways, both features amount to "emergency exits," enabling groups to sidestep a direct confrontation with apparent failure.

During the height of movement mobilization, peace groups had very few successes in attaining the policies they sought. By the late 1980s, however, many of their policy objectives had been adopted, though for reasons apparently unrelated to movement activities.[9] Thus, the movement's efforts to pursue legislative changes were widely labeled as ineffective. The abandonment of seemingly futile activities by individuals seeking political change is hardly surprising. Groups pursuing vaguer goals, such as promoting personal peace or social justice, could more easily construct a rationale for continuing even as legislative votes failed to go in their favor and movement decline became obvious.

Although groups with vague goals have more options in dealing with failure than those pursuing concrete goals, those with a generalist issue focus can avoid issue failure completely. The fortunes of specialist groups are tied to the vagaries of particular issue attention cycles, but a generalist focus permits a group to hop from issue to issue as the attention cycle shifts. Multimovement groups take this adaptive capability a step further by being able to shift to another issue domain altogether.[10] As peace organizing seems to become less fruitful or more problematic for the organization, it can pursue its other objectives. For some groups we studied, this meant a return to their earlier issue focus. In a sense, these already existing groups from other movements or organizational sectors had been co-opted to peace action during the movement's surge. They could place peace organizing on a back burner and return to their other concerns, which is especially important for large PMOs that may need the resource pools of several issues to carry their overhead. By contrast, small PMOs with a multimovement focus experienced higher mortality, leading us to speculate that such small PMOs are overextended. In a local movement sector with limited carrying capacity, claiming a distinct issue niche with a minimalist structure may be a more durable strategy.

Only among small PMOs was professionalization associated with organizational mortality. Compared to small PMOs that relied entirely on volunteer labor, those that had taken on the overhead of paid staff yet still relied substantially on member volunteers were very vulnerable to disbanding. Among small PMOs, the minimalist strategy of keeping overhead low and relying entirely on volunteers proved to be rather durable.[11]

Tactical Repertoires and Playlists

Charles Tilly's (1979) conception of tactical repertoires has been widely cited to denote the constraints on tactical utilization imposed by political context and locality. Like musical repertoires, they are limited by the experience, knowledge, and technical capabilities of the group, and only novices play everything they know in a single performance. Collective actors cannot use tactics unavailable to them, nor can they perform their entire repertoire all the time. Rather, the specific tactical "playlists" performed during a given year are selected from the larger repertoire to fit the group's perceptions of political opportunity, issue framing, and other environmental considerations. Specific situations may favor particular playlists, thereby conferring survival advantages on some SMOs but not others.

Political tactics are commonly divided into either conventional or unconventional categories, with an electoral and nonelectoral division within the conventional category (Rusk 1976; Kaase and Marsh 1979; Dalton 1988). With regard to social movements, John Lofland (1993) distinguishes between "polite" and unconventional protest and William Gamson (1975) between "ruly" and "unruly" tactics. Recent analyses of interest groups have made a second cut along an insider/outsider axis (Gais and Walker 1991; Schlozman and Tierney 1986). Outsider tactics attempt to influence policymakers indirectly through citizen lobbying or public pressure, whereas insider tacticians seek direct polity access.

From the data used here, we have no way of directly determining the entire repertoire of tactics available to PMOs. However, a factor analysis of responses to questions of whether or not PMOs engaged in thirty-eight separate activities allowed us to identify seven distinct tactical playlists performed by PMOs during 1987. Three of the seven can be considered conventional insider tactics: national legislative activities, such as helping to draft legislation, planning legislative strategy, or testifying at official hearings; state or local legislative activities of the same kind; and party electoral activities such as member involvement in political party organizations, caucuses, or campaigns. Two other playlists were conventional outsider activities: national outsider activities, which include monitoring congressional voting records and peace-related legislation; and grassroots electoral activities, which include participating in voter registration drives, sponsoring public meetings and forums for political candidates, and getting people to the polls on election day. The sixth playlist, citizen action, includes participation in a rally, demonstration, vigil, prayer service, or letter-writing campaign. The seventh, nonviolent direct action, was the only unconventional playlist used. This included boycotts, civil disobedience, tax resistance during times of war, nonviolence training, and draft counseling. In addition to these seven dimensions of tactics, some PMOs organized citizen exchange programs, which do not load on any of the seven playlists. We therefore consider citizen exchange activities separately in our analysis.

SMOs' actions do indeed have a bearing on their survival. Insider legislative politics at the state or local level or both and citizen exchange activities were consistently associated with PMO survival. By contrast, groups engaging in partisan electoral politics were more likely to disband. This suggests that groups able to establish access to the polity acquire legitimacy and thus have a better chance of surviving. As Gamson notes, they may be around to win a battle at a later time. The importance among small PMOs of access to state or local polities is consistent with survival advantages conferred by the external legitimacy indicators of broad cosponsorship and network embeddedness discussed previously.

However, this need for access could also be interpreted to mean that only those who are willing to accept the rules and legitimacy of the current institutional arrangements can get insider access and manage to survive. Radical groups and those that specialize in disruptive tactics are actively repressed and denied participation in the political arena. They generally eschew insider access in the first place. The effects of local insider access, broad cosponsorship, and partisan politics are also consistent with the broad-based, confrontational, yet nonpartisan strategy typical of neo-Alinsky groups affiliated with nationwide community organizing networks like the Industrial Areas Foundation, the Pacific Institute for Community Organizing (PICO), and the Gamaliel Foundation for Direct Action Research and Training (DART) (Reitzes and Reitzes 1987; Rogers 1990). By mobilizing broad community support and refraining from partisan, especially electoral, politics, many groups whose advocacy strategy was influenced by the career of Saul Alinsky have successfully juxtaposed local insider access and confrontational activities.

The benefits of avoiding partisan activity becomes especially obvious when we contrast the negative survival impact of political activities with the positive impact of running citizen exchange programs. When an organization provides a concrete service to its members and the surrounding community by participating in exchange programs, its chances of disbanding are significantly reduced (cf. Lofland 1989). Participants are provided with travel experiences and opportunities to meet with visiting foreigners at social and cultural affairs in their own community. Subsequently, these participants experience a sense of loyalty to the sponsoring organization, thereby improving its chances of continued support and survival.

Survivor Profiles and Movement Transformation

In this concluding section, we profile surviving PMOs in each domain and consider their possible impact on subsequent peace movement mobilizations. First, we profile survivors across the entire movement, as indicated in the first row of Table 9.4. We then consider survival profiles separately in each of the domains.

PMOs Movementwide

The peace movement "industry" grew rapidly from 1980 to 1983. Nearly half the PMOs active in 1988 were founded during the movement's surge in the early 1980s. Following any such "boom" in SMO foundings, a shaking-out period occurs during which groups from that founding cohort disband more frequently than either more established or brand-new groups. The decline associated with this shaking-out period coincided in the late 1980s with a period of declining public support for the movement even before the Gulf War. This created a more competitive and inhospitable political and resource environment for PMOs that most undoubtedly exacerbated the "normal" postsurge shakeout.

The groups most likely to persevere until 1992 had surpassed threshold levels of size and organizational structure. In other words, they had mobilized a membership base in excess of 100 members and had taken on some, but not necessarily all, characteristics of formal organizations. Furthermore, surviving PMOs pursued a broad range of peace-related issues, enabling them to recruit support from a wider cross-section of the peace community. Similarly, groups with higher perceptions of the legitimacy accorded them by outsiders were more robust. Survivors also played insider legislative politics at the local and state levels. In prior research, gaining such polity access has been treated as an indicator of success in its own right (Gamson 1975; Tilly 1979). It may not, then, be surprising that one type of success is associated with another.

Access to state and local officials, but not national legislators, is associated with PMO survival. This does not suggest that national PMOs, which were less likely to disband than small and large PMOs, should shift to lobbying local and state officials in order to increase durability. Rather, it means that among the more vulnerable large and especially small PMOs, those that had insider access to officials appropriate to their scope of operations were more likely to survive the movement's decline. This raises the question of differences in the dynamics of survival across PMO domains. We consider this matter beginning with small PMOs.

Table 9.4 Survival Profiles Among PMO Domains, 1988-1992

PMO Domains	Demographics and Legitimacy	Structure and Operations	Tactical Playlists
All PMOs (N = 411)	− PMOs founded 1979–1984 + More than100 members + Perceived legitimacy	− Informal organizational structure + Broad issue focus	+ State/local insider politics − Partisan electoral
Small PMOs (N = 128)	− PMOs founded 1979–1984 + Event cosponsorship + Member empowerment − Positive media relations	+ Organizational evaluation + Broad issue focus − Moderate volunteerism	+ State/local insider politics
Large PMOs (N = 147)	+ Perceived legitimacy − Event cosponsorship − Member empowerment	+ Centralized financial tasks + Multimovement issue focus − Individual members only + Vague goals	+ State/local insider politics + Citizen exchanges − Partisan electoral
National PMOs (N = 135)	− Event cosponsorship	− Semiformal organizational structure + Broad issue focus	+ Citizen exchanges

Note: + indicates a factor associated with PMO survival; − indicates those associated with demise.

Small PMOs

The liability of "adolescence" was strongest among small PMOs and accounts for most of the populationwide, postsurge, shaking-out effect discussed previously. Small PMOs were most vulnerable to disbanding. The survival effect of cosponsoring events with a wide range of other groups suggests the importance for small PMOs to be integrated into local movement and civic networks. Being an active player in local networks facilitates access to local officials. Such activities undoubtedly enhance the PMO member's sense of efficacy and empowerment. Neither the resource base nor the issue attention cycle of localized arenas can easily carry PMOs focused on a single issue, narrowly defined. Support for such groups would likely be episodic and the group would go into hibernation, to reemerge as its issue cycled back.

Besides breadth of issue focus, three aspects of organizational agency affected survival among small PMOs. First, only fourteen of the small PMOs entered this period of movement decline while attempting to field paid staff with budgets of $30,000 or less. Three of these are what John McCarthy and Mayer Zald (1977) call "professionalized" SMOs, and all three survived this period of decline. Apparently full professionalization, or paid staff with no member volunteers, is a viable operating strategy for small PMOs. However, augmenting member labor by employing even one staffer increased mortality for community-based groups with such limited resources. Second, small PMOs in which leaders regularly evaluated the group and its activities had a survival advantage over those that did not.

Third, the negative impact of cultivating positive relations with members of the news media may be due to increased vulnerability to internal conflict and jealousy. In both formal and informal interviews with local and regional leaders in another social movement, media attention has been described as both desirable and hard to handle (L. Wilson 1993). Once reporters have developed a source, they tend to return repeatedly to that one leader for subsequent quotes or sound bites about the group's activities. Over time the public identification of the group with that one source became the occasion for internal conflicts between other leaders and the one who had emerged as spokesperson. Despite their particular issue focus, there is no reason to think peace movement groups would be any less inclined toward such internal conflicts. In the large and national PMO domains, media coverage per se may bring fund-raising advantages that offset its potential for divisiveness. Large and national groups may also have become more savvy in dealing with the mixed blessing of media coverage.

Large and National PMOs

Legitimacy appears to confer survival advantages for PMOs movement-wide, but its dynamics vary between small PMOs and large and national ones. Among small PMOs, the emphasis is on being a credible group with a broadly defined issue niche in the eyes of local movement and civic constituencies. For large and national PMOs, legitimacy appears to relate more to credibility in the eyes of such elites as institutional funders, legislators, or government officials. The emphasis is on resource acquisition and polity access. The negative survival impact of event cosponsorship underscores this point.

Among large and national PMOs, cosponsorships are rather political and can tie a group to one constituency while distancing it from others. The positive impact of rather apolitical activities like citizen exchanges, in contrast to the negative impact of partisan electoral activities, are consistent with this interpretation. Both insider politics and citizen exchanges are respectable, polite, and likely to be considered legitimate by external elites. Insider politics is more confrontational, yet the confrontation is directed through conventional, system-affirming channels. Only groups that tacitly affirm the existing system of interest intermediation gain the entrée to legislators that enables them to help draft legislation. Citizen exchanges are not overtly political and pursue an alternative social change strategy through the promotion of positive interpersonal relations and solidarity across lines of geopolitical conflict. Such citizen diplomacy is rarely controversial and goes generally unnoticed by those who make U.S. foreign policy.

Citizen exchanges, insider politics, and the avoidance of damaging public affiliations all bespeak the survival benefit of gaining and maintaining legitimacy as conferred by mainstream elites. Even the survival advantage of maintaining a membership base comprising both individuals and organizations can be interpreted in this vein. By having organizational members, large PMOs can maintain "private" relations with groups with which they would rather not be publicly affiliated.

For large and national PMOs, matters of organizational operations and structure were less important than issue focus and vague goals. A narrow issue focus was a liability movementwide because groups need to surf the attention cycles of a broad array of issues. This situation seems to be most acute for large PMOs. To carry the significant overhead they have taken on in localized or regional spheres of operation, they need to adopt a multi-movement profile. Entering a period of political fluctuation with a multi-movement track record allows a group to redirect its efforts without appearing to drop one agenda and lurch toward the issue of the day. In a time of movement decline, this would be a clear survival advantage over otherwise comparable groups that must crank up a new issue focus from scratch. The benefit of vague rather than concrete goals also fits this interpretive line.

When the remnant of PMOs founded during the peace surge of the early 1980s joins their persevering counterparts from prior founding cohorts to mobilize and shape the next peace campaign, what sort of influence will they exert? A number of peace activists will bring strong ties to their PMOs from other movements because of their multimovement activities. Most of the PMOs will be peace generalists with experience and contacts on a broad range of issues. These persevering groups will begin the campaign with insider access to state and local officials and with international contacts to PMO leaders abroad built up from their citizen exchange activities. The importance of mainstream legitimacy among the large and national groups may motivate some of them to advocate restraint and moderation. They may try to quell the use of confrontational tactics in order to conserve their access and legitimacy. Those that do so will most certainly become the rhetorical foils of newly emerging leaders and groups with a greater sense of urgency about the issue at hand.

Notes

1. This differs from the hazard rate approach used in organizational ecology analyses in two ways: (1) we do not have several data points over a relatively long period, and (2) we do not have representative samples from both of our periods. Therefore, we cannot determine if organizational changes intermediate to our two periods were responsible for 1992 mortality status, and we cannot generalize about the peace movement population in 1992 because only the survivors (and not newly created organizations) are included in the 1992 data. Despite these limitations, however, the richness of the SMO data enables us to examine the organizational characteristics that affect the likelihood of their survival.

2. Five of the 139 groups that reported 1986 budgets of less than $30,000 (and were therefore included in the 5 percent random sample of small PMOs) subsequently reported on our survey that their 1987 budget exceeded $30,000. The PMO domain categories described below and portrayed in Table 9.1 were derived from budgets reported in the survey. These five groups are therefore included in the "large, nonnational domain" in our analysis.

3. The sampling and data collection procedures are discussed in greater detail by Mary Anna Colwell and Doug Bond (1994). Issues of potential response bias and validity are assessed by Smith (forthcoming). The derivation and reliability of specific measures discussed here are described by Bob Edwards (1994 and 1995a) and by Sam Marullo, Ron Pagnucco, and Jackie Smith (1996). The multivariate results of the PMO mortality analysis are reported in Edwards and Marullo (1995).

4. Ninety-three percent of the 7,700 PMOs listed in the *Grassroots Peace Directory* in 1987 had budgets smaller than $30,000 per year. The preponderance of PMOs are small, semiformally organized, nonnational groups (Edwards 1995a).

5. The concept of minimalist organizations has been used, with mixed

results, in analyses of mortality among groups as large as national trade associations averaging fourteen staff members and budgets of $623,000 (Aldrich et al. 1990) and as small as local chapters of Mothers Against Drunk Driving (Weed 1987).

6. Groups were considered to be formally organized if they had all five of the following: a governing committee, a written budget, paid staff, incorporation, and tax-exempt status. Groups with one or more (but not five) were considered semiformal in structure. Informally organized PMOs, which make up approximately 14 percent of the population, had none of these.

7. Debra Minkoff (1993) tested this membership format and found it unrelated to mortality among national SMOs over a thirty-year period of movement surging and abeyance.

8. We constructed a standardized scale from responses regarding eighteen major goals, each of which was scored as being either vague (1) or concrete (-1). A positive score thus indicates that a group pursues a preponderance of vague goals.

9. We would argue that movement lobbying and organizing on behalf of policies such as a comprehensive test ban, cutting defense spending, stopping NATO weapons modernization, and limiting SDI and ASAT weapons development were in fact successful and contributed to achieving these outcomes (Cortright 1993; Marullo 1994; Jeffrey Knopf, Chapter 7, this book). However, there has been very little visibility for these efforts and even less attribution of efficacy for them.

10. In our data, alternative goals in the area of the environment, economic justice, and civil rights were the most common. Roughly one-fifth of the groups had a multimovement focus.

11. Three small PMOs in the sample were fully professionalized (relied entirely on paid staff), and none of them disbanded between 1988 and 1992. Though this operating strategy is quite rare among small PMOs, it also appears to be rather durable.

10

Peace Movement Adaptation at the State Level: The Case of Maine

JOHN MACDOUGALL

The goal of this chapter is to describe and explain a case of successful freeze movement adaptation at the state level in the late 1980s and early 1990s. The case is that of Maine, where the successor organizations to the freeze campaign developed innovative and successful programs, a stable and committed membership base, and effective cooperation within and between peace organizations.

Studies of movement decline have focused on various organizational factors. These include the movement's inability to relate to day-to-day real concerns experienced by members of the public who could at least potentially support the movement (Bean 1988), having too narrow a middle-class base (Young 1984: 13), excessive concern with organizational survival in times of decline (Meyer 1990), interorganizational rivalry (see Will Hathaway and David S. Meyer, Chapter 4, this book; Robert Kleidman and Thomas R. Rochon, Chapter 3 this book), and a fixation on the policies of the national government together with a blindness to how the government may in the long term vitiate movement goals (Young 1984: 14; cf. Huberts 1989; Joseph 1993).

I will argue that the peace movement in Maine in the late 1980s and early 1990s generally avoided these pitfalls.[1] I focus on the most important statewide successor organizations to the freeze campaign. These are the groups that concentrated on disarmament and economic conversion, topics most closely related to the original goals of the freeze. I did not study in depth groups concerned with less closely related issues such as Central America. However, it should be noted that people in the latter organizations often took action in the cause of disarmament or economic conversion without the knowledge of the freeze campaign and its successors (Feinstein 1993).

My main sources of data were interviews with fourteen leaders of the peace, economic conversion, and labor movements. This kind of information can be biased, but my interviewees were aware of this and tried to be realistic about the significance of their work. Additional sources of information were movement newsletters and other internal documents.

This chapter focuses on how peace movement leaders in Maine kept their organizations viable at a time when the national movement was declining and the national political climate was less favorable to mobilization. In the following pages, I focus on conscious mobilization choices by peace movement organizations. My analysis is located primarily within the resource mobilization tradition of social movement research (for example, Jenkins 1983; McCarthy and Zald 1977; cf. Oliver 1989). I contend that the peace movement in Maine succeeded in adapting to the post–Cold War environment primarily because of organizational strategies. Although the political opportunity structure in the state was not particularly favorable, movement organizations were skillful at sustaining and mobilizing their resources. Peace leaders in Maine made and then successfully implemented a number of intelligent decisions that enabled their organizations to husband their resources, devise creative programs, and forge constructive intra- and interorganizational relationships. As a result, some organizations flourished, in particular those concerned with economic conversion. The "traditional" peace organizations that succeeded the freeze campaign, while not growing in the late 1980s and early 1990s, also remained viable and adaptable.

In the following section, I spell out my argument about the political opportunity structure in Maine. I then outline the history of the Maine freeze campaign and its successor organizations. Next I discuss the main dimensions of the peace movement's resource maintenance and mobilization process and its responses to the changing political opportunity structure. In the concluding section I assess the various factors that contributed to the movement's survival and adaptation and also compare this assessment with other analyses of movement maintenance and change.

The Political Opportunity Structure in Maine

As I document below, the peace movement in Maine was stable in the late 1980s and early 1990s, at a time when movement organizations collapsed at the national level and in other states and regions. How can we account for this? Two general explanations deserve attention: the political opportunity structure and resource mobilization maintenance. Although these are not necessarily mutually exclusive, I argue that in Maine the opportunity structure was not particularly benign.

Before going into detail, I should point out that the term "political opportunity structure" is not used here in the precise sense used by Sidney Tarrow (1989a) to spell out dimensions of relationships between elite players and challenging groups. Perhaps the term "political environment" is preferable in this section; however, I will stick to "political opportunity structure" because the variables cited here all have a close bearing on the power relationship between elites and challengers. I contend that the opportunity structure is strongly shaped by economic structures and fluctuations, by continuities and changes in political cultures and institutions, by the behavior of the mass media, by demographic trends, and by cultural values and assumptions. Let us look at each of these areas.

In Maine the economic situation became much worse in the late 1980s and early 1990s. Prior to that—in the 1970s and early 1980s—the state made a major and successful shift from its historical dependence on tourism and extractive industries to an economy based more on high technology and oriented more to world markets. But in the late 1980s and early 1990s the boom turned into a severe recession. Military cutbacks played a major role here, and the number of workers laid off at bases and by defense contractors from 1990 to 1992 constituted 1 percent of the state's workforce (Judd, Churchill, and Eastman 1995: 557–561; Maine State Planning Office 1993).

The recession and military cutbacks could potentially have caused severe problems for peace organizers. Citizens may, and sometimes do, seek to preserve military jobs through desperate pursuit of defense contracts and fierce opposition to base closures. In addition, in a recession the discretionary income and energy available for peace activism are diminished.

Two major changes in national and international politics also hampered the peace movement's work in Maine. The first was the softening of Reagan's rhetoric on arms control and his advocacy of Star Wars (the Strategic Defense Initiative) as an alternative to the freeze. The second change was the end of the Cold War. These changes no doubt made it harder for peace organizations to generate opposition to militaristic national policies. Because of all these reasons, for many progressives the concerns of the peace movement could now take a back seat to other issues.

The media are another important part of the political landscape. Here the situation is not particularly favorable. In Maine as elsewhere television, radio, and newspaper reporters lost interest in nuclear weapons protests after 1984 (cf. Ryan 1991; Andrew Rojecki, Chapter 6, this book).

A final aspect of the political opportunity structure that needs to be mentioned are demographic and cultural trends. Here the situation was somewhat favorable to the peace movement and became rather more so in the course of the 1980s. Maine has a small population and no large metropolitan areas. Partly because of this, people active on public issues can readily develop close ties with each other. If they are smart and able to cooperate, they can quite easily wield considerable influence.

The economic boom of the 1970s and early 1980s, together with the desire by many residents of other states to avoid the pressures and pollution of urban life, also generated a considerable influx of well-educated, liberal people likely to support causes like peace. The new migrants generally developed respectful relations with their "old-timer" neighbors, who were usually less progressive. In addition, there is something of a culture of tolerance in the state. As a result, in-migration did not usually lead to divisive political debates (Judd, Churchill, and Eastman 1995: 557).

In general, Mainers are tolerant compared to residents of many states. They take pride in their state's uniqueness and have a strong tradition of independent thinking on public issues. In addition, the state's political institutions seem relatively free of corruption, and public officials profess to be concerned with community welfare and good public policy rather than just personal or parochial gain (Barone and Ujifusa 1993: 554–556; Hanson 1993).

These demographic and cultural tendencies in Maine mean that although the opportunity structure is not very hospitable, it can nonetheless be harnessed to the peace movement's advantage. Movement organizations that recognize the obstacles presented by the opportunity structure and adapt to the favorable demographic and cultural trends are likely to become significant players in shaping state policy and even values (cf. Rochon and Mazmanian 1993). In the following sections, I discuss how and to what extent this took place in the late 1980s and early 1990s.

The Maine Freeze Campaign and Its Successors

Before the freeze proposal was put before the public, there had been a careful organizing effort in Maine on related topics. In the late 1970s, a multi-issue coalition was created to raise awareness of how peace and other issues, such as nuclear weapons and nuclear power, were related. Maine peace organizations were also involved in some of the early planning for the national freeze campaign (Hibbard 1993).

The state's freeze campaign was established in 1981. A three-stage strategy was employed during the first half of 1982. First, a delegation of diverse Mainers made a well-publicized visit to Washington, bringing signatures on the freeze petition to the state's senators and representatives. Second, resolutions approving the freeze were passed by eighty-one cities and towns. Third, the state legislature endorsed the freeze (Hibbard 1993; Peace Action Maine [n.d.]: 1). The freeze campaign encouraged groups supportive of the freeze idea to work in their own communities and con-stituencies. The main allies of the freeze turned out to be legislators, orga-nized labor, and religious groups (Hibbard 1993; cf. Cortright 1993: 43).

There was also much activism on related issues. There was widespread grassroots opposition to the MX missile (MacDougall 1991). A widely dis-tributed booklet showing how nuclear war would harm Maine included a message from Governor Joseph Brennan. The state officially rejected the federal government's plans for crisis relocation in the event of nuclear war (Cortright 1993: 38; Hibbard 1993; Peace Action Maine [n.d.]).

There soon began a process of organizational adaptation, innovation, bifurcation, and merger. In 1984 the Maine Peace Mission (PM) was found-ed by churches and other organizations as a way to influence national legis-lation on disarmament and other issues. The goal was dialogue with the legislators, rather than confrontation (Schweppe 1994).

Though the momentum of the freeze movement was clearly diminish-ing after 1984, several major initiatives were launched by peace organiza-tions in the later 1980s. In 1985, 18,000 signatures of Mainers were gath-ered on a petition calling for a comprehensive nuclear test ban to be delivered to the Reagan-Gorbachev summit meeting (see David Cortright and Ron Pagnucco, Chapter 5, this book).

A campaign was launched in 1988 to end the Navy's testing of cruise missiles, which may have been nuclear-armed, over northern and western Maine. Activists secured enough signatures to put the cruise issue on the ballot, and the referendum was passed. Cruise missile tests were not entire-ly stopped over the state, but this campaign gave the peace movement added visibility and credibility (Davis 1993; Sharp 1994).

An organizational shift took place in 1988, when PM was merged with the Nuclear Weapons Freeze Campaign to form the Maine Peace Campaign (MPC). The MPC became the state affiliate of SANE/FREEZE, which had merged at the national level in 1987.

Soon afterward the PM was discontinued, but its director, Susie Schweppe, seeing that the Cold War was winding down and military spend-ing was being cut, believed that economics should become a key concern for the peace movement. The MPC agreed to establish a new suborganiza-tion called the Peace Economy Project (PEP), whose goal was to convince the public and policymakers of the need for economic conversion and for redirecting national priorities away from military spending (Schweppe 1994).

Local groups working with the PEP studied the impact of military spending on their own communities, and a well-publicized study examined the benefits to Maine of a 7 percent annual cutback in military spending over four years (Anderson and Bischak 1990). In 1992 the PEP orchestrat-ed local resolutions calling for military cutbacks and shifting national priorities, which were passed by over 150 municipalities and the state legislature. In 1992 the PEP was renamed the Economic Conversion Project (ECP). After several energetic and well-funded years, the ECP disbanded in 1996, to some extent because external grants ended but mainly because the board felt the project had accomplished its goals. Some of its work was taken over by Maine Businesses for Social Responsibility, the Maine Transportation Initiative, and Sustainable Maine (ECP 1992 and 1996; MacDougall 1996; Schweppe 1994; R. Wilson 1993).

The MPC went through a difficult period after the cruise missile campaign, but it ultimately made a successful transition to the post–Cold War world. With the Cold War clearly ending in 1990, many supporters and even some board members thought there was no further need for the organization. A major financial crisis ensued. A separate coalition was formed to coordinate protests against the Gulf War, and some MPC board members suggested this coalition should take over as the statewide peace organization. This proposal was rejected by the board, and a new campaign called Real Security 1992 was launched. It had goals similar to those of the PEP and proved effective. A particularly successful event was a forum held in April 1992 in Portland, the state's largest city. Leaders of government, business, labor, and the elderly and representatives of the environmental, women's, and other movements joined a call for a major reorientation of national policy toward domestic needs (Johnson 1993; Schweppe 1994).

In 1993 the MPC changed its name to Peace Action Maine (PAM).[2] Between 1993 and 1996, PAM's disarmament activities centered on nuclear testing, arms exports, land mines, and military spending. In addition, the organization added a second dimension to its work, a concern with local conflicts. Many fresh leaders were recruited through this initiative.

A final instance of organizational bifurcation in the peace movement occurred when much of the lobbying work was taken over by the two Maine chapters of 20/20 Vision, founded in 1988. 20/20 is a network of local groups organized within congressional districts that focuses on disarmament and the environment. "Subscribers" pay $20 per year and are expected to spend twenty minutes a month writing or calling policymakers about an issue selected by a core local group. The two Maine 20/20 chapters work closely with MPC/PAM.

Strategies, Resources, and Leadership

If a movement organization is to survive, let alone grow, in an inhospitable political environment, it must deal successfully with several problems having to do with maintaining and mobilizing resources. First, it must devise strategies and specific activities that mobilize its supporters and have a fair chance of success. Second, it must preserve and if possible increase its physical and financial resources and have sufficient tangible facilities such as office space and computer equipment. Third, the organization must have appropriate structures and procedures for making and implementing decisions in order to ensure optimal cooperation, innovation, and efficiency. These structures and procedures include a sufficient number of paid staff; a productive relationship among board members, staff, and active volunteers; the representation of relevant constituencies on boards and committees; and communication with allied organizations and socioeconomic groups. Fourth, there should be structures and procedures to promote interorganizational coordination and creativity. Finally, the organization must be flexible yet also persistent in implementing these processes (cf. Jenkins 1983: 532–542; McAdam, McCarthy, and Zald 1988: 714–718).

In Maine the peace movement performed excellently in all these areas in the later 1980s and 1990s. It adapted to the political opportunity structure in the state by centering its campaign on economic conversion. At a major forum organized by the ECP in Portland in 1992, the slogan endorsed by all of the very diverse speakers was "Cut military spending—rebuild America" (ECP 1992: 1).

Strategies and Campaigns

Long-term mobilization of peace movement supporters took various forms in different periods after 1981. Since the late 1970s, many peace activists in the state sought to empower people in their own communities and constituencies and to encourage people to incorporate peace principles into their own lives. These ideas were well received in many circles. In the early 1980s some activists saw the freeze as part of a wider project of profound social transformation, while others in the movement were more narrowly focused on the freeze itself. By the mid-1980s, significant numbers of activists in Maine set out to bridge these and other ideological gaps, both within the movement and between activists and members of the wider society. For instance, the Maine Peace Mission consciously sought to listen respectfully to the concerns of people who might oppose or be indifferent to the freeze campaign. This sometimes resulted in new energies becoming available to the movement (Hibbard 1993).

Several specific campaigns were seen by the peace movement as furthering the principles just cited and contributing to significant disarmament and demilitarization. Generally speaking, these campaigns were innovative, focused on local grievances, and took advantage of local institutions and local political/economic trends. For instance, the MPC board decided that a campaign to end local cruise missile tests would be an excellent way to bring the arms race home to Mainers. When people were invited to sign petitions to place the question on the ballot, many were distressed to learn that preparations for nuclear war were going on literally over their heads. Maine's entire congressional delegation, the governor, and most major newspapers in the state all favored continuation of the tests. Considering the degree of elite opposition the referendum campaign encountered, victory at the polls was a significant testimony to the movement's organizing skills and popular support (Johnson 1993; Sharp 1994; Stein 1993).

A creative and popular educational tool called the Priorities Poll was developed for the campaigns to reduce U.S. military spending. Members of the public were given twenty nickels representing the federal budget and were then invited to put them into different tubes representing spending on defense, education, deficit reduction, and so on.[3] Most people allocated to defense far less than it in fact received, and they were surprised to learn the size of the defense budget (Peace Action Maine [n.d.]; Sharp 1996; Staley-Mays 1996).

Since 1993, PAM's activities focusing on local conflicts have included training in conflict resolution, sponsoring Peaceful Planet Toy Fairs, and being the lead organization in Maine promoting gun control laws. These campaigns are seen as valuable in their own right, but each is also a way to attract a new type of member. This work is an adaptive response to widespread and growing concern with violence in communities, homes, and workplaces (Dormody 1996; Hart 1993; Staley-Mays 1996). These campaigns have been especially effective in reaching young professionals and parents.

One area of work that often attracts peace activists but can prove frustrating is election campaigns. The ECP was unable to endorse candidates because of its tax status, but it disseminated much information on candidate positions. Members of the MPC and PAM were very visible in the state's presidential caucuses in 1988 and 1992, mostly on the Democratic side. In 1994 PAM vigorously campaigned for U.S. Senate candidate Tom Andrews, who had been a strong supporter of the movement's positions. Not only did Andrews lose by a big margin, but his campaign made little use of grassroots activists. Partly because of this perceived debacle, PAM did not endorse any candidates in 1996 but worked hard to publicize their positions on peace issues. These actions were part of a new nationally coordinated campaign called Peace Voter. The campaign helped moderate Democrat Tom Allen to defeat conservative Republican James Longley, Jr., in the race for the 1st U.S. congressional district. Allen highlighted defense spending more than most candidates, largely because of PAM's efforts. In all its electoral work, MPC/PAM focused on issues rather than candidates. This surely reduces the feeling of helplessness many activists feel when their candidate fails (Dormody 1996; Johnson 1993; Peace Action Maine 1994; Schweppe 1994).

According to several informants, the campaigns described in the preceding paragraphs earned MPC/PAM and PEP/ECP a solid reputation among the public and elites. They are seen as organizations that can devise and implement effective programs, that speak for major segments of the public, and that mean what they say. After working closely for years with leaders of business, labor, and government and having highlighted the practical problems of conversion, the ECP has persuaded many Mainers that conversion is an economic development issue, not just a peace issue (Hart 1993; Schweppe 1994; Sharp 1996).

Money and Tangible Resources

The peace movement in Maine has established a reasonably stable financial and membership base thanks to its persistence and flexibility. In the early 1990s, MPC/PAM's annual spending held steady at about $62,000, but in 1996 it jumped to $73,000 (Sharp 1996).

In 1984 Enid Sharp, a member of the Maine freeze steering committee, proposed that the freeze start having dues-paying members. For some on the committee such an idea was anathema, but since the state freeze campaign was out of money at the time, Sharp's suggestion was adopted. In the ensuing years, subsequent peace organizations have maintained membership rolls of between 700 and 1,000. Most members are quite well educated but not particularly affluent. MPC/PAM calls on members once a year to renew and does one other telephone fund-raising drive per year. However, many members and supporters request phone calls every few months. It has been found that written information is a useful complement to phone calls in sustaining enthusiasm as well as recruiting people for particular activities. MPC/PAM leaders "sell" membership as a commitment to the range of issues embraced by the organization (Sharp 1996).

In 1996 PAM received $3,000 from Maine Share, which takes payroll deductions from many employers in the state and directs them to more radical organizations than those generally supported by the state's United Way. PAM hopes this will become an annual donation. In addition, in 1996 PAM launched its first serious campaign to solicit major donations from individuals, using trained volunteers. This generated an additional $4,000 (Sharp 1996; Staley-Mays 1996).

MPC/PAM held several successful sales and fund-raising events. Buttons and bumper stickers have netted thousands of dollars each year since the mid-1980s. Tens of thousands of dollars have been earned by sales of Give Peas a Chance (pun no doubt intended), a dry soup mix made of donated ingredients. Since 1994 the organization earned several thousand dollars from its conflict resolution workshops, and some of these earnings went to the general treasury (Sharp 1996).

The peace movement in Maine tailors its projects and campaigns to its financial and human resources, in line with the frugal cultural values prevalent in the state. By the late 1980s, the MPC leadership recognized that although the movement could not make big demands of its members, it could still get a lot done by making small demands on many people (Schweppe 1994; Stein 1993).

Leadership Within Organizations

Another key resource that has been successfully maintained and adopted has been leadership, both volunteer and paid staff. By 1988 MPC saw itself as an umbrella organization that coordinated the efforts of various local and statewide peace groups as well as an initiator of its own activities (Feinstein 1993). The steering committee of the freeze campaign and the MPC/PAM, later renamed the board, has all along had many extraordinarily dedicated and persistent members. Since the late 1970s the goal has always been grassroots participation and consensus decisionmaking, but the way in which this was implemented has changed over time.

As popular interest in the freeze declined after 1985, the MPC board became somewhat more formal in its proceedings. Since the late 1980s consensus procedures could be replaced by majority voting on an urgent issue, if two-thirds of the board agrees. This procedure has rarely been used, but its availability reportedly promotes expeditious decisionmaking. There is also an acceptance of leadership autonomy. For instance, Enid Sharp is granted considerable leeway in membership and fund-raising (Hibbard 1993; Johnson 1993).

There was a conscious effort in 1993 to expand and intensify the work done by board members. The reinvigorated board added several new members, enabling half of the existing board to retire, because for the first time in several years they became convinced that they were not indispensable (Hart 1993; Peace Action Maine [n.d.]: 3).

For the MPC, the shift from an all-volunteer organization to one employing paid workers required significant attitudinal and policy changes. After a difficult transition in 1990–1991, the board recognized the importance of paying its executive director a tolerably decent salary, and this has attracted good candidates.[4] Because its budget increased in 1996, PAM has had two half-time codirectors (Davis 1993; Johnson 1993; Sharp 1996).

MPC/PAM has also taken advantage of leadership training courses provided by the Peace Development Fund's Exchange Project (located in Amherst, Massachusetts). Courses covering fund-raising and strategic planning were taken by PAM's executive director and several board members (Hart 1993). Participants learn that major goals cannot be attained overnight but can be successfully reached in the long term if the necessary steps are taken in sequence. The result has been an increase in the organization's energy, creativity, and cohesiveness.

Interorganizational Collaboration

The two main organizations in Maine's peace movement, MPC/PAM and PEP/ECP, have collaborated well. They differ in goals and style, with MPC/PAM reflecting a more oppositional set of values and beliefs that contrast with PEP/ECP's efforts to stay close to the mainstream. PAM opposes U.S. arms exports, whereas the ECP took no position on the issue. Nevertheless, there was much fruitful collaboration between the two organizations (Peace Action Maine 1994; Schweppe 1994). There has also been collaboration in the broader "peace movement sector" in Maine. The leaders of PEP/ECP and MPC/PAM left Central America and other causes to other organizations but assisted those organizations when help was requested. Such support has been reciprocated, for instance, during the cruise missile campaign. In 1996, long-term efforts were begun to build closer ties between PAM and such organizations as the National Association for the Advancement of Colored People and a major homeless shelter in Portland. These organizations helped distribute PAM's 1996 voter guide (Staley-Mays 1996; Stein 1993).

Peace organizations in Maine also seem to demonstrate considerable tolerance when they have divergent views. For instance, PAM is vocally opposed to U.S. arms exports, whereas the ECP has confined itself to public education on this issue in deference to the fact that some of its contributors work for arms exporting companies. This difference has not, however, hampered collaboration between the two organizations (Peace Action Maine 1994; Schweppe 1994).

In the area of financial and tangible resources, there has also been considerable sharing and cooperation. When PEP was set up within MPC, the latter decided to let PEP have a parallel structure and fund-raising efforts so as to broaden the resources available to the MPC as a whole. For several years PAM shared office space with Physicians for Social Responsibility. In October 1996 these two organizations moved to the new Peace and Justice Center of Southern Maine, which houses about thirteen groups and makes it much easier for the organizations to share equipment, ideas, and information. Membership lists are also shared on an ad hoc basis for mobilizing people, though not for fund-raising (Davis 1993; Sharp 1996).

Adaptability, Persistence, and Political Opportunity

The many examples of peace movement flexibility and persistence cited in the preceding pages suggest that movement organizations in Maine responded effectively to reduced political opportunity for mobilization. Despite Reagan's increasing moderation in his second term, the end of the Cold War, and the waning of media interest in nuclear disarmament after 1985, MPC/PAM devised a series of campaigns that focused on Mainers' own concerns. Peace groups thought carefully about how their work must change in the post–Cold War environment. They picked activities accordingly, focusing on such issues as national budget priorities and the arms trade. Thanks to these efforts, Maine peace organizations were successful in developing a core of members with a long-run commitment to peace activism unaffected by recessions or political fads. It helped that MPC/PAM was not heavily dependent on foundation grants, since these funders are particularly vulnerable to economic shifts and liable to abandon peace projects if they are no longer fashionable.

Political opportunity was, if anything, more bleak in Maine than elsewhere. In the late 1980s and 1990s, Maine's economy soured, with major base closures and cutbacks at military contractors. Yet the PEP/ECP persuaded many citizens and elites that conversion was necessary and that sufficient governmental and other resources must be directed to a sustainable civilian economy. In 1993, a year in which the state's fiscal situation was grim, the ECP helped persuade the legislature to fund a state Office of Economic Conversion, framing it as a vital program for economic development. One favorable and idiosyncratic circumstance was that (at least until 1996) the ECP had some unusual allies in the corporate leadership at Bath Iron Works, the largest private employer in the state and a builder of navy destroyers. The company's former president, Buzz Fitzgerald, was vocal in his support for conversion and tried to carry out the necessary shifts in corporate policies and culture (Schweppe 1994).

To counter media distortion and indifference, peace activists in Maine cultivated local media leaders, for instance, newspapers' editorial boards, with some success. Where possible, peace groups sought to involve local leaders and to frame their efforts as seeking to help local communities. The MPC deliberately avoided a shrill tone in its public statements on various issues. These efforts paid off. After meeting with PAM's assistant director, for example, the *Portland Press-Herald* (the state's most widely circulated newspaper) published an editorial expressing PAM's viewpoint on arms exports (Davis 1993; Johnson 1993; Sharp 1996).

Peace organizations in the state have taken advantage of Maine's demographic and cultural features. For instance, they stressed the local relevance of national budget priorities and cruise missile testing, thus appealing to the widespread sentiment that outsiders do not understand Maine's special problems and assets. Many peace leaders, who are themselves recent immigrants, have taken pains to develop respectful relationships with state politicians and business and labor leaders, whose families have often lived in Maine for many generations. With these efforts, Maine peace organizations seek to arouse people's feeling of hope, believing that positive sentiments are more potent in the long term than the fears that were the prime motivators of the freeze campaign.

Conclusion

The peace movement in Maine has adapted successfully to the post–Cold War era, an era dominated by economic and local concerns. All of this has happened at a time when peace organizations have disbanded in many states and regions. I have argued that peace movement organizations in Maine have been able to make this transition primarily because of conscious choices in several key areas rather than a locally favorable political opportunity structure.

Maine's peace organizations did the following, all of which were needed for a successful transition. First, they undertook a series of activities that were sharply focused on Mainers' concerns and the current political environment. Second, movement organizations carefully husbanded their human, financial, and tangible resources. Third, decisionmaking structures within organizations were efficient yet participatory, enhancing organizational cohesion and adaptability. As a result, there was much interorganization cooperation. And fourth, peace organizations displayed great persistence but also great creativity. These characteristics of peace organizations in Maine are quite similar to those found in a national sample of small peace groups that survived in this period (see Sam Marullo and Bob Edwards, Chapter 9, this book).

Although the political opportunity structure has not been particularly benign in Maine, the peace movement has adapted to it skillfully. For instance, the economy deteriorated in the late 1980s and early 1990s, aggravated by a major downturn in the military sector. This was turned to the movement's advantage through successful organizing on the issue of economic conversion. Today most Mainers believe that conversion is a key part of the state's economic revitalization. In addition, there are some favorable aspects of the opportunity structure, such as the arrival of generally articulate and liberal immigrants, the state's relatively small population, and its traditions of local independence and political tolerance. Peace organizations took advantage of these conditions, for instance, by stressing the local nature of peace issues and their advocates.

How do these findings compare with analyses of organizations in other movements that have survived and adapted in periods of major political or economic change? Unfortunately, there is not very much literature on this topic at the level of state, regional, or local groups. Still, there appear to be similarities in several areas. One important factor is the ability of a movement to develop programs that large numbers of people can readily appreciate and to persuade potential supporters that particular communities face serious threats (McAdam 1983). Successful movements also create local settings in which members of the public come together routinely to discuss public problems and movement solutions (McAdam, McCarthy, and Zald 1988: 710 and 715; cf. Downton and Wehr 1991: 123). The freeze movement encountered a major hurdle because nuclear weapons are not "naturally" part of people's lives in the way that (say) jobs, education, or health care are. However, this problem was creatively addressed in Maine, especially through the cruise missile referendum campaign (cf. Jenkins 1983: 542).

Another finding from studies of other movements is that regional coalitions are more likely to endure if they can successfully persuade their constituents that there is a real chance of overcoming their political adversaries. Regional coalitions are more likely to survive if they have a clear and narrow focus and can secure outside funding or bring into their ranks organizations with a solid membership and financial base of their own (Staggenborg 1986). Here too peace groups in Maine have an excellent record.

The Maine peace movement in the 1980s and 1990s consisted primarily of campaign-specific coalitions, working on such issues as cruise missile testing. Even such organizations as PEP/ECP were to some degree coalitions, since they deliberately sought support, donations, and board members from diverse constituencies. By contrast, MPC/PAM was by the late 1980s no longer a coalition, since it launched most of its initiatives on its own rather than responding to requests by affiliated organizations.

McAdam, McCarthy, and Zald (1987: 716–717) suggest that when the political environment is unfavorable, movement organizations may usefully adopt a semiprofessional structure whereby paid leaders mobilize members periodically. In such situations it is essential to choose tactics and goals that retain members yet also keep the organization visible. The latter is, of course, a difficult balancing act, but in Maine the MPC/PAM has addressed these problems effectively. It has created a division of labor between those working on organizational maintenance by sustaining membership on the one hand and those carrying out innovative and visible programs on the other hand.

Maine peace organizations have not only survived the decade between 1985 and 1995, but they have thrived. In this period, the Peace Mission and PEP were launched. PAM added violence prevention activities to its action portfolio in 1993, enabling it to recruit new kinds of members. Skilled mobilization of the sort seen in Maine can create and sustain a "critical mass" of interest and energy even when the national political environment is inhospitable to mobilization.

Notes

I am especially grateful to Enid Sharp and Susie Schweppe for providing much useful information. Thanks are also due to the following for comments and help with data collection: Mary Anna Colwell, Judy Feinstein, Eric Johnson, Peter MacDougall, Fred Rose, Jack Thompson, and all my other informants. Research for this article was supported in part by a grant from the Council for Industrial Development at the University of Massachusetts at Lowell.

1. I call the successor to the freeze movement the peace movement rather than the disarmament movement or the demilitarization movement. Despite the presence in Maine of other movements working for peace (e.g., in Central America), "peace movement" was the term used most often by movement activists, the press, and other elite actors (not to mention most scholars).

2. At the national level, SANE/FREEZE also became Peace Action. PAM remained the state affiliate of the national organization.

3. A category called "Pentagon Pork" was added in 1996.

4. The salary was in the middle $20,000 range, plus health benefits.

11

The Development & Maintenance of Activism in Anti–Nuclear Weapons Movements

TODD C. EDWARDS

Research on participation in social movements has generally been guided by one of two major conceptual approaches: the social-psychological approach or the resource mobilization approach. From the social-psychological perspective, intrapsychic factors such as grievances, personality, and alienation drive movement participation. From the resource mobilization perspective, the critical factors are structural, such as money, prestige, influence, social networks, and disposable time.

Past attempts to explain movement participation have made it abundantly clear that each approach has its own particular merits (McAdam 1986; Turner 1981; Walsh and Warland 1983). However, the majority of this research has held a static view of activism, not considering the relative roles of these factors over time. This is a significant weakness in the literature, considering that movements must overcome the free rider problem not only to mobilize activists but also to maintain activism once it is initiated. In this chapter I focus on the role played by psychological factors such as grievances and ideology, as well as contextual factors such as social networks, in the development and maintenance of participation in the anti–nuclear weapons movement.

Methodology

Because of a lack of relevant theory for explaining how participation in social movements develops and changes over time, a "grounded theory" approach was taken in this study. Barney Glaser and Anselm Strauss (1967: 4) developed the method of grounded theorizing to "forestall the opportunistic use of theories that have dubious fit and working capacity" for the setting(s) at hand. The primary objective of the grounded theory method is the development of conceptually rich and integrated theories of social phenomena that are derived from systematic data analysis.

The grounded theory method is sometimes criticized on logico-deductive grounds because data are not representatively sampled from a population. However, the primary objective of the method is the specification of social phenomena at a conceptual level. The sampling of concepts is most essential, not the sampling of cases. Anselm Strauss and Juliet Corbin (1990: 191) describe the logic of conceptual sampling: "In terms of making generalizations to a larger population, we are not attempting to generalize as such but to specify. We specify the conditions under which our phenomena exist, the action/interaction that pertains to them, and the associated outcomes or consequences." The grounded theory method produces rich findings that can then be fed into a logico-deductive process of verification and generalization. The grounded theoretical approach is, in short, appropriate for the kind of exploratory analysis of a topic such as that undertaken here.

Data Collection and Research Design

Data were collected primarily through in-depth interviewing and to a lesser extent through participant observation and document analysis. One formal interview was conducted with each participant, lasting approximately one hour. The interviews were semistructured and explored factors that prompted or hindered involvement in movement activities.

With the assistance of the leader of a large anti–nuclear weapons (ANW) organization in the Los Angeles area, thirty-three ANW activists were selected to participate in the study. Eleven respondents were drawn from each of the following groups:

1. High-Active: Those members who were judged to be consistently (for a significant period of time) among the core of most active members in the organization and its activities. They were veteran movement leaders.

2. Reduced-Active: Those members who were judged to have been, at one time, among the core of most active members in the organization and its activities, but whose involvement has since dropped off substantially. This category also includes members who have never been highly involved with the current organization but were significantly involved with another ANW organization prior to their involvement with this one.

3. Low-Active: Those members who were judged to be substantially less active in the organization and its activities than the core of most active members. This group includes those members whose level of involvement has consistently been greater than token contributions (for example, those restricted to membership dues) but that has never been consistently as high as the most active members.[1] This group does not include members who were significantly involved with another ANW organization prior to their

involvement with this one; such respondents fall into the "reduced-active" category.

These activism categories were purposively selected to study the development of movement involvement. First, by including only veterans of the movement, a baseline of activism development was ensured.[2] Second, by including a low-active and a high-active group, the difference between being an active member in the organization and being, in essence, a movement leader could be investigated. Finally, by including a high-active and a reduced-active group, the transition from movement leader to movement dropout could be charted.

The assignment of organization members to these groups was based upon the judgment of the organization's leader, who had been deeply involved in the movement (as well as this particular organization) for several years. His perception of how well the members fit into the respective activism categories was confirmed with an ANW activism scale (Werner and Roy 1985) administered to each respondent. Also, in order to check for selection biases on the part of the leader (such as might occur as a result of organizational infighting), the first several respondents were asked to name other activists whom they considered to be movement veterans. There was a high degree of overlap between these respondents' selections and the movement leader's, reducing the likelihood that selection biases were operating. This high degree of overlap also indicates that a large percentage of the population of veteran activists from this organization was included in the study.

Since the primary purpose of the study was to focus upon social-psychological factors instrumental in the development of activism, the three groups of activists were matched on the demographic variables of age, gender, marital status, and family stage.[3] Further, in order to ensure that a representative sample of core activists was attained, the high-active group members were selected according to a core activist demographic profile developed from a survey study the author conducted with the same organization approximately five years earlier (Edwards and Oskamp 1992). The reduced-active and low-active members were then matched to the high-active members who had been selected (see Appendix, Table 11.2, for a demographic breakdown and comparison). In general, the participants in this study reflected the broader membership's homogeneity. They are highly likely to be white, to have at least a bachelor's degree, have a relatively high income, and be liberal in politics.

Limitations of the Methodology

There are at least five limitations inherent in the methodology employed in this study. First, the data collected were self-reported and therefore not subject to outside verification. Second, some of the data collected were retrospective in nature and are subject to memory biases. However, since virtually all of the study participants had been involved in the ANW movement for several years, these biases have probably been roughly constant across the activism groups (see Appendix, Table 11.3). Third, the interviews were conducted over a span of one year, so those interviewed near the end of the study were subject to different historical factors than those interviewed near the beginning. However, the interviews were staggered across the activism groups in order to hold this variable constant across the groups. Fourth, it is unclear to what degree these findings are generalizable to other settings and other social movements. Finally, since this study did not include longitudinal data, any theoretical conclusions with regard to causal processes must be considered tentative.

Findings

In describing the likelihood that any particular characteristic is to be found in an activism group (high, reduced, or low), the following scale was adopted based upon the number of group members who exhibited the characteristic.

10–11 members (91–100%)	=	"very likely"
8–9 members (73–82%)	=	"likely"
5–7 members (45–64%)	=	"tend to"
3–4 members (27–36%)	=	"tend not"
0–2 members (0–18%)	=	"unlikely"

When one of these descriptors appears in the text, the reader may refer back to this scale to determine the magnitude of the empirical finding to which it relates. The findings for each activism group are presented as a composite, and quotations from the interviews are used to demonstrate the points being made. In order to focus on the most robust variables, the emphasis has generally been on characteristics exhibited by a minimum of five members (45 percent) from one of the groups.

The usual criteria of statistical significance are hard to apply to small samples. In deciding what constitutes a meaningful difference between the groups on any particular variable, a criterion of "greater than or equal to four group members" was adopted. If there was a between-group difference of four or more group members on any variable, it is reported as a difference between the groups.[4] Since there are eleven members in each activism group, a difference of four members represents 36 percent of the entire group, a relatively large proportion. Although this criterion is decidedly arbitrary, it is nonetheless useful for mapping out distinctions between the activism groups. The processes by which members of the three activism groups came to be involved in the ANW movement will be examined in the areas of grievance and ideology, personal efficacy, contextual factors, and social relations (see Table 11.1).

Table 11.1   Comparison of Activism Groups on Key Variables

Variables	High-Active		Reduced-Active		Low-Active	
Grievance and Ideology						
ANW ideology broaden/evolve	8	(73%)	3	(27%)	4	(36%)
Illegitimate defense policy	9	(82%)	3	(27%)	5	(45%)
ANW issue is primary	8	(73%)	4	(36%)	3	(27%)
Remain highly committed	11	(100%)	6	(55%)	5	(45%)
Personal Efficacy						
Personal effectiveness strategy	11	(100%)	10	(91%)	7	(64%)
Personal policy impact	8	(73%)	4	(36%)	3	(27%)
Increasing personal efficacy	6	(55%)	3	(27%)	1	(9%)
"Long-run" view	7	(64%)	3	(27%)	1	(9%)
Contextual Factors						
Personal factors lead to involvement	9	(82%)	10	(91%)	5	(45%)
Social Relations						
Self-initiate into ANW SMO	7	(64%)	8	(73%)	3	(27%)
Family support: low level	2	(18%)	6	(55%)	2	(18%)
Friend support: low level	2	(18%)	3	(27%)	6	(55%)
Social ties with ANW activists	10	(91%)	8	(73%)	4	(36%)

Note: The numbers and percentages of members in each group exhibiting the characteristic are presented.

Grievance and Ideology

Although all participants had a tendency to be involved in other liberal social movement organizations (SMOs) prior to participating in the ANW movement and all were very likely to hold an ANW stance prior to their first initiation into an ANW SMO, the high-active participant's ideological stance was most likely to broaden and evolve over the course of her involvement. There were at least three ways in which this evolution occurred. First, when some participants began their involvement in the movement they believed that the manufacture of nuclear weapons should be stopped immediately. After having been involved with the issue for a period of time, they began to understand the practical difficulties inherent in this position. As a result, they eventually redefined their position in terms of the need for a process of economic conversion from military to civilian production. Some participants developed an understanding of the economic reasons for the arms buildup and of the way in which the military-industrial complex perpetuates itself through a campaign of misinformation in which massive numbers of nuclear arms are justified for national security purposes. Finally, some participants came to perceive an interconnection between the issue of nuclear weapons and other social issues such as ecology and economic justice.

By contrast, the reduced-active participant's ideological stance tended not to evolve and broaden over the course of involvement and was also the least likely to have been affected in general by participation in the movement.

The high-active participant was also most likely to believe that the U.S. government's policy with regard to the production and deployment of nuclear weapons was illegitimate, or even that the policymaking process itself was illegitimate:

> The most important reason [I decided to become active at that point] is that Mikhail Gorbachev had been in power in the Soviet Union for a little over a year by the summer of 1986 and he had already instituted a unilateral moratorium on nuclear weapons testing on the part of the Soviet Union and there had been *no reciprocation whatsoever on the part of the United States*.[5] (interviewee 3)

This finding lends support to Myra Ferree and Frederick Miller's (1985) assertion that an attribution of stable external causality is necessary for sustained collective action to occur. In order for a collectivity to work for change, its members must believe that the target of the proposed change exists independently in the external environment (is not construed) and that the target's action is not purposive. Such an attribution is most likely to occur in consensus situations in which individuals can exchange information and compare perceptions (Kelley 1967). These considerations are also reflected in David Snow et al.'s (1986) assertion that an understanding of the ways in which grievances are interpreted by movement participants is necessary for understanding activism.

Another important difference between the participants is that the high-active participant was most likely to view the ANW issue as primary and to believe that all other social issues are irrelevant unless the ANW issue is dealt with first:

> 300 years ago the same problems existed but not on this scale. Man did not have the capacity to completely annihilate the entire planet. So it could be that in the future there would not be this kind of crisis situation, hopefully. That there will be something that will cause this crisis situation to be alleviated so that it's a safer planet. So no, I don't think that it's going to stay at this crisis peak forever. I think that *if it doesn't get resolved and go to less of a crisis, there won't be any planet.* (interviewee 10)

The high-active participant held this view despite political changes then under way in the former Soviet Union, which were widely thought to have reduced the threat of nuclear war. Indeed, the high-active participant was less likely than the reduced-active participant to attribute any reduction in her involvement to a reduction in the threat of nuclear war.[6] Accordingly, the high-active participant was also the most likely to remain highly committed to the ANW effort and the least likely to experience a reduced level of issue salience over time. The high-active participant was also more likely than the low-active participant to intend to remain involved in the movement. The reduced-active participant was the least likely to express concern with regard to issues of nuclear weapons testing and proliferation.

Personal Efficacy

The high-active and reduced-active participants were very likely to adopt strategies for increasing their personal effectiveness within the movement, more so than the low-active participant. A personal effectiveness strategy is a course of action carried out by an individual in order to maximize the probability that her efforts will have an impact on the achievement of movement goals. Following is a list of the personal effectiveness strategies found among the activists, along with explanations and examples of each.

1. Social engagement. This is an effort to engage the attention of those outside the movement so that an attempt can be made to influence them toward an ANW position. An example of this strategy is setting up information tables near post offices during tax time to inform people mailing their tax forms about the percentage of their taxes being used for building nuclear weapons. Some members reflect upon their own experience of becoming aware of the ANW issue and then use this experience to influence others. One member, who struggled at first to understand the technical information related to nuclear weapons, later developed a strategy of "lay interpretation" in which she translated this information into nontechnical terms and related it to others outside of the movement:

> So I try to keep it as simple as possible on my end. . . . I'll have a plane and I'll tell them this plane cost this, and that to me works real well. Money always works real well. When you talk about money. And people say, Oh God. (interviewee 5)

2. Politically based change. This is a strategy in which change is pursued through the existing political system. For instance, some members shifted their attention and efforts to the United Nations due to unresponsiveness on the part of the U.S. government. Some members also talked

about the need to strike a balance between idealism and pragmatism in selecting political candidates to work with:

> *There's no use being [so] pure ideologically that you can't be effective.* . . . There have to be those spokesmen who are out front speaking truth to power and there also have to be those people who get into office who at least do better things, if not best. (interviewee 8)

3. Counter social control. This is a strategy in which members respond to attempted social control by the power elite. Several members spoke of the use of alternative media to get their message out, through community access cable, computer networks, and roadside placards:

> People would just stand with placards at the offramps of some of the free-ways. So all you needed for that was maybe a dozen people and people would see your placard. In other words *what you were trying to do was to bring the issue to the public and keep it in front of the public eye because we knew that the newspapers and the radio and the television just didn't report anything.* (interviewee 7)

4. Direct recruitment. With this strategy, an attempt is made to bring others into the movement. Sometimes there is an effort to target groups per-ceived as having been excluded in the past. For example, some members worked on bringing young people into the movement because they per-ceived that the movement was aging. Strategies were specifically designed for young people, such as involving them in video production.

5. Critique of movement/SMO. Finally, with this strategy an assess-ment is made of the needs or shortcomings of the movement or SMO, and appropriate action is taken. For instance, one member, perceiving an insu-larity on the part of the ANW activist community, decided to work on pub-lic outreach strategies. Other members worked only on activities that they felt were unattended to by the rest of movement:

> I was looking for a way to get involved which would not be completely in the shadow of what was happening at All Saints' Church. . . . I guess it was just sort of egoistic but I wanted to find some way to do something that would not get totally sucked in to what they were already doing. And *maybe to accomplish a few things which they couldn't accomplish in terms of what they were doing.* (interviewee 12)

Still other members shifted from traditional methods of mobilization, such as marches or speakers, to methods they believed to be more cost-effective, such as television/video, radio, and computer networks:

> *People who are under 50 understand that TV reaches people.* Over 50 they think that events really are important, or the print media is important.

The print media is totally unimportant. . . . That's not what changes public opinion any more. . . . It's an establishment type of thing. . . . It's the way we always have done it . . . And it's going to have to change. . . . *Method is as important as issue.* (interviewee 10)

These findings regarding personal effectiveness strategies are interesting in light of Pamela Oliver and Gerald Marwell's (1988) contention that the free rider is one who feels unable to make a difference in outcome large enough to overcome personal costs. It appears that the most active participants employ strategies intended to turn this result around. Indeed, the high-active participant was most likely to believe that her past efforts had had an impact upon policy or policymakers and accordingly was more likely than the low-active participant to experience an increasing sense of personal efficacy over time:

I've seen some successes in issues I've been involved with. And then you get setbacks again, but I think *overall I'm more optimistic.* I'm more optimistic about getting a test ban treaty; I'm more optimistic about the country being more and more aware of the need for economic conversion. People are open to the message. . . . We were working on lobbying the Congress and *we finally got a vote that went our way* for the first time in the ten years that they had voted to cut military budgets. . . . Dancing around my house. . . . The B2 . . . bomber funding seems to be way down from what they wanted . . . so I think we beat them on the B2. . . . I feel real good about that. (interviewee 4)

This high-active participant was also most likely to conceive of her efficacy in terms of a long-run view and was more likely than the low-active participant to believe that she had influenced or recruited others to the movement. A long-run view means that she does not expect her efforts to pay dividends tomorrow or next year. But she does believe that her efforts are contributing to the achievement of a positive outcome, which will occur someday. It is not uncommon for her to describe the benefits of her efforts even in terms of future generations. The high-active participant was also more likely than the low-active participant to cite past instances of effectiveness:

I think we've had a lot of success. We've accomplished a lot. The weapons have been reduced and some programs have even been halted. At one time they were going to have some kind of mobile weapons running around the desert on a track. I mean it's ridiculous, the stuff they would think of. *So I think the public's more educated and some of the harebrained schemes that were in people's minds aren't really taking off.* (interviewee 1)

By focusing on moments of past success and maintaining hope for future success, the most active participants developed a rational justification for their involvement in the movement. In addition, the high-active participant tended to express the belief "If I don't do it, then no one else will" (echoing Oliver 1984) when explaining her participation in the movement, whereas the reduced-active participant was unlikely to do so.

Contextual Factors

The high-active and reduced-active participants were approximately one and one-half times as likely to have personal factors that disposed them toward activism, but for the low-active participant the opposite was true. One common example of a personal factor that served as a catalyst to movement participation was having an occupation directly relevant to the issue of nuclear weapons, such as being a nuclear engineer, physicist, environmental scientist, or defense industry worker. An example of a personal factor that served as a barrier to movement participation was a low amount of free time due to competing responsibilities such as raising children. Another example was poor health or physical problems associated with old age.

However, high-active and reduced-active participants were also more likely than members of the low-active group to discuss issues of coping with the demands of involvement. Coping mechanisms include setting limits on one's level of involvement or working through frustrations associated with involvement:

> *I started questioning whether mine was the kind of personality who could go out and demonstrate and do all this stuff without getting all upset about it.* . . . So I still listen to them and I still make contributions through the mail and I still go to some events but not very many. I want to have a healthy family life too. (interviewee 22)

The high-active participant was about as likely to experience political and movement-related catalyzers to her involvement as she was to experience barriers, whereas the reduced-active and low-active participants experienced twice as many barriers as catalyzers. Examples of these catalyzers and barriers are as follows.

1. Political catalyzer. Some participants talked about an accumulation of events that led to their involvement in the movement, such as the arms race, Chernobyl, and nuclear proliferation.

2. Political barrier. Several participants expressed disillusionment over how the Gulf War seemed to negate their past efforts in working toward nonviolent political change.

3. Movement-related catalyzer. An example of this type of catalyzer is a "flat" SMO structure in which new recruits are quickly "promoted" to prominent positions in the organization.

4. Movement-related barrier. Examples here include a general decline in the movement itself or tension between personalities within the SMO. Some participants also discussed the technical complexity of the nuclear weapons issue as a barrier to their participation, and others cited the low profile and insularity of the movement during the last several years.

Social Relations

Contrary to what David Snow, Louis Zurcher, Jr., and Sheldon Ekland-Olson (1980) say, both the high-active and reduced-active participants tended to join ANW organizations on their own initiative rather than being recruited by movement members (as the low-active participants were). This is especially interesting in light of the fact that the period in which first recruitment or initiation occurred was more similar for the high-active and low-active participants than it was for the reduced-active participants (see Appendix, Table 11.3). This rules out the possibility that the high-active and reduced-active participants signed up more often due to the common political or social context in which their first initiation occurred. The high-active participant was also more likely than the low-active participant to become immersed in movement activities immediately following initiation into an ANW organization: "I went down and volunteered and *I spent from April until November [as a] full time volunteer.* I usually worked 8 or 10 hours a day on the [California Bilateral Nuclear Freeze] initiative itself" (interviewee 11).

Although all participants generally received a moderate to high level of social support for their involvement, only the high-active participant escaped almost entirely from experiencing low support. The reduced-active participant tended to experience low support from family members:

My wife is pretty nonpolitical. We hold the same values politically and feel the same way. But *she does not go out to marches and she doesn't go to meetings* and that kind of thing. *I always had a conflict with my father about this over the years.* (interviewee 12)

The low-active participant tended to experience low support from friends:

[My friends and I] *just can't talk about anything.* We keep the conversation very neutral. . . . *It is made more difficult with my friendships* because I think since I became involved in politics. . . . I probably see things more in a political way. (interviewee 23)

The reduced-active participant was unlikely to have family members who participated in the ANW movement, and the low-active participant was unlikely to have friends who did. Furthermore, although all participants were likely to experience at least a moderate level of social support from fellow ANW activists, the low-active participant was the least likely to develop social ties as a result of her involvement, and the reduced-active participant was more likely than the high-active participant to experience a low level of support. These findings support the already considerable evidence of the importance of solidary relations in sustaining activist behavior (Edwards and Oskamp 1992; Ferree and Miller 1985; Fireman and Gamson 1979; Klandermans 1984; Klandermans and Oegema 1987; McAdam 1986).

Finally, whereas all participants tended to experience a sense of deviancy or marginalization as members of the movement, the reduced-active participant was the least likely to experience a sense of social validation for her efforts from those outside of the movement (apart from family and friends). An example of outside validation is the experience of one activist, who said:

> *Sometimes you really are surprised cause you find people saying yeah, I was thinking about that.* Closet people who believe like you do but they're like I used to be—just sit back. Talking to your family and close friends but kind of embarrassed to say anything publicly. (interviewee 5)

This reaction may be due to this participant's having become involved earlier in the course of the movement and having been involved for a significant period of time before the idea of a nuclear weapons freeze was popular. This reduced-active participant was in a better position to perceive change with regard to the widening appeal of the ANW message and perhaps may have overestimated the likelihood that others would become involved in the movement. By the same token, having been involved for a significant period of time following the large freeze mobilizations of the early 1980s, the high-active participant was more aware of the subsequent decrease in movement participation.

Conclusion

A complex myriad of intrapsychic and structural factors appear to interact with one another in the developmental process of participation in the ANW movement. Some of these factors are common to all of the participants (high, reduced, low), but some clearly distinguish between them. The following factors are common to the high-active and reduced-active participants, but distinguish them from the low-active participants: (1) both tend to join ANW organizations on their own initiative rather than being recruited by a movement member, (2) both are very likely to adopt strategies for increasing their personal effectiveness within the movement, (3) both are likely to experience personal factors that dispose them toward involvement, and (4) both are likely to develop social ties with fellow ANW activists as a result of their involvement in the movement.

The following factors are even more revealing in that they distinguish the high-active participants from the others: (1) their ideological stance is likely to broaden and evolve over the course of their involvement in the movement, (2) they are likely to believe that the U.S. government's policy with regard to the production and deployment of nuclear weapons is illegitimate or even that the policymaking process itself is illegitimate, (3) they are likely to view the ANW issue as primary and to believe that all other social issues are irrelevant unless nuclear weapons are dealt with first, (4) they are very likely to remain highly committed to the ANW cause, (5) they are unlikely to attribute any reduction in their involvement in the movement to a reduced threat of nuclear war, (6) they are likely to believe that their past efforts have had an impact on policy or policymakers, (7) they tend to experience an increasing sense of personal efficacy over time, (8) they tend to conceive of their personal efficacy in terms of a long-run view, and (9) they are unlikely to experience a low level of support or even resistance to their ANW activities from family members or friends.

In order to best understand participation in the anti–nuclear weapons movement, it is essential that close attention be paid to the developmental aspects of activism. As I have shown in this chapter, the ways in which grievance and ideology, personal efficacy, contextual factors, and social support evolve and change over the course of movement involvement are intimately related to the type and level of involvement. Although the development of personal effectiveness strategies distinguishes the high-active and reduced-active participant from the low-active participant, a belief in the continuing threat of nuclear war, the development of a sense of personal efficacy, and an absence of low levels of social support from family and friends further distinguish the high-active from the reduced-active participant. These factors can only be understood within a developmental framework.

The practical implications of these findings are several. First, despite a dramatic decline in the anti–nuclear weapons movement in the wake of reduced East-West tensions, there are a substantial number of people who have continued to work toward a worldwide reduction in the number of nuclear weapons. This is probably best explained by the finding in this chapter that those who have continued to work on these issues also continue to perceive the threat of nuclear war as significant. Many of these interviewees spoke of how the overall number of nuclear weapons worldwide continues to increase despite arms control agreements. One of the greatest challenges of keeping movement members mobilized may lie in convincing them that a credible threat continues to exist.

However, the participants who continue to remain highly active also believe that their past efforts have had an impact upon policy or policymakers, and they experience an increasing sense of personal efficacy over time. Although both the high-active and reduced-active participants developed strategies for increasing their personal effectiveness, only the high-active participants experienced an increasing sense of efficacy. This may be explained by the finding that the high-active participants conceived of their effectiveness in terms of a long-run view and did not expect their efforts to pay immediate dividends. It may be that, objectively, the high-active and reduced-active participants' efforts were equally effective but that only the high-active participants perceived them as such.

Personal factors such as the amount of social support one receives from family and friends also affect level of participation. Personal factors that serve as catalyzers to involvement distinguish the high-active and the reduced-active participant from the low-active participant, whereas the absence of low levels of social support from family and friends distinguishes the high-active participant from the reduced-active and low-active participants.

Some factors can be manipulated by movement leaders in order to increase the probability of recruiting and maintaining commitment among movement members. However, there are also some factors that are for all intents and purposes beyond the reach of movement organizers. An increased understanding of activists' participation in cycles of mobilization and demobilization will not necessarily lead to increased control over those cycles.

Appendix

Table 11.2   Demographic Matching of Samples

	1989 Study		1993 Study		
	High (N = 32)	Low (N = 180)	High (N = 11)	Reduced (N = 11)	Low (N = 11)
Age					
18–24	3%	2%	0 (0%)	0 (0%)	0 (0%)
25–34	3%	9%	1 (9%)	0 (0%)	3 (27%)
35–44	28%	33%	3 (27%)	2 (18%)	3 (27%)
45–54	19%	15%	4 (36%)	3 (27%)	1 (9%)
55–64	12%	12%	0 (0%)	3 (27%)	0 (0%)
65–74	25%	18%	3 (27%)	1 (9%)	3 (27%)
75–84	9%	12%	0 (0%)	2 (18%)	0 (0%)
85+	0%	1%	0 (0%)	0 (0%)	1 (9%)
Mean	53	52	50	58	51
SD	16	17	13	14	19
Sex					
Female	63%	69%	7 (64%)	7 (64%)	7 (64%)
Male	38%	32%	4 (36%)	4 (36%)	4 (36%)
Marital status					
Married	53%	61%	6 (55%)	7 (64%)	9 (82%)
Single	13%	16%	2 (18%)	0 (0%)	1 (9%)
Divorced	25%	14%	1 (9%)	3 (27%)	1 (9%)
Widowed	9%	10%	2 (18%)	1 (9%)	0 (0%)
ANW activist couple	36%	36%	3 (27%)	3 (27%)	5 (45%)
Number of children at home for 1993 study					
0	19%	31%	7 (64%)	9 (82%)	8 (73%)
1	9%	13%	2 (18%)	0 (0%)	0 (0%)
2	31%	30%	1 (9%)	1 (9%)	3 (27%)
3	22%	13%	1 (9%)	1 (9%)	0 (0%)
4	13%	9%	0 (0%)	0 (0%)	0 (0%)
5+	6%	3%	0 (0%)	0 (0%)	0 (0%)

Table 11.3   First Recruitment to an Anti–Nuclear War SMO

	High		Reduced		Low		Total
Year of occurrence							
1950s	2	(29%)	4	(57%)	1	(14%)	7
1960s	—		1	(100%)	—		1
1970s–1982	2	(20%)	4	(40%)	4	(40%)	10
post-1982	7	(47%)	2	(13%)	6	(40%)	15
Age at time of occurrence							
<18	—		—		—		0
18–25	1	(33%)	2	(67%)	—		3
26–35	3	(25%)	3	(25%)	6	(50%)	12
36–45	6	(55%)	4	(36%)	1	(9%)	11
46–55	1	(25%)	1	(25%)	2	(50%)	4
56–65	—		1	(50%)	1	(50%)	2
>65	—		—		1	(100%)	1

Notes

The author would like to thank John Grula and the other members of SANE/FREEZE who so graciously donated their time to this study, as well as Stuart Oskamp for his invaluable guidance.

1. This group may also include members whose level of involvement has been only sporadically high for relatively short periods of time.

2. A selection criterion of having been involved in the movement for at least two years was adopted. One exception to this rule was made for a member who had been consistently highly involved for approximately one year.

3. In an earlier study, few demographic variables were found to predict significant and independent portions of the variance in level of ANW activism (Edwards and Oskamp 1992).

4. In a few cases, differences of three or more group members were used to qualify the differences of four or more.

5. Italics were added to emphasize the points being made.

6. Although members of the high-active group were consistently the most active members of the organization, several members of this group did report a general reduction in their involvement corresponding to decline in the movement itself.

PART 4

Conclusion

12

Toward a Coalitional Theory of Social & Political Movements

DAVID S. MEYER & THOMAS R. ROCHON

In Akira Kurosawa's classic film *Rashomon,* the story of a robbery-murder-rape-seduction is told three times by three different participants and witnesses. Although the central facts of the tale are recognizable in each retelling, the emphases, motivations, and meanings vary strikingly depending on the observer. In the same way, the views of the nuclear freeze movement presented in this book vary according to the theoretical perspective and substantive interests of the author or authors of each chapter, even as some elements of the story are repeated consistently. Seemingly basic issues of the origins, impacts, and legacies of the freeze movement turn out to have complicated answers, indeed different answers depending upon the vantage point of the observer.

In this concluding chapter, we will draw from the views of the nuclear freeze movement presented in the previous chapters to develop a more comprehensive view of that movement. As we noted in the Introduction, scholars frequently adopt perspectives that restrict their view of the full range of movement activities and effects. In the preceding chapters of this volume, the authors have brought to bear the insights of particular theoretical approaches on the collection of events and challenges that constitute the nuclear freeze movement. Such partial perspectives may be unavoidable, for the observer of any set of events selects which traits and relationships to feature as central to the phenomenon while other details and stories get pushed to the background. In order to have a comprehensive view of the freeze, or any movement for that matter, we need to do more. In this final chapter, we want to offer a more synthetic perspective of movements that recognizes the interplay of their social and political processes and purposes.

The nuclear freeze movement was about the foreign policy of the United States, international arms control, and, for many activists, domestic political priorities. Freeze activists also claimed to be motivated by a democratic ethos; they sought to bring people to the fore in a defense policy debate and to bring to the village square the issues normally confined to expert discussion. On one level, it is critical to allow the freeze (or any social movement) to define its own terms. If we take activists at their word, then we understand the movement by looking at the issues it addressed.

Like other movements, however, the nuclear freeze was about more than the concerns explicitly articulated by its advocates. In mobilizing citizens at the grassroots level across the United States, freeze activists seized upon an exploitable political issue to make much broader claims about participation and democracy. The freeze movement was animated by numerous activists and communities with no previous interest in nuclear weapons issues or foreign policy, and its adherents moved on to new issues after the peak of freeze mobilization passed. Drawing on different kinds of evidence, John MacDougall and Todd C. Edwards find that participation in the freeze movement was one phase—and for many activists the initial mobilizing phase—of an ongoing commitment to oppose U.S. foreign policies.

How, then, do we make sense of a phenomenon that captured media attention and the public imagination so intensely but for such a brief time? Above all, the chapters in this book make clear the multifaceted nature of social change efforts pursued through popular movements. Activists draw their grievances from the failures of established political institutions, they phrase those grievances in terms taken from a community of counter-experts, and they use extra-institutional or nonconventional protest as a lever to gain a hearing within policymaking institutions. As they gain access to political institutions, activists adjust their demands and activities in response to their changing resources and opportunities. By their efforts, movement activists alter the grievances, resources, and opportunities available to them and to other dissident movements. In addition, the experience of calling for procedural and substantive change in government policy is a profoundly transformative process for those who undertake it. Movement activists both change the world and are themselves changed by their involvement.

In what follows, we focus particularly on three stages of the freeze movement cycle, stages that arise in the context of any movement. The first phase was the coalescence of the freeze, in which amorphous public concerns and diverse peace organizations came to focus on the freeze proposal. The second issue facing the freeze was defining its relationship to established political institutions and ultimately the decision by the Nuclear Weapons Freeze Campaign (NWFC) to focus on passage of a congressional resolution. The final issue is assessment of the freeze legacy to the continually evolving network of peace movement organizations.

For each of these stages in the cycle of movement activity, we find it useful to think of movements as temporary and shifting coalitions involving both movement organizations and external allies. Therefore, we maintain a focus on the dynamics of the movement coalition throughout this chapter.

Origins and Organization

We begin with the definition offered in the Introduction, in which we claimed that movements are "episodic campaigns that lodge challenges against the state and mainstream society, using both conventional and nonconventional means of making claims." In other words, movements combine lobbying activity and coalition building intended to influence policy with pedagogical activity designed to influence cultural values. Movement strategies and action are thus aimed at both the political and social arenas. The women's movement, for example, works to affect legislation concerning women and to change cultural values about the roles of women in society. The environmental movement seeks changes in public policy and in people's ecological awareness. The freeze movement sought negotiation of a particular arms control proposal and the spread of new thinking about the relationship between armaments and security. These movements are, then, both social and political.

From this perspective, it follows that the process of organizing a challenging movement is one of building networks and coalitions that are intended to have multiple purposes, including influence on political institutions and on the wider society. The groups and individuals who are primarily concerned with one or another of these arenas of movement activity do not always have the same goals, and they need not always act in concert. By examining the contrasts between movement activity in the social and political arenas, it is possible to see the partial truths contained in each of the major approaches to the study of movements. Whereas new social movement approaches describe the grander social processes that give rise to dissent, they do not tell us why a particular set of issues arises at a particular time. Resource mobilization approaches direct our attention to the changes in political opportunities that give specific demands a wide popular and political appeal at a particular point in time. But an exclusive focus on the external resources and opportunities available to a movement tends to conceal the ways in which cooperating groups and individuals create resources by defining their goals in a particular way.

Older research mobilization approaches would have us presume that there is a constant and essentially irreducible supply of grievances upon which activist entrepreneurs may draw in mobilizing popular support (cf. McCarthy and Zald 1977). In its crudest form, such an approach is profoundly ahistorical. In Chapter 3, Robert Kleidman and Thomas R.

Rochon's comparison of three cycles of peace activism shows that each was centered on a particular issue whose significance had grown in the immediately preceding years. The Emergency Peace Campaign of 1936–1937 cannot be understood in isolation from the increased tensions in Europe at that time, and the test ban campaign of 1957–1963 could not have been undertaken prior to the increase in the number of atomic tests and the discovery of milk contaminated with strontium 90 by radioactive fallout. Similarly, the freeze movement fed upon the confluence of Soviet and U.S. nuclear overkill capacities, new information about the possibility that nuclear war could create a "nuclear winter" that would end life on earth, and the accelerating arms race between the United States and the Soviet Union. The importance of political resources and opportunities for movements is undeniable, but each wave of peace movement activity is also predicated upon the ability of movement leaders to phrase their issues in ways that strike a resonant chord with the concerns of potential activists and of the general public.

That said, it is obviously a matter of considerable importance to understand the circumstances that cause an issue to develop resonance in a wide audience. In the case of the nuclear freeze movement, the sudden surge in popular support was not the product of a profound social transformation or a new dissident identity, as the new social movement approach would suggest. Rather, as Rochon and Stephen P. Wood show in Chapter 2, the surge of public support for a nuclear freeze was predicated on the clash between a worsening climate of U.S.-Soviet relations and unchanged public beliefs about the necessity of maintaining a stable (if vigilant) relationship between the nuclear superpowers. Public concern about nuclear war and distrust of the Soviet Union were both constant features of the Cold War era. What did change was the belief that the superpower relationship was degenerating to such an extent that the possibility of nuclear war was becoming too real. The freeze proposal promised to allay that threat, but so could any number of other arms control proposals and for that matter so could the Star Wars program. The rapid spread of support for the nuclear freeze, including among the great majority of Republican party identifiers, was possible precisely because the movement did not rely upon an alteration of fundamental social or political values. The hasty exit of the freeze from public discourse after 1984 was also a consequence of the lack of change in social values.

What, then, did happen to make the freeze mobilization possible? Changes in U.S. foreign policy, begun during the Carter administration but dramatically crystallized with the election of President Ronald Reagan in 1980, altered the context in which activist appeals for action were received. Movement leaders, supported by arms control experts and prominent

Democratic politicians, could credibly claim that the Reagan administration's foreign policy was a departure from the existing relationship with the Soviet Union and a threat to global peace.

As the foreign policy establishment exited (or was pushed out of) the institutional arenas of national security policymaking, the ranks of those ready to add their voices to a plan that would restart the arms control process grew. Peace movement activists were ready to exploit this opportunity because leaders saw nuclear weapons as a powerful issue around which to demonstrate Americans' concerns with U.S. national security policy and to press the demand for greater public participation in setting the goals of foreign policy. As Will Hathaway and David S. Meyer point out in Chapter 4, a wide variety of movement organizations chose to cooperate on a focused campaign for the nuclear freeze, though in many instances the goal of negotiating a freeze was only one aspect of a wider agenda for change in the process and substance of policy. The early successes of the freeze campaign encouraged these organizations to suspend their broader agendas in order to concentrate on the freeze proposal.

Collaboration between long-established peace organizations was crucial to the rapid spread of the movement, for it provided a social and political network through which information could be quickly disseminated and actions could be coordinated. What seemed to outsiders to be a spontaneous rising of the American people across the country was in fact possible only because of the coordinated efforts of thousands of community groups that had previously embraced a wide range of issues. This network of community groups, many of them affiliated with such institutions as churches, schools, or other national organizations, was itself a legacy of previous movement mobilizations. The 1970s witnessed an unprecedented growth of interest-oriented groups at both the national and community levels (Berry 1989). These organizations were the product of ongoing popular and community struggles to seize control of issues that affect the quality of people's lives. National movements for civil rights and against the Vietnam War in the 1960s and for women's rights and against nuclear power in the 1970s also helped create this dense network of voluntary organizations. That network was one of the prime legacies bequeathed by prior movement campaigns to the organizers of the freeze movement.

Chapters 3 and 4 both find that the unity of the freeze coalition was greatest during the growth phase of the movement. The impulse to cooperate was strong because any organization that did not jump on the freeze bandwagon at that point was almost sure to be left behind. The movement was strengthened by the distinctive contributions of each organization in the coalition. Physicians for Social Responsibility provided medical expertise, the Interfaith Council for Peace and Justice offered a moral perspective on the arms race, the Committee for a Sane Nuclear Policy (SANE) provided a generation's worth of movement experience, and other organizations contributed volunteers and knowledge of the local political terrain.

Differences between the various freeze organizations, broadly characterized by Hathaway and Meyer as the arms control faction and the disarmament faction, emerged more prominently as the lobbying of Congress began to consume the NWFC. As the practical limits of this institutional and instrumental orientation became clearer, organizational leaders found it increasingly difficult to maintain an exclusive focus on the freeze. Differences between organizations reliant on professional staff and oriented to national lobbying on the one hand and organizations composed of volunteers and oriented to local action on the other exacerbated the tensions between organizational leaders.

Our understanding of the limits of coalitional possibilities within the freeze movement is deepened by David Cortright and Ron Pagnucco's account in Chapter 5 of the international contacts made by the NWFC. International organizations and events provided the setting for some of the most memorable freeze movement activities, such as the rally in New York during the UN Second Special Session on Disarmament and the meeting of a joint delegation of peace movement organizations with U.S. and Soviet negotiators at the 1985 Geneva summit. Despite the occasional cooperation of powerful movement organizations in the United States and Europe, a truly international movement for nuclear disarmament did not emerge.

Cortright and Pagnucco point out that this reflected in part strategic differences between the continents. The U.S. movement emphasized a bilateral freeze on existing U.S. and Soviet nuclear weapons, whereas the European peace movements emphasized opposition to the planned NATO deployment of U.S. Pershing II and cruise missiles. Equally important were the differences between existing movement networks and political opportunities in each country. Some European movements (including those in Denmark and the Netherlands) had powerful parliamentary allies and could thus place their hopes on a legislative strategy similar to that of the freeze movement. Others, including the movements in France and Germany (after 1983), had no hope of gaining majority support in parliament and so defined a more oppositional stance. Had the NWFC embraced European movement organizations employing direct action or focusing their critiques primarily on U.S. weapons and conduct, it would have been a critical blow to its standing with the American public. Contact with the French movement, whose largest wing was closely associated with the French Communist Party, would have been suicidal. Cortright and Pagnucco demonstrate the all but insurmountable difficulties in forming a truly international movement in an issue area so heavily entangled with distinctively defined national security interests.

In sum, a coalitional perspective on movements helps explain the rapidity of movement response to the opportunities created in the United States by the foreign policies of the late Carter and early Reagan administrations and in Europe by the NATO decision to deploy a new generation of intermediate-range nuclear missiles. The nature of prior generations of movement mobilizations in each setting enables us to account for the specific form and ideological focus taken by each movement. The nuclear freeze campaign could draw on the success of the test ban campaign for inspiration in its effort to shape the arms control agenda. European movements, lacking that experience, relied on a network of organizations formed during prior "ban the bomb" and pacifist campaigns. Finally, the coalitional perspective on movement campaigns helps us understand movement decline as a result of tensions internal to the coalition. This is a valuable addition to the conventional wisdom about the preeminence of external changes in the issue or about political opportunity structures as reasons for movement decline. At the same time, those elements of the external political climate, including erstwhile allies and the institutional settings in which movements seek to wield influence, are also important in shaping the trajectory of movement mobilization. It is to that topic that we now turn.

Institutionalizing Dissent

Movement coalitions, when successful, straddle the boundaries between institutional politics and extra-institutional protest. In the case of the nuclear freeze, the relationship between the movement as a whole and its ostensible allies within mainstream politics proved critical to the movement's rapid development and quick demise. To appreciate the extent to which political and social elites allied to the freeze movement were able to control it, we must recognize that the movement meant very different things to its key actors and supporters. Activist organizations, based both in Washington, D.C., and in communities across the country, saw nuclear weapons as a powerful issue around which to demonstrate not only concern with security issues but also the demand for a more effective public role in defining U.S. foreign policy. Andrew Rojecki shows in Chapter 6 that the mass media were cooperative in their portrayal of the freeze as a movement with an exceptionally broad base of grassroots support, one that went beyond the usual coalition of pacifist groups. But portrayal of the movement as expressing the concerns of the American heartland was linked to the assumption that, at the end of the day, nuclear strategy and arms control negotiations are the province of the experts. The freeze proposal itself was viewed as a symbol of popular concern rather than as a substantive proposal to be treated on its own merits. Activist demands for a more direct public role in arms control policies were never refuted so much as they were ignored.

The reason that institutional allies are so problematic for a movement is that the alliances in question are frequently not generated at the initiative of movement strategists. The mass media and political elites are typically the ones who determine whether a movement is newsworthy, whether it offers a promising vehicle for political ambitions, and—most important—just what the movement is about (see the chapters in Part 2). In the case of the freeze, initiative for a congressional resolution came from Senator Edward Kennedy and from Representatives Jonathan Bingham and Edward Markey. This initiative certainly represented a political opportunity for the freeze movement, and the publicity generated by congressional sponsorship in the spring of 1982 coincided with the movement's fastest period of growth. Yet, congressional allies redefined and refashioned the freeze proposal so as to serve their own ends—ends at odds with those pursued by grassroots activists.

The politicians who decided in 1982 to support the freeze also had their own spin on the meaning of the proposal. As Jeffrey W. Knopf points out in Chapter 7, "members of Congress . . . [said] they had to vote for it or get creamed on Main Street." But the "it" for which they voted was not the "it" for which the national freeze organizations were campaigning. The legislative process in the House, from Foreign Affairs Committee to floor debate, introduced greater and greater deviations from the simple and clear language of the freeze. The final version passed in the House said nothing more than what the average representative wanted it to say, which was that more effort should be put into arms control. The freeze debate dramatically demonstrated how a popular movement could alter the symbolic context of policymaking, but it also showed that even sympathetic elites would not permit a popular movement to define the specific content of an international arms control negotiation.

Politicians and other public figures had a growing interest in drawing attention to *their version* of the nuclear freeze and the nuclear freeze movement. As the stake in defining the nuclear freeze proposal and movement increased, so did conflicts about the goals and meanings of the freeze both within the movement (Benford 1993) and between the movement and a wide range of authorities (Meyer 1995). During the course of its career as a congressional resolution, the freeze proposal became a bid to jump-start the arms control efforts of the Reagan administration. The movement behind the proposal was stripped of its ambition to define a new role for the public in national security policy. The nuclear freeze came to be viewed solely as a symbolic statement of the need to repair the U.S.-Soviet relationship.

Essentially, activists were playing on a field with more powerful, more sophisticated, more experienced, and more enduring competitors. Loss of control over their own movement led to difficulties in maintaining an issue focus that could sustain mobilization. At the same time, movement organizations could hardly afford to turn their backs on the possibility of access to the mass media or to congressional allies if they expected to have any chance for real political influence.

The Impact of the Freeze

Do movements matter? Did the nuclear freeze movement change anything? Activists and opponents of the movement certainly acted as if the freeze mobilization was important. The late-night strategy sessions and heated disputes on all sides would not have taken place if participants believed that their choices were of no consequence. In retrospect, the matter of impact often seems to be less clear. Decades later, scholars dispute the relative weight of court decisions and social movements in changing politics and policy on abortion and civil rights (for example, Rosenberg 1991) and whether the movement against U.S. involvement in Vietnam affected the duration of that war (see Joseph 1993). The influence of a protest movement on international affairs is particularly complicated. Today, a decade after the end of the nuclear freeze challenge, the freeze movement's central demands for an end to the nuclear arms race remain elusive. At the same time, virtually everything else surrounding the nuclear arms race has changed. The United States and Russia have substantially reduced their nuclear arsenals, both unilaterally and through negotiations. More significantly, the Cold War that drove and legitimated the arms race is over.

Looking at incremental aspects of policy changes or the recognition of nuclear weapons movement activists hardly does justice to these global changes. Part of the problem is that a movement may have many different types of impacts. Our thinking about movement impacts is indebted to the work of William Gamson (1975), whose study of fifty-three "challenging groups" in the United States prior to World War II incorporated two distinct measures of movement success: acceptance of the group as a legitimate participant in the policy process (through consultation, negotiations, or formal inclusion), and the winning of policy changes benefiting a group's constituency. Particular movement challenges may succeed in one area and fail in the other.

Gamson's distinction between influence on policy and influence on the policy process usefully disentangles two types of impact that political movements may have. But this important work did not even purport to examine the larger social changes that may be brought about by movement activity. Movement activists do not just lobby and contest elections; they also develop alternative policies, stage demonstrations, write songs, and hold potluck dinners. Such changes in cultural values, social norms, and the demarcation between public and private spheres are all significant elements of potential movement influence that escape any analysis restricted to the achievement of success in the political arena (Rochon and Mazmanian 1993; Whittier 1995; Rochon forthcoming).

What can the chapters in this book say about the impact of the freeze movement? The chapters by Knopf and Rochon in Part 2 help us rethink the critical issues of movement impacts. Knopf argues that looking for movement impacts exclusively in terms of the substance of policy outcomes, as Gamson (1975) did, is problematic. In foreign policy, which responds to so many exogenous influences, such an approach may attribute to movements an influence they do not have or miss out on influence that the movement did have. Knopf promotes a more nuanced understanding of movement influence by focusing on the processes by which policy is made. He finds that the freeze movement, by activating public opinion on the subject of arms control, caused a shift in the politics of nuclear weapons in Washington, D.C. Congressional leaders and presidential aspirants championed the freeze, and the Reagan administration, which had to that point shown no interest in arms control, began to develop a set of negotiating principles. Public support for the freeze did not result in adoption of the freeze itself, but it did cause the issue of arms control to take on a new urgency in Washington. The freeze movement emboldened administration advocates of arms control to argue their case more vocally.

The result, Knopf shows us, is that the political impact of the freeze movement should not be measured in terms of the fate of the freeze proposal itself. Indeed, Knopf barely discusses the congressional freeze resolutions. The freeze movement instead provided the context in which elites fought their battles over arms control. The impact of the movement in swinging the balance in the direction of arms control may be seen in President Reagan's May 1982 Strategic Arms Reduction Talks (START) proposal, in the proliferation of congressional and administration nuclear build-down proposals, and perhaps above all in the president's conversion to the idea that "nuclear war cannot be won and must never be fought."

Viewed in these terms, the freeze movement had a significant impact on the politics of nuclear weapons in the United States in the 1980s, even if it was not the specific policy impact sought by freeze activists. The possibility of nuclear war was arguably reduced because of pressures created by the freeze movement, despite the fact that the freeze proposal itself was never even brought up by U.S. arms control negotiators.

Rochon's chapter on the impact of the freeze movement widens our perspective still further by viewing these policy demands as only one "face" that a movement puts forward. The other two faces of movement influence are alteration of the policy process and changes in social values.

The focus of the nuclear freeze movement was clearly on changing administration policy on arms control, but its greatest resource as a movement was the extent of its grassroots support. The dilemma of the freeze movement was that its strengths (public support) did not align well with its aspirations (influencing arms control negotiations). An enormous amount of effort in the 1982 congressional elections did translate public support into a Congress more favorable to the freeze proposal, but even that shift produced only a symbolic resolution of support for the freeze, which the administration was invited to ignore and which it in fact chose to ignore.

Rochon argues in Chapter 8 that a more appropriate goal for the freeze movement, given its grassroots resources, would have been to focus on changing the arms control policy process. The disjuncture between public abhorrence of the possibility of nuclear war and the seemingly casual escalation of tensions between the United States and the Soviet Union provided a setting in which movement leaders could have argued that arms control is too vital a subject to be the exclusive province of the executive branch. An arms control policy developed through cooperation between the Reagan administration and the Senate would be a policy process over which grassroots movements might hope for more influence in the future.

The freeze movement might also have concentrated on efforts to influence cultural values related to nuclear deterrence. Fear that the arms race could spiral into nuclear war meant that there was widespread public support not only for the nuclear freeze but also for build-down proposals. By focusing more on public education than on congressional lobbying, the freeze movement might have been able to make clear the distinction between proposals that reduce the number of nuclear missiles but increase their explosive magnitude and other proposals that reflect a genuine move toward minimal deterrence. Such efforts might not have paid off in the short term, but with the end of the Cold War a significant reduction in the size of nuclear arsenals has become a realistic possibility. That there is no public demand for such reductions may be due to the lost opportunity to cultivate ideas of minimal deterrence among the public during the course of the freeze movement.

We have found that a coalitional or network-oriented approach to the study of movements is helpful in understanding both their rise and their decline. There are several stages in the translation of popular concern about an issue into a protest movement. The policies of the Reagan administration toward the Soviet Union were at variance with long-held public understandings of what constituted a secure relationship between the two nuclear superpowers. Those policies and public concerns constituted an opportunity for the revitalization of the peace movement network, a network that had been refashioned in the course of popular organizing and protest during the test ban treaty campaign and the movement against the Vietnam War. Party politics in Congress, rivalries within the Reagan administration, and the images generated by the news media were additional forces that gave shape and direction to the freeze campaign. The rise, progress, and decline of the freeze movement cannot be understood without reference both to its internal tensions and external constraints.

The Movement After the Movement

We have emphasized the importance of the legacy of prior mobilizations in creating an organizational network that helped shape the freeze movement. Logically, then, any assessment of the impact of the freeze must include consideration of the network of organizations and alliances left behind by the freeze mobilization itself. The third section of this book addresses precisely that issue.

The framing of issues and the selection of tactics within a movement campaign is not just a matter of expressing a grievance but also of defining one's political and social identity. In the case of the freeze movement, both the issue and the focus on electoral politics generated the active support of a wide segment of the population. The effect was to reach back, beyond the movement against the Vietnam War, to the mainstream support enjoyed by the movement against nuclear testing. Media portrayals of the freeze constituted a kind of ratification of this movement image. The freeze enjoyed a synergistic "bandwagon effect" (cf. Granovetter 1978; Chong 1991), as an amazingly wide variety of groups signed onto the freeze proposal.

If we are correct in our emphasis on the importance of campaign coalitions in shaping the postmobilization organizational network, then the pragmatic nature of the freeze movement should remain visible today as a legacy of the activists and organizations mobilized at that time. In Chapter 9, Sam Marullo and Bob Edwards find that surviving peace movement organizations are disproportionately likely to embrace a broad issue focus and to engage in "insider tactics," including the lobbying of local or state legislatures. The eclecticism of goals and tactics found among peace movement organizations by John MacDougall in Chapter 10 is also precisely the kind of legacy one would expect the freeze to leave behind. Rather than retrenchment to a militant core of supporters, MacDougall finds that peace movement organizations in Maine have adopted a pragmatic flexibility in their subsequent campaigns. Maine peace activists emphasize the connections between their concerns and issues of immediate importance to the state, such as jobs. MacDougall's chapter is instructive in showing us how movement organizations highlight the connections between defense issues and such broader social concerns as economic conversion, the maintenance of jobs, and environmental preservation. The peace movement has broad-

TOWARD A COALITIONAL THEORY 249

ened its appeal by developing links with unions, churches, and prominent politicians and by developing activities with a wide appeal, such as international citizen exchanges. Chapters 9 and 10 both demonstrate that the organizational network of the freeze movement has largely survived, but with a transformed focus that is eclectic and pragmatic. This network provides the basis for future peace campaigns; what is missing is a unifying issue with the capacity to mobilize broadly in the population.

Todd C. Edwards gives us yet another view of the same problem in Chapter 11, this time from the perspective of the activists. Compared to those who are active only during a campaign, continuous activists are able to broaden their range of interests by connecting an anti–nuclear weapons stance to other issues of social justice. MacDougall demonstrates that this pattern assists the development of new organizational alliances; Edwards shows that the same pattern enables activists to tackle fresh challenges and to connect their involvement to emerging public concerns.

The image left by this body of research into the aftermath of the freeze campaign is of a movement that continues to operate as a network of organizations. The postcampaign movement also continues to innovate in its issue focus and in its development of new policy targets and activities. The meetings are smaller, and the bright lights of media attention have been turned off. But these are matters simply of scale. The sole difference between the peace movement during the freeze campaign and today that is *not* a matter of scale is the diversification of organizational goals and tactics characteristic of the postfreeze movement. As we have noted, that diversity is a means of preparing the ground for the concentration of effort that will again be needed in the next peace campaign.

Lessons and Legacies: Beyond the Freeze Movement

Kurosawa's *Rashomon* reminds us that even "true" narratives of historical events vary according to the vantage point of the observer. By iterating several versions of the same story, we have tried to give the reader a clearer sense of the multiple layers of experience in the nuclear freeze movement. Every theoretical perspective carries with it a frame that defines both the central conceptual issues and the boundaries of significant evidence. Such perspectives are needed to give order to events and their causes. As Bertrand Russell once said, "A person with a completely open mind has no mind at all."

The selection of a theoretical approach to use in understanding movements is, in other words, not a bad thing. It becomes problematic only when that theoretical approach is seen to represent something larger than a partial perspective on movements. Overcoming the "*Rashomon* effect" in the study of movements requires above all a recognition that each analytical approach is constructed to throw light on a particular aspect of a social or political protest.

In this book we have brought together a series of scholarly efforts that focus on the freeze movement's relationship with the polity and society. Simply by juxtaposing these diverse treatments of the freeze, we gain a fuller understanding not only of this movement, but also of the broad spectrum of causes, activities, and potential effects of any movement. We have seen that it is only an analytically useful fiction to speak of "the" nuclear freeze movement. Rather than being unitary actors, movements are composed of diverse elements cooperating and competing on different issues at a given time. The range of activists and organizations that make up a movement also vary over time. A movement is not only bigger during a phase of mass mobilization than it is either before or after, but it is also different. Nor does the constellation of movement organizations, activists, goals, and strategies look the same after a campaign as it did before the mobilization began.

When we examine the freeze movement as a constantly shifting field of internal and external coalitions, two broad conclusions emerge. First, tensions among the organizations sponsoring the movement campaign are an important cause of movement growth and decline. Second, expansion of the movement is accompanied by a widening circle of attention from the mass media, politicians, and other public figures such as arms control experts. Each newcomer to the debate seeks to draw attention to his or her own version of what the nuclear freeze is about. This is a matter not only of the nuances of language ("the president *should* freeze" versus "the president *shall* freeze") but also of the very meaning of the movement.

The outcome was a substantial drift in the meaning of the freeze proposal and the direction of the freeze movement over time. Initially, the freeze was tied to a much broader analysis of foreign policy and often to an alternative domestic economic policy as well. These broader analyses were conveyed in movement publications, limited in reach but widely circulated among activists. As the movement made inroads in the mass media and came to be championed by political figures outside of the movement core itself, the definition of the freeze narrowed. Conversely, the breadth of the movement expanded once again at the end of the freeze campaign. With relaxation of the discipline of participating in a campaign, the organizational pattern of diversity and flexibility in issue focus reasserted itself.

If we pull back from the freeze campaign's struggles to define itself in the media, in the halls of Congress, and with its social and political allies, we see a still wider pattern in which the freeze developed in a particular cultural context, made its mark on that culture, and then left behind an altered network of opposition to nuclear weapons. Cultural ideas about nuclear weapons, the Soviet Union, and past peace mobilizations represent a cognitive and evaluative context that provides both a resource and an arena for dissident politics (Swidler 1986; Rochon 1998). The symbols of nuclear weapons, communism, and peace protest define a set of cultural boundaries that delimit the strategic choices of movement leaders and institutional leaders alike. Movements may effect a change in public policy or in the policymaking process, but they are more frequently able to make incremental changes in the field of meanings and procedures through which policy is made.

At first blush one would think that the nuclear freeze movement, unusually specific in its goals and particularly meteoric in its life, would provide a fairly easy case for understanding movement growth and decline, organization, and influence. That a campaign expressly concerned with international politics would owe clear debts to civil rights and feminist movements and would contribute to subsequent campaigns on economic justice shows how complex and interconnected the process of social change is. By focusing on organizational networks and policy cultures both during successive campaigns and in the periods between them, we can better understand the array of political, social, and cultural changes produced by movement activism.

REFERENCES

Adams, Tom (1991) *Grass Roots: How Ordinary People Are Changing America* (New York: Citadel Press).

Adelman, Kenneth (1989) *The Great Universal Embrace: Arms Summitry—A Skeptic's Account* (New York: Simon and Schuster).

Aldrich, Howard, and Ellen Auster (1986) "Even Dwarfs Started Small: Liabilities of Age and Size and Their Strategic Implications," pp. 165–198 in Barry Staw and L. L. Cummings (eds.), *Research in Organizational Behavior,* vol. 8 (Greenwich, CT: JAI Press).

Aldrich, Howard, Udo Staber, Catherine Zimmer, and John Beggs (1990) "Minimalism and Mortality: Patterns of Disbanding Among U.S. Trade Associations, 1900–1983," pp. 21–52 in Jitendra Singh (ed.), *Organizational Evolution: New Directions* (Newbury Park, CA: Sage).

Aldrich, John, John Sullivan, and Eugene Borgida (1989) "Foreign Affairs and Issue Voting: Do Presidential Candidates 'Waltz Before a Blind Audience?'" *American Political Science Review* 83 (March): 123–141.

Allison, Graham (1971) *Essence of Decision: Explaining the Cuban Missile Crisis* (Boston: Little, Brown).

Anderson, Marion, and Greg Bischak (1990) *A Shift in Federal Spending: What the Peace Dividend Can Mean to Maine* (Lansing, MI: Employment Research Associates).

Anderson, Martin (1990) *Revolution: The Reagan Legacy* (rev. ed.) (Stanford, CA: Hoover Institution Press).

Atwood, David (1997) "Mobilizing Around the United Nations Special Sessions on Disarmament," in Jackie Smith, Charles Chatfield, and Ron Pagnucco (eds.), *Transnational Social Movements and World Politics: Solidarity Beyond the State* (Syracuse, NY: Syracuse University Press).

Barone, Michael, and Grant Ujifusa (1993) *Almanac of American Politics 1993* (Washington, DC: National Journal).

Baumgartner, Frank, and Bryan Jones (1993) *Agendas and Instability in American Politics* (Chicago: University of Chicago Press).

Bean, Kevin (1988) "Reconversion in Connecticut," *Social Policy* 18 (Winter): 46–49.

Benford, Robert (1993) "Frame Disputes Within the Nuclear Disarmament Movement," *Social Forces* 71 (March): 677–701.

Bennett, W. Lance (1990) "Toward a Theory of Press-State Relations in the United States," *Journal of Communication* 40 (Spring): 103–126.

Bentley, Judith (1984) *The Nuclear Freeze Movement* (New York: Franklin and Watts).

Berry, Jeffrey (1977) *Lobbying for the People: The Political Behavior of Public Interest Groups* (Princeton, NJ: Princeton University Press).

——— (1989) *The Interest Group Society* (2nd ed.) (New York: HarperCollins).

Bjork, Rebecca (1989) *The Strategic Defense Initiative: Symbolic Containment of the Nuclear Threat*. Ph.D. dissertation, University of Southern California, Los Angeles.

Bobo, Kim, Jackie Kendall, and Steve Max (1991) *Organizing for Social Change: A Manual for Activists in the 1990s* (Washington, DC: Seven Locks Press).

Boulding, Elise (1990) "The Early Eighties Peak of the Peace Movement," pp. 19–36 in Sam Marullo and John Lofland (eds.), *Peace Action in the Eighties* (New Brunswick, NJ: Rutgers University Press).

Browne, Eric (1973) *Coalition Theories: A Logical and Empirical Critique* (London: Sage).

Buechler, Steven (1990) *Women's Movements in the United States: Woman Suffrage, Equal Rights, and Beyond* (New Brunswick, NJ: Rutgers University Press).

Bullard, Robert (1995) "The Quest for Environmental Equity: Mobilizing the African-American Community for Social Change," pp. 39–50 in Riley Dunlap and Angela Mertig (eds.), *American Environmentalism: The U.S. Environmental Movement, 1970–1990* (Washington, DC: Taylor and Francis).

Bundy, McGeorge, Gerard Smith, Robert McNamara, and George Kennan (1982) "Nuclear Weapons and the Atlantic Alliance," *Foreign Affairs* 60 (Spring): 753–768.

Burgin, Eileen (1993) "The Influence of Constituents," pp. 67–88 in Randall Ripley and James Lindsay (eds.), *Congress Resurgent: Foreign and Defense Policy on Capitol Hill* (Ann Arbor: University of Michigan Press).

Bürklin, Wilhelm (1985) "Cycles in Politics: Dimensions, Ranges, and Variable Classification." Paper prepared for the European Consortium for Political Research Joint Sessions, Barcelona, Spain, March 25–30.

Carmichael, Stokely, and Charles Hamilton (1967) *Black Power: The Politics of Liberation in America* (New York: Vintage Books).

Carroll, Glenn (1983) "A Stochastic Model of Organizational Mortality: Review and Reanalysis," *Social Science Research* 12 (December): 303–329.

Chappell, Henry W., Jr., and William Keech (1986) "Policy Motivation and Party Differences in a Dynamic Spatial Model of Party Competition," *American Political Science Review* 80 (September): 881–899.

Chatfield, Charles (1997) "Intergovernmental and Nongovernmental Organizations to 1945," in Jackie Smith, Charles Chatfield, and Ron Pagnucco (eds.), *Transnational Social Movements and World Politics: Solidarity Beyond the State* (Syracuse, NY: Syracuse University Press).

Chatfield, Charles, with Robert Kleidman (1992) *The American Peace Movement* (New York: Twayne).

Chilton, Patricia (1994) "Mechanics of Change: Social Movements, Transnational Coalitions, and the Transformation Processes in Eastern Europe," *Democratization* 1, no. 1: 151–181.

Chong, Dennis (1991) *Collective Action and the Civil Rights Movement* (Chicago: University of Chicago Press).

―――― (1993) "How People Think, Reason, and Feel About Rights and Liberties," *American Journal of Political Science* 37 (August): 867–899.

Clark, Kenneth (1966) "The Civil Rights Movement: Momentum and Organization," *Daedalus* 95 (Winter): 239–267.

Cohen, Jean (1985) "Strategy or Identity: New Theoretical Paradigms and Contemporary Social Movements," *Social Research* 52 (Winter): 663–716.

Cohen, Michael, James March, and Johan Olsen (1972) "A Garbage Can Model of Organizational Choice," *Administrative Science Quarterly* 17 (March): 1–25.

Cole, Paul (1983) "The Reagan Administration's Reaction to the Nuclear Freeze Movement," pp. 93–106 in Paul Cole and William Taylor (eds.), *The Nuclear Freeze Debate* (Boulder, CO: Westview Press).

Collins, Barry, and Bertram Ravin (1969) "Group Structure: Attraction, Coalitions, Communication, and Power," pp. 102–204 in Gardner Lindzey and Elliott Aronson (eds.), *The Handbook of Social Psychology,* 2nd ed. (Reading, MA: Addison Wesley Publishing).

Collins, John (1985) *U.S.-Soviet Military Balance, 1980–1985* (Washington, DC: Pergamon-Brassey).

Colwell, Mary Anna (1988) "The 1988 Survey of Groups and Organizations Working for Peace." Available from Colwell at 1628 Jaynes St., Berkeley CA 94703.

―――― (1989) "Organizational and Management Characteristics of Peace Groups." San Francisco: Institute for Nonprofit Organization Management, Working Paper no. 8, University of San Francisco.

Colwell, Mary Anna, and Doug Bond (1994) "American Peace Movement Organizations: The 1988 and 1992 Surveys." San Francisco: Institute for Nonprofit Organization Management, Working Paper no. 21, University of San Francisco.

Colwell, Mary Anna, Doug Bond, Sam Marullo, John McCarthy, Michelle Markley, Ron Pagnucco, Bob Edwards, and Jackie Smith (1992) "The 1992 Peace Movement Organization Survey." Available from Doug Bond, Program on Nonviolent Sanctions, 1737 Cambridge St., Cambridge, MA 02138.

Conetta, Carl (1988) *Peace Resource Book: 1988/1989* (Cambridge, MA: Ballinger).

Cortright, David (1993) *Peace Works: The Citizen's Role in Ending the Cold War* (Boulder, CO: Westview Press).

Covert, Margaret (1990) *The Reproductive Rights Movement: Translating Ideology into Action.* Master's thesis, Tufts University, Boston.

Crumm, Eileen (1995) "The Value of Economic Incentives in International Politics," *Journal of Peace Research* 32 (August): 313–330.

Dalton, Russell (1988) *Citizen Politics in Western Democracies* (Chatham, NJ: Chatham House Publishers).

―――― (1994) *The Green Rainbow* (New Haven, CT: Yale University Press).

Davis, Jeanne (1993) Interview with John MacDougall.

Deuce, Nick (1983) "Legislators for the Freeze," *Freeze Newsletter* (April/May): 9.

Dormody, Sheila (1996) Interview with John MacDougall.

Downs, Anthony (1957) *An Economic Theory of Democracy* (New York: Harper and Row).

Downton, James, and Paul Wehr (1991) "Peace Movements: The Role of Commitment and Community in Sustaining Member Participation," pp. 113–134 in Metta Spencer (ed.), *Research in Social Movements, Conflicts and Change,* vol. 13 (Greenwich, CT: JAI Press).

Drew, Elizabeth (1983) "A Political Journal," *The New Yorker* 49 (June 20): 39–75.

Dwyer, Judith (1983) "The Role of the American Churches in the Nuclear Weapons Debate," pp. 77–92 in Paul Cole and William Taylor (eds.), *The Nuclear Freeze Debate* (Boulder, CO: Westview Press).

Economic Conversion Project (ECP) (1992) "We've Got Some News," May/June.

———— (1996) Letter to supporters, January 15.

Eder, Klaus (1985) "The 'New Social Movements': Moral Crusades, Political Pressure Groups, or Social Movements?" *Social Research* 52 (Winter): 869–890.

Edwards, Bob (1994) "Semiformal Organizational Structure Among Social Movement Organizations: An Analysis of the U.S. Peace Movement," *Nonprofit and Voluntary Sector Quarterly* 23 (Winter): 309–333.

———— (1995) *Organizational Style in Middle-Class and Poor People's Social Movement Organizations: An Empirical Assessment of New Social Movements Theory.* Ph.D. dissertation, Catholic University of America, Washington, DC.

———— (1995b) "With Liberty and Environmental Justice for All: The Emergence and Challenge of Grassroots Environmentalism in the United States," pp. 35–55 in Bron Taylor (ed.), *Ecological Resistance Movements* (Albany, NY: SUNY Press).

Edwards, Bob, and Sam Marullo (1995) "Organizational Mortality in a Declining Social Movement: The Demise of Peace Movement Organizations in the End of the Cold War Era," *American Sociological Review* 60 (December): 908–927.

Edwards, Bob, and John McCarthy (1992) "Social Movement Schools," *Sociological Forum* 7 (September): 541–550.

Edwards, Todd, and Stuart Oskamp (1992) "Components of Antinuclear War Activism," *Basic and Applied Social Psychology* 13 (June): 217–230.

Eldersveld, Samuel (1956) "Experimental Propaganda Techniques and Voting Behavior," *American Political Science Review* 50 (March): 154–165.

Ellsberg, Daniel (1981) "Introduction: Call to Mutiny," pp. i–xxviii in E. P. Thompson and Dan Smith (eds.), *Protest and Survive* (New York: Monthly Review Press).

Enelow, James, and Melvin Hinich (eds.) (1990) *Advances in the Spatial Theory of Voting* (Cambridge: Cambridge University Press).

Ennis, James, and Richard Schreuer (1987) "Mobilizing Weak Support for Social Movements: The Role of Grievance, Efficacy, and Cost," *Social Forces* 66 (December): 390–409.

Entman, Robert (1993) "Framing: Toward Clarification of a Fractured Paradigm," *Journal of Communication* 43 (Autumn): 51–58.

Entman, Robert, and Andrew Rojecki (1993) "Freezing Out the Public: Elite and Media Framing of the U.S. Anti-Nuclear Movement," *Political Communication* 10 (April-June): 155–173.

Epstein, Barbara (1991) *Political Protest and Cultural Revolution* (Berkeley: University of California Press).

Erickson Nepsted, Sharon (1995) "Indignation and Action: The Development of Insurgent Consciousness in the Central America Peace Movement." Paper presented at the American Sociological Association annual meetings, Washington, DC, August.

Faludi, Susan (1991) *Backlash: The Undeclared War Against American Women* (New York: Crown).

Feighan, Edward (1983) "The Freeze in Congress," pp. 29–55 in Paul Cole and

William Taylor (eds.), *The Nuclear Freeze Debate: Arms Control Issues for the 1980s* (Boulder, CO: Westview Press).

Feinstein, Judy (1993) Interview with John MacDougall.

Ferree, Myra, and Frederick Miller (1985) "Mobilization and Meaning: Toward an Integration of Social Psychological and Resource Perspectives on Social Movements," *Sociological Inquiry* 55 (Winter): 38–61.

Fichman, M., and D. A. Levinthal (1988) "Honeymoons and the Liability of Adolescence: A New Perspective on Duration Dependence in Social and Organizational Relationships." Paper presented at the annual meetings of the Academy of Management, Anaheim, CA.

Fine, Melinda (1983) "Political Delegations from Europe," *Freeze Newsletter* (December): 6.

——— (1984) "Introduction from the International Coordinator," *Freeze Focus* (June): 3.

Finn, James (1985) "The Peace Movement in the United States," pp. 162–172 in Werner Kaltefleiter and Robert Pfaltzgraff (eds.), *The Peace Movement in Europe and the United States* (London: Croom Helm).

Fireman, Bruce, and William Gamson (1979) "Utilitarian Logic in the Resource Mobilization Perspective," pp. 8–44 in Mayer Zald and John McCarthy (eds.), *The Dynamics of Social Movements* (Cambridge, MA: Winthrop).

Fischhoff, Baruch (1983) "Strategic Policy Preferences: A Behavioral Decision Theory Perspective," *Journal of Social Issues* 39 (Fall): 133–160.

Fisher, Louis (1990) *American Constitutional Law* (New York: McGraw-Hill).

Fiske, Susan, Felicia Pratto, and Mark Pavelchak (1983) "Citizens' Images of Nuclear War: Content and Consequences," *Journal of Social Issues* 39 (Fall): 41–65.

Forsberg, Randall, Richard Garwin, Paul Warnke, and Robert Dean (1983) *Seeds of Promise: The First Real Hearings on the Nuclear Arms Freeze* (Andover, MA: Brick House).

Freeman, Jo (1975) *The Politics of Women's Liberation* (New York: David McKay).

——— (1979) "Resource Mobilization and Strategy: A Model for Analyzing Social Movement Organization Actions," pp. 167–189 in Mayer Zald and John McCarthy (eds.), *The Dynamics of Social Movements* (Cambridge, MA: Winthrop).

Freeze Newsletter (1982) "The West German Peace Movement Appeals to the American People," *Freeze Newsletter* (July): 20–21.

Friedman, Debra, and Doug McAdam (1992) "Collective Identity and Activism: Networks, Choices, and the Life of a Social Movement," pp. 156–173 in Aldon Morris and Carol Mueller (eds.), *Frontiers in Social Movement Theory* (New Haven, CT: Yale University Press).

Gais, Thomas, Mark Peterson, and Jack Walker, Jr. (1984) "Interest Groups, Iron Triangles, and Representative Institutions in American National Government," *British Journal of Political Science* 14 (April): 161–185.

Gais, Thomas, and Jack Walker, Jr. (1991) "Pathways to Influence in American Politics," pp. 103–120 in Jack Walker, *Mobilizing Interest Groups in America: Patrons, Professions, and Social Movements* (Ann Arbor: University of Michigan Press).

Gallup, George (1984) *Public Opinion 1983* (Wilmington, DE: Scholarly Resources).

Gallup Poll Monthly, October 1984 (Princeton, NJ).

Gallup Report, no. 188, May 1981 (Princeton, NJ).

Gamson, William (1964) "Experimental Studies of Coalition Formation," pp. 82–100 in L. Berkowitz (ed.), *Advances in Experimental Social Psychology,* vol. 1 (New York: Academic Press).

——— (1975) *The Strategy of Social Protest* (Homewood, IL: Dorsey Press).

——— (1992) *Talking Politics* (New York: Cambridge University Press).

Gamson, William, and David Meyer (1996) "Framing Political Opportunity," pp. 275–290 in Doug McAdam, John McCarthy, and Mayer Zald (eds.), *Comparative Perspectives on Social Movements: Mobilizing Structures and Cultural Framings* (Cambridge: Cambridge University Press).

Gamson, William, and André Modigliani (1989) "Media Discourse and Public Opinion on Nuclear Power: A Constructionist Approach," *American Journal of Sociology* 95 (July): 1–37.

Garfinkle, Adam (1984) *The Politics of the Nuclear Freeze* (Philadelphia: Foreign Policy Research Institute).

Garthoff, Raymond (1985) *Détente and Confrontation: American-Soviet Relations from Nixon to Reagan* (Washington, DC: Brookings Institution).

Gitlin, Todd (1980) *The Whole World Is Watching* (Berkeley: University of California Press).

Glaser, Barney, and Anselm Strauss (1967) *The Discovery of Grounded Theory: Strategies for Qualitative Research* (Chicago: Aldine De Gruyter).

Gore, Albert, Jr. (1983) "Beyond the Freeze," *Washington Post* (May 9): 11.

Granovetter, Mark (1978) "Threshold Models of Collective Behavior," *American Journal of Sociology* 83 (May): 1420–1443.

Gray, Robert (1984) "Congress, Arms Control, and Weapons Modernization," in U.S. House of Representatives, Committee on Foreign Affairs, *Congress and Foreign Policy, 1983,* a Congressional Research Service report (Washington, DC: Government Printing Office).

Greider, William (1992) *Who Will Tell the People: The Betrayal of American Democracy* (New York: Simon and Schuster).

Groennings, Sven, E. W. Kelley, and Michael Leiserson (eds.) (1970) *The Study of Coalition Behavior* (New York: Holt, Rinehart, and Winston).

Grofman, Bernard (ed.) (1993) *Information, Participation, and Choice: An Economic Theory of Democracy in Perspective* (Ann Arbor: University of Michigan Press).

Gurevitch, Michael, and Mark Levy (1985) *Mass Communication Review Yearbook,* vol. 5 (Beverly Hills, CA: Sage).

Gusfield, Joseph (1981) "Social Movements and Social Change: Perspectives of Linearity and Fluidity," pp. 317–339 in Louis Kriesberg (ed.), *Research in Social Movements, Conflict, and Change,* vol. 4 (Greenwich, CT: JAI Press).

Habermas, Jürgen (1981) "New Social Movements," *Telos* 49 (Fall): pp. 33–37.

Haig, Alexander (1984) *Caveat: Realism, Reagan, and Foreign Policy* (New York: Macmillan).

Halliday, Terence, Michael Powell, and Mark Granfors (1987) "Minimalist Organizations: Vital Events in State Bar Associations, 1870–1930," *American Sociological Review* 52 (August): 456–471.

Hallin, Daniel (1986) *The Uncensored War* (New York: Oxford University Press).

Halperin, Morton, with the assistance of Priscilla Clapp and Arnold Kanter (1974) *Bureaucratic Politics and Foreign Policy* (Washington, DC: Brookings Institution).

Hannan, Michael, and Glenn Carroll (1992) *Dynamics of Organizational Populations* (New York: Oxford University Press).

Hanson, John (1993) Interview with John MacDougall.

Harris, Louis (1984) "Public Opinion and the Freeze Movement: Public Attitudes Toward the Freeze," pp. 39–40 in Steven Miller (ed.), *The Nuclear Weapons Freeze and Arms Control* (Cambridge, MA: Center for Science and International Affairs of Harvard University and Ballinger Press).

Hart, David (1993) Interview with John MacDougall.

Hathaway, William (1990) *Long-Term Arms Control and Disarmament Coalitions.* Master's thesis, Tufts University, Boston.

Heclo, Hugh (1978) "Issue Networks and the Executive Establishment," pp. 87–124 in Anthony King (ed.), *The New American Political System* (Washington, DC: American Enterprise Institute).

Hertsgaard, Mark (1989) *On Bended Knee: The Press and the Reagan Presidency* (New York: Schocken Books).

Hibbard, Deb (1993) Interview with John MacDougall.

Hinckley, Barbara (1972) "Coalitions in Congress: Size and Ideological Distance," *Midwest Journal of Political Science* 16 (May): 197–207.

Hogan, Michael (1994) *The Nuclear Freeze Campaign: Rhetoric and Foreign Policy in the Telepolitical Age* (East Lansing: Michigan State University Press).

Hogan, Michael, and Leroy Dorsey (1991) "Public Opinion and the Nuclear Freeze: The Rhetoric of Popular Sovereignty in Foreign Policy Debate," *Western Journal of Speech Communication* 55 (Fall): 319–338.

Hogan, Michael, and Ted Smith (1991) "Polling on the Issues: Public Opinion and the Nuclear Freeze," *Public Opinion Quarterly* 55 (Winter): 534–569.

Huberts, Leo (1989) "The Influence of Social Movements on Government Policy," pp. 395–426 in Bert Klandermans (ed.), *International Social Movement Research,* vol. 2 (Greenwich, CT: JAI Press).

Jasper, James, and Dorothy Nelkin (1992) *The Animal Rights Crusade: The Growth of a Moral Protest* (New York: Free Press).

Jenkins, J. Craig (1983) "Resource Mobilization Theory and the Study of Social Movements," pp. 527–553 in Ralph Turner and James Short (eds.), *Annual Review of Sociology,* vol. 9 (Palo Alto, CA: Annual Reviews).

Johnson, Eric (1993) Interview with John MacDougall.

Johnson, Loch (1989) "Covert Action and Accountability: Decision-Making for America's Secret Foreign Policy," *International Studies Quarterly* 33 (March): 81–109.

Johnston, Carla (1986) *Reversing the Nuclear Arms Race* (Cambridge, MA: Schenkman Books).

Joseph, Paul (1993) *Peace Politics* (Philadelphia: Temple University Press).

Judd, Richard, Edwin Churchill, and Joel Eastman (eds.) (1995) *Maine, the Pine Tree State* (Orono: University of Maine Press).

Kaase, Max, and Alan Marsh (1979) "Political Action Repertoires: Changes over Time and a New Typology," pp. 137–176 in Samuel Barnes, Max Kaase et al. (eds.), *Political Action: Mass Participation in Five Western Democracies* (Beverly Hills, CA: Sage).

Kahn, Si (1982) *Organizing: A Guide for Grassroots Leaders* (New York: McGraw-Hill).

Katz, Milton (1986) *Ban the Bomb: A History of SANE, the Committee for a Sane Nuclear Policy* (New York: Praeger).

Kazin, Michael (1984) "The Freeze: From Strategy to Social Movement," pp. 445–461 in Paul Joseph and Simon Rosenblum (eds.), *Search for Sanity* (Boston: South End Press).

Kehler, Randy (1993) Interview with David Cortright, September 24.

Keller, Bill (1982) "Coalitions and Associations Transform Strategy, Methods of Lobbying in Washington," *Congressional Quarterly Weekly Report* (January 23).

Kelley, Harold (1967) "Attribution Theory in Social Psychology," pp. 192–240 in David Levine (ed.), *Nebraska Symposium on Motivation* (Lincoln: University of Nebraska Press).

Kennan, George (1982) *The Nuclear Delusion* (New York: Pantheon).

Kent, Bruce (1995) Interview with Ron Pagnucco, August 9.

Key, V. O., Jr. (1961) *Public Opinion and American Democracy* (New York: Knopf).

——— (1966) *The Responsible Electorate* (Cambridge, MA: Harvard University Press).

Kingdon, John (1984) *Agendas, Alternatives, and Public Policies* (Boston: Little, Brown).

Kitschelt, Herbert (1986) "Political Opportunity Structures and Political Protest: Anti-Nuclear Movements in Four Democracies," *British Journal of Political Science* 16 (January): 57–85.

Klandermans, Bert (1984) "Mobilization and Participation: Social-Psychological Expansions of Resource Mobilization Theory," *American Sociological Review* 49 (October): 583–600.

Klandermans, Bert, and Dirk Oegema (1987) "Potentials, Networks, Motivations, and Barriers: Steps Towards Participation in Social Movements," *American Sociological Review* 52 (August): 519–531.

Klandermans, Bert, and Sidney Tarrow (1988) "Mobilization into Social Movements," pp. 1–38 in Bert Klandermans, Hanspeter Kriesi, and Sidney Tarrow (eds.), *From Structure to Action: Comparing Social Movement Research Across Cultures,* vol. 1, *International Social Movement Research* (Greenwich CT: JAI Press).

Kleidman, Robert (1993) *Organizing for Peace: Neutrality, the Test Ban, and the Freeze* (Syracuse, NY: Syracuse University Press).

——— (1994) "Volunteer Activism and Professionalism in Social Movement Organizations," *Social Problems* 41 (May): 257–276.

Knopf, Jeffrey (1993) "Beyond Two-Level Games: Domestic-International Interaction in the Intermediate-Range Nuclear Forces Negotiations," *International Organization* 47 (Autumn): 599–628.

Korb, Lawrence, and Linda Brady (1984–1985) "Rearming America: The Reagan Administration Defense Program," *International Security* 9 (Winter): 3–18.

Kotz, Nick (1988) *Wild Blue Yonder: Money Politics and the B-1 Bomber* (New York: Pantheon Books).

Kramer, Bernard, S. Michael Kalick, and Michael Milburn (1983) "Attitudes Toward Nuclear Weapons and Nuclear War, 1945–1982," *Journal of Social Issues* 39 (Fall): 7–24.

Kuechler, Manfred, and Russell Dalton (1990) "New Social Movements and the Political Order," pp. 277–300 in Russell Dalton and Manfred Kuechler (eds.), *Challenging the Political Order* (New York: Oxford University Press).

Ladd, Everett Carll (1982) "The Freeze Framework," *Public Opinion* 5 (August/September): 20–46.

Ladd, Steve, Nora Hallett, and Rev. Tony Martin (1983) "National Freeze Tour of Germany (November 1982)," *Freeze Newsletter* (January): 9–11, 22.

Leavitt, Robert (1983) "Freezing the Arms Race: Public Opinion (Supplement)." Case Program, John F. Kennedy School of Government, Harvard University, Cambridge, MA.

Lewis, John, and Coit Blacker (1983) "Forming Coalitions for Arms Control," *Sierra* 68 (May/June): 60–61.

Lifton, Robert Jay, and Richard Falk (1982) *Indefensible Weapons* (New York: Basic Books).

Lipsky, Michael (1968) "Protest as a Political Resource," *American Political Science Review* 62 (December): 1144–1158.

Lofland, John (1989) "Consensus Movements: City Twinning and Derailed Dissent in the American Eighties," pp. 163–196 in Louis Kriesberg (ed.), *Research in Social Change, Conflict, and Social Movements,* vol. 11 (Greenwich, CT: JAI Press).

——— (1993) *Polite Protesters: The American Peace Movement of the 1980s* (Syracuse, NY: Syracuse University Press).

Lofland, John, Mary Anna Colwell, and Victoria Johnson (1990) "Change Theories and Movement Structure," pp. 87–105 in John Lofland and Sam Marullo (eds.), *Peace Action in the Eighties* (New Brunswick, NJ: Rutgers University Press).

Lofland, John, and Sam Marullo (1993) "The Soaring Phase of Social Movements: American Peace Activism, 1981–1983," pp. 223–272 in John Lofland (ed.), *Polite Protesters: The American Peace Movement of the 1980s* (Syracuse, NY: Syracuse University Press).

MacDougall, John (1991) "Congress, the M-X Missile and the Nuclear Freeze Movement," pp. 263–282 in Bert Klandermans (ed.), *International Social Movement Research,* vol. 3 (Greenwich, CT: JAI Press).

——— (1996) "Conversion Without Doctrinal Debate: Maine, USA," pp. 59–66 in Bjorn Moeller and Lev Voronkov (eds.), *Defense Doctrines and Conversion* (Aldershot, UK: Dartmouth).

Maine State Planning Office (1993) *A Defense Adjustment Action Plan for Maine* (Augusta, ME: State Planning Office).

Mansbridge, Jane (1992) "A Deliberative Theory of Interest Representation," pp. 32–57 in Mark Petracca (ed.), *The Politics of Interests* (Boulder, CO: Westview Press).

Martin, Patricia (1990) "Rethinking Feminist Organizations," *Gender and Society* 4, no. 2: 182–206.

Marullo, Sam (1990) "Patterns of Peacemaking in the Local Freeze Campaign," pp. 246–263 in Sam Marullo and John Lofland (eds.), *Peace Action in the Eighties* (New Brunswick, NJ: Rutgers University Press).

——— (1994) *Ending the Cold War at Home: From Militarism to a More Peaceful World Order* (New York: Lexington).

Marullo, Sam, Ron Pagnucco, and Jackie Smith (1996) "Frame Changes and Social Movement Contraction: U.S. Peace Movement Framing after the Cold War," *Sociological Inquiry* 66 (Winter): 1–28.

McAdam, Doug (1982) *Political Process and the Development of Black Insurgency, 1890–1970* (Chicago: University of Chicago Press).

——— (1983) "Tactical Innovation and the Pace of Insurgency," *American Sociological Review* 48 (December): 735–754.

—— (1986) "Recruitment to High-Risk Activism: The Case of Freedom Summer," *American Journal of Sociology* 92 (July): 64–90.

McAdam, Doug, John McCarthy, and Mayer Zald (1988) "Social Movements," pp. 695–737 in Neil Smelser (ed.), *Handbook of Sociology* (Beverly Hills, CA: Sage).

McCarthy, John (1987) "Pro-Life and Pro-Choice Mobilization: Infrastructural Deficits and New Technologies," pp. 49–66 in Mayer Zald and John McCarthy (eds.), *Social Movements in an Organizational Society* (New Brunswick, NJ: Transaction Books).

McCarthy, John, David Britt, and Mark Wolfson (1991) "The Institutional Channeling of Social Movements by the State in the United States," pp. 45–76 in Louis Kriesberg (ed.), *Research in Social Movements, Conflicts and Change,* vol. 13 (Greenwich, CT: JAI Press).

McCarthy, John, and Mayer Zald (1977) "Resource Mobilization and Social Movements: A Partial Theory," *American Journal of Sociology* 82 (May): 1212–1241.

McCrea, Frances, and Gerald Markle (1989) *Minutes to Midnight: Nuclear Weapons Protest in America* (Newbury Park, CA: Sage).

McFadden, Robert (1983) "Atomic War Film Spurs Nationwide Discussion," *New York Times* (November 22): A27.

Meese, Edwin (1992) *With Reagan* (Washington, DC: Regnery Gateway).

Melucci, Alberto (1988) "Getting Involved," pp. 329–348 in Bert Klandermans, Hanspeter Kriesi and Sidney Tarrow (eds.), *From Structure to Action: International Social Movement Research,* vol. 1 (Greenwich, CT: JAI Press).

Meyer, David (1990) *A Winter of Discontent: The Nuclear Freeze and American Politics* (New York: Praeger).

—— (1993a) "Political Process and Protest Movement Cycles," *Political Research Quarterly* 46 (September): 451–479.

—— (1993b) "Institutionalizing Dissent: The United States Political Opportunity Structure and the Nuclear Freeze Movement," *Sociological Forum* 8 (June): 157–179.

—— (1995) "Framing National Security: Elite Public Discourse on Nuclear Weapons During the Cold War," *Political Communication* 12 (June): 173–192.

Meyer, David, and Douglas Imig (1993) "Political Opportunity and the Rise and Decline of Interest Group Sectors," *Social Science Journal* 30 (July): 253–270.

Meyer, David, and Sam Marullo (1992) "Grassroots Mobilization and International Politics: Peace Protest and the End of the Cold War," pp. 99–140 in Louis Kriesberg and David Segal (eds.), *Research in Social Movements, Conflicts, and Change,* vol. 14 (Greenwich, CT: JAI Press).

Meyer, John, and Brian Rowan (1977) "Institutionalized Organizations: Formal Structure as Myth and Ceremony," *American Journal of Sociology* 83 (September): 340–363.

Milbrath, Lester (1963) *The Washington Lobbyists* (Chicago: Rand McNally).

Milburn, Michael, Paul Watanabe, and Bernard Kramer (1986) "The Nature and Sources of Attitudes Toward a Nuclear Freeze," *Political Psychology* 7 (December): 661–673.

Miller, Steven (1984a) "Politics over Promise: Domestic Impediments to Arms Control," *International Security* 8 (Spring): 67–90.

Miller, Steven (ed.) (1984b) *The Nuclear Weapons Freeze and Arms Control* (Cambridge, MA: Ballinger).

Minkoff, Debra (1993) "The Organization of Survival: Women's and Race-Ethnic Voluntarist and Activist Organizations, 1955–1985," *Social Forces* 71, no. 4: 887–908.

Molander, Earl, and Roger Molander (1990) "A Threshhold Analysis of the Antinuclear War Movement," pp. 37–52 in Sam Marullo and John Lofland (eds.), *Peace Action in the Eighties* (New Brunswick, NJ: Rutgers University Press).

Morris, Aldon (1984) *The Origins of the Civil Rights Movement: Black Communities Organizing for Change* (New York: Free Press).

Morris, Aldon, and Carol Mueller (eds.) (1992) *Frontiers in Social Movement Theory* (New Haven, CT: Yale University Press).

Mueller, Dennis (1989) *Public Choice II* (Cambridge: Cambridge University Press).

Nacht, Michael (1985) *The Age of Vulnerability: Threats to the Nuclear Stalemate* (Washington, DC: Brookings Institution).

Neal, Mary (1993) "Rhetorical Styles of the Physicians for Social Responsibility," pp. 167–179 in Sam Marullo and John Lofland (eds.), *Peace Works* (Boulder, CO: Westview Press).

Newhouse, John (1990 [1988]) *War and Peace in the Nuclear Age* (New York: Vintage Books [Alfred Knopf]).

Nincic, Miroslav (1988) "The United States, the Soviet Union, and the Politics of Opposites," *World Politics* 40 (July): 452–475.

Oberschall, Anthony (1973) *Social Conflict and Social Movements* (Englewood Cliffs, NJ: Prentice Hall).

Offe, Claus (1984) *Contradictions of the Welfare State* (London: Hutchinson).

——— (1985) "New Social Movements: Challenging the Boundaries of Institutional Politics," *Social Research* 52 (Winter): 817–868.

O'Heffernan, Patrick (1991) *Mass Media and American Foreign Policy* (Norwood, NJ: Ablex Publishing).

Oliver, Pamela (1984) "If You Don't Do It, Nobody Else Will": Active and Token Contributors to Local Collective Action," *American Sociological Review* 49 (October): 601–610.

——— (1989) "Bringing the Crowd Back In," pp. 1–30 in Louis Kriesberg (ed.), *Research in Social Movements, Conflicts and Change,* vol. 11 (Greenwich, CT: JAI Press).

Oliver, Pamela, and Gerald Marwell (1988) "The Paradox of Group Size in Collective Action: A Theory of the Critical Mass II," *American Sociological Review* 53 (February): 1–8.

Ordeshook, Peter (1986) *Game Theory and Political Theory: An Introduction* (Cambridge: Cambridge University Press).

Ornstein, Norman, and Shirley Elder (1978) *Interest Groups, Lobbying and Policymaking* (Washington, DC: Congressional Quarterly Press).

Oskamp, Stuart (1991) *Attitudes and Opinions,* 2nd ed. (Englewood Cliffs, NJ: Prentice-Hall).

Overby, L. Marvin, and Sarah Ritchie (1990) "Mobilized Masses and Strategic Opponents: A Resource Mobilization Analysis of the Clean Air and Nuclear Freeze Movements." Paper presented at the meetings of the Southern Political Science Association, Atlanta.

Page, Benjamin (1978) *Choices and Echoes in Presidential Elections* (Chicago: University of Chicago Press).

Page, Benjamin, Robert Shapiro, and Glenn Dempsey (1987) "What Moves Public Opinion," *American Political Science Review* 81 (March): 23–43.

Pagnucco, Ronald (1992) *Tactical Choice by Groups Working for Peace in the Contemporary United States: The Ruly/Unruly Divide*. Ph.D. dissertation, Catholic University of America, Washington, DC.

Pagnucco, Ron, and Jackie Smith (1993) "The Peace Movement and the Formulation of U.S. Foreign Policy," *Peace and Change* 18 (April): 157–181.

Paine, Christopher (1985) "Lobbying for Arms Control," *Bulletin of Atomic Scientists* 41 (August): 125–130.

Peace Action Maine (PAM) (1994) "Peace Talk," Summer.

——— [n.d.] "Final Draft," unpublished manuscript.

Peace III, Roger (1991) *A Just and Lasting Peace: The U.S. Peace Movement from the Cold War to Desert Storm* (Chicago: Noble Press).

Pertschuk, Michael (1986) *Giant Killers* (New York: W. W. Norton).

Petracca, Mark (1992) "The Rediscovery of Interest Group Politics," pp. 3–31 in Mark Petracca (ed.), *The Politics of Interests* (Boulder, CO: Westview Press).

Pipes, Richard (1995) "Misinterpreting the Cold War," *Foreign Affairs* 74 (January/February): 154–160.

Piven, Frances Fox, and Richard Cloward (1977) *Poor People's Movements: Why They Succeed, How They Fail* (New York: Pantheon).

Powell, Walter, and Paul DiMaggio (1991) *The New Institutionalism in Organizational Analysis* (Chicago: University of Chicago Press).

Reagan, Ronald (1990) *An American Life* (New York: Simon and Schuster).

Reitzes, Donald, and Dietrich Reitzes (1987) *The Alinsky Legacy: Alive and Kicking* (Greenwich, CT: JAI Press).

Riker, William (1962) *The Theory of Political Coalitions* (New Haven, CT: Yale University Press).

Rivers, Douglas, and Nancy Rose (1985) "Passing the President's Program: Public Opinion and Presidential Influence in Congress," *American Journal of Political Science* 29 (May): 183–196.

Rochon, Thomas (1988) *Mobilizing for Peace: The Antinuclear Movements in Western Europe* (Princeton, NJ: Princeton University Press).

——— (1990) "Political Movements and State Authority in Liberal Democracies," *World Politics* 42 (January): 299–313.

——— (forthcoming) *Culture Moves: Ideas, Activism, and Changing Values* (Princeton, NJ: Princeton University Press).

Rochon, Thomas, and Daniel Mazmanian (1993) "Social Movements and the Policy Process," *Annals of the American Academy of Political and Social Science* 528 (July): 75–87.

Rogers, Mary Beth (1990) *Cold Anger: A Story of Faith and Power Politics* (Denton, TX: University of North Texas Press).

Rosenberg, Gerald (1991) *The Hollow Hope: Can Courts Bring About Social Change?* (Chicago: University of Chicago Press).

Rozell, Mark, and Clyde Wilcox (1995) "The Past as Prologue: The Christian Right in the 1996 Elections," pp. 253–263 in Mark Rozell and Clyde Wilcox (eds.), *God at the Grass Roots* (Lanham, MD: Rowman and Littlefield).

Rupp, Leila, and Verta Taylor (1987) *Survival in the Doldrums: The American Women's Rights Movement* (New York: Oxford University Press).

Rusk, Jerrold (1976) "Political Participation in America: A Review Essay," *American Political Science Review* 70 (June): 583–591.

Russett, Bruce (1990) *Controlling the Sword* (Cambridge: Harvard University Press).

Ryan, Charlotte (1991) *Prime Time Activism: Media Strategies for Grassroots Organizing* (Boston: South End Press).

Salisbury, Robert (1990) "The Paradox of Interest Groups in Washington—More Groups, Less Clout," pp. 203–229 in Anthony King (ed.), *The New American Political System,* 2nd ed. (Washington, DC: AEI Press).

Sampson, Tim (1984) "Coalitions and Other Relations," pp. 207–212 in Lee Staples (ed.), *Roots to Power: A Manual for Grassroots Organizing* (New York: Praeger).

Sandman, Peter, and JoAnn Valenti (1986) "Scared Stiff—or Scared into Action," *Bulletin of the Atomic Scientists* 42 (January): 12–16.

Scarce, Rik (1990) *Eco-Warriors: Understanding Radical Environmentalism* (Chicago: Noble Press).

Schattschneider, E. E. (1960) *The Semisovereign People: A Realist's View of Democracy in America* (New York: Holt, Rinehart, and Winston).

Scheer, Robert (1982) *With Enough Shovels: Reagan, Bush, and Nuclear War* (New York: Random House).

Schennink, Ben (1994) Interview with Ron Pagnucco (June 5).

Schlozman, Kay Lehman, and John Tierney (1986) *Organized Interests and American Democracy* (New York: Harper and Row).

Schneider, Barry (1984) "The Nuclear Freeze Proposal: Background and Rationale," pp. 1–14 in Keith Payne and Colin Gray (eds.), *The Nuclear Freeze Controversy* (Lanham, MD: University Press of America and Abt Books).

Schneider, William (1984) "Public Opinion," pp. 11–35 in Joseph Nye (ed.), *The Making of America's Soviet Policy* (New Haven, CT: Yale University Press).

Schweppe, Susie (1994) Interview with John MacDougall.

Scott, W. Richard (1992) *Organizations: Rational, Natural, and Open Systems* (Englewood Cliffs, NJ: Prentice-Hall).

Seidman, Helen (1991) Interview with David Cortright (November 20).

Sharp, Enid (1994) Interview with John MacDougall.

———— (1996) Interview with John MacDougall.

Sherry, Michael (1995) *In the Shadow of War* (New Haven, CT: Yale University Press).

Shultz, George (1993) *Triumph and Turmoil: My Years as Secretary of State* (New York: Macmillan).

Silberman, Eve (1985) "Who Is Carl Pursell?" *Ann Arbor Observer* (September).

Singh, Jitendra, and Charles Lumsden (1990) "Theory and Research in Organizational Ecology," pp. 161–195 in Richard Scott and Judith Blake (eds.), *Annual Review of Sociology* (Palo Alto, CA: Annual Reviews).

Smith, Christian (1996) *Resisting Reagan* (Chicago: University of Chicago Press).

Smith, Hedrick (1988) *The Power Game: How Washington Really Works* (New York: Random House).

Smith, Jackie (1997) "Characteristics of the Modern Transnational Social Movement Sector," in Jackie Smith, Charles Chatfield, and Ron Pagnucco (eds.), *Transnational Social Movements and World Politics: Solidarity Beyond the State* (Syracuse, NY: Syracuse University Press).

———— (forthcoming) "Nonresponse Bias in Organizational Surveys: Evidence from a Survey of Groups and Organizations Working for Peace," *Nonprofit and Voluntary Sector Quarterly.*

Smith, Richard (1984) "Advocacy, Interpretation, and Influence in the U.S. Congress," *American Political Science Review* 78 (March): 44–63.

Snow, David, and Robert Benford (1988) "Ideology, Frame Resonance, and Participant Mobilization," pp. 197–217 in Bert Klandermans, Hanspeter Kriesi, and Sidney Tarrow (eds.), *From Structure to Action: International Social Movement Research,* vol. 1 (Greenwich, CT: JAI Press).

Snow, David, E. Burke Rochford, Steven Worden, and Robert Benford (1986) "Frame Alignment, Micromobilization, and Movement Participation," *American Sociological Review* 51 (August): 464–481.

Snow, David, Louis Zurcher, Jr., and Sheldon Ekland-Olson (1980) "Social Networks and Social Movements: A Microstructural Approach to Differential Recruitment," *American Sociological Review* 45 (October): 787–801.

Solo, Pam (1988) *From Protest to Policy: Beyond the Freeze to Common Security* (Cambridge, MA: Ballinger).

——— (1993) Interview with David Cortright (September 20).

Staggenborg, Suzanne (1986) "Coalition Work in the Pro-Choice Movement," *Social Problems* 33 (June): 374–389.

——— (1988) "The Consequences of Professionalization and Formalization in the Pro-Choice Movement," *American Sociological Review* 53 (August): 585–605.

——— (1991) *The Pro-Choice Movement* (New York: Oxford University Press).

Staley-Mays, Wells (1996) Interview with John MacDougall.

Stein, Bob (1993) Interview with John MacDougall.

Strauss, Anselm, and Juliet Corbin (1990) *Basics of Qualitative Research: Grounded Theory Procedures and Techniques* (Newbury Park, CA: Sage).

Swidler, Ann (1986) "Culture in Action: Symbols and Strategies," *American Sociological Review* 51 (April): 273–286.

Szegedy-Maszak, Marianne (1989) "The Movement: Rise and Fall of the Washington Peace Industry," *Bulletin of the Atomic Scientists* 45 (January/February): 18–23.

Talbott, Strobe (1984) *Deadly Gambits: The Reagan Administration and the Stalemate in Nuclear Arms Control* (New York: Vintage Books).

Tarrow, Sidney (1989a) Struggle, Politics, and Reform: Collective Action, Social Movements, and Cycles of Protest (Ithaca, NY: Cornell University, Western Societies Program, Occasional Paper no. 21).

——— (1989b) *Democracy and Disorder* (New York: Cambridge University Press).

——— (1994) *Power in Movement* (New York: Cambridge University Press).

Taylor, Verta (1989) "Social Movement Continuity: The Women's Movement in Abeyance," *American Sociological Review* 54 (October): 761–775.

Taylor, Verta, and Nancy Whittier (1992) "Collective Identity in Social Movement Communities: Lesbian Feminist Mobilization," pp. 104–129 in Aldon Morris and Carol Mueller (eds.), *Frontiers of Social Movement Theory* (New Haven, CT: Yale University Press).

Tetlock, Philip (1983) "Policy-Makers' Images of International Conflict," *Journal of Social Issues* 39 (Fall): 67–86.

Thomas, David (1985) "Apocalypse Now: The American Peace Movement in the 1980s," pp. 402–433 in Walter Laqueur and Robert Hunter (eds.), *European Peace Movements and the Future of the Western Alliance* (New Brunswick, NJ: Transaction Books).

Tierney, John (1992) "Organized Interests and the Nation's Capitol," pp. 201–220 in Mark Petracca (ed.), *The Politics of Interests* (Boulder, CO: Westview Press).

Tilly, Charles (1975) *From Mobilization to Revolution* (Reading, MA: Addison-Wesley).

—— (1979) "Repertoires of Contention in America and Britain, 1750–1830," pp. 126–155 in Mayer Zald and John McCarthy (eds.), *The Dynamics of Social Movements* (Cambridge, MA: Winthrop).

—— (1993–1994) "Social Movements as Historically Specific Clusters of Political Performances," *Berkeley Journal of Sociology* 38: 1–30.

Topsfield Foundation (1987) *Grassroots Peace Directory* (Pomfert, CT: Topsfield).

Towell, Pat (1984) "Reagan Faces Squeeze on Nuclear Arms Policy: Liberal Coalition Plans Strategy for Hill, Polls," *Congressional Quarterly Weekly Report* 42 (January 21): 101–108.

Turner, Ralph (1981) "Collective Behavior and Resource Mobilization as Approaches to Social Movements: Issues and Continuities," pp. 1–24 in Louis Kriesberg (ed.), *Research in Social Movements, Conflict, and Change,* vol. 4 (Greenwich, CT: JAI Press).

Tydeman, Ann (1981) *Putting the Pieces Together: A Guide to Coalition Building* (Washington, DC: National Citizens' Coalition for Nursing Home Reform).

Tyler, Tom, and Kathleen McGraw (1983) "The Threat of Nuclear War: Risk Interpretation and Behavioral Response," *Journal of Social Issues* 39 (Fall): 25–40.

U.S. Helsinki Watch Committee (1987) *From Below: Independent Peace and Environmental Movements in Eastern Europe and the USSR* (New York: U.S. Helsinki Watch Committee).

Van Voorst, L. Bruce (1982) "The Critical Masses," *Foreign Policy* 48 (Fall): 82–93.

Walker, Jack (1977) "Setting the Agenda in the U.S. Senate: A Theory of Problem Selection," *British Journal of Political Science* 7 (October): 423–445.

—— (1981) "The Diffusion of Knowledge, Policy Communities and Agenda Setting," pp. 75–96 in John Tropman, Milan Dluhy, and Roger Lind (eds.), *New Strategic Perspectives on Social Policy* (New York: Pergamon Press).

—— (1991) *Mobilizing Interests Groups in America: Patrons, Professions, and Social Movements* (Ann Arbor: University of Michigan Press).

Waller, Douglas (1987) *Congress and the Nuclear Freeze* (Amherst: University of Massachusetts Press).

Walsh, Edward, and Rex Warland (1983) "Social Movement Involvement in the Wake of a Nuclear Accident: Activists and Free Riders in the TMI Area," *American Sociological Review* 48 (December): 764–780.

Weed, Frank (1987) "Grass-roots Activism and the Drunk Driving Issue: A Survey of MADD Chapters," *Law and Policy* 9 (July): 259–278.

—— (1991) "Organizational Mortality in the Anti–Drunk Driving Movement: Failure Among Local MADD Chapters," *Social Forces* 69 (March): 851–868.

Werner, Paul, and Paul Roy (1985) "Measuring Activism Regarding the Nuclear Arms Race," *Journal of Personality Assessment* 49 (April): 181–186.

Whittier, Nancy (1995) *Feminist Generations: The Persistence of the Radical Women's Movement* (Philadelphia: Temple University Press).

Wilson, James Q. (1973) *Political Organizations* (New York: Basic Books).

Wilson, Larry (1993) Interview by Bob Edwards, Washington, DC.

Wilson, Randy (1993) "Making Peace Practical," *In These Times,* July 12.

Wiltfong, Gregory, and Doug McAdam (1991) "The Costs and Risks of Social Activism," *Social Forces* 69 (June): 987–1010.

Wirls, Daniel (1992) *Buildup: The Politics of Defense in the Reagan Era* (Ithaca, NY: Cornell University Press).

Wittner, Laurence (1984) *Rebels Against War: The American Peace Movement, 1933–1983* (Philadelphia: Temple University Press).

Yankelovich, Daniel, and John Doble (1984) "The Public Mood: Nuclear Weapons and the U.S.S.R." *Foreign Affairs* 63 (Fall): 33–46.

Yankelovich, Daniel, Robert Kingston, and Gerald Garvey (1984) *Voter Options on Nuclear Arms Policy: A Briefing Book for the 1984 Elections* (Providence, RI: Public Agenda Foundation and the Center for Foreign Policy Development at Brown University).

Young, Nigel (1984) "Why Peace Movements Fail: An Historical and Social Overview," *Social Alternatives* 4, no. 1: 9–16.

Zald, Mayer, and John McCarthy (1987) "Social Movement Industries: Competition and Conflict Among SMOs," pp. 161–180 in Mayer Zald and John McCarthy (eds.), *Social Movements in an Organizational Society* (New Brunswick, NJ: Transaction).

Zald, Mayer, and Bert Useem (1987) "Movement and Countermovement Interaction: Mobilization, Tactics, and State Involvement," pp. 247–272 in Mayer Zald and John McCarthy (eds.), *Social Movements in an Organizational Society* (New Brunswick, NJ: Transaction).

Zaller, John (1992) *The Nature and Origins of Mass Opinion* (New York: Cambridge University Press).

THE CONTRIBUTORS

David Cortright is president of the Fourth Freedom Forum in Goshen, Indiana, and former president of the Nuclear Weapons Freeze Campaign.

Bob Edwards is assistant professor of sociology at East Carolina University. He is author of a number of articles on social movements and editor of a special issue of *American Behavioral Scientist* devoted to the theory and measurement of social capital.

Todd C. Edwards has a Ph.D. in psychology from Claremont Graduate University. He currently works as a research consultant with Rain City Associates in Seattle, Washington.

Will Hathaway is currently director of human resource development at Eastern Michigan University.

Robert Kleidman is associate professor of sociology at Cleveland State University and author of *Organizing for Peace: Neutrality, the Test Ban, and the Freeze* (Syracuse University Press).

Jeffrey W. Knopf is assistant professor of international relations at the University of Southern California and the author of *Domestic Society and International Cooperation: The Impact of Protest on U.S. Arms Control Policy* (forthcoming from Cambridge University Press).

John MacDougall is professor of sociology and codirector of the Peace and Conflict Studies Institute at the University of Massachusetts at Lowell. He is currently working on a project on regional sustainability.

Sam Marullo is professor of sociology at Georgetown University, coeditor of a number of books on peace movements and politics, and author of *Ending the Cold War at Home: From Militarism to a More Peaceful World Order* (Lexington Books).

David S. Meyer is associate professor of political science at the City University of New York. He is the author of *A Winter of Discontent: The Nuclear Freeze and American Politics* (Praeger).

Ron Pagnucco is assistant professor in the Department of Sociology at Mount Saint Mary's College. He is coeditor of *Transnational Social Movements and World Politics: Solidarity Beyond the State* (Syracuse). His (1992) Ph.D. dissertation was on the strategy of tactical choice among movement organizations.

Thomas R. Rochon is professor and director of the Center for Politics and Economics at Claremont Graduate University. He is the author of *Culture Moves: Ideas, Activism, and Changing Values* (forthcoming from Princeton University Press).

Andrew Rojecki is assistant professor of journalism at the University of Indiana and author of a forthcoming book on media images of antinuclear movements and the Cold War. His current project is on the link between television and interracial trust.

Stephen P. Wood received his Ph.D. in political science in 1997 from Claremont Graduate University. His dissertation was on the relationship between political institutions, property rights, and economic diversification in the less developed countries.

INDEX

Carter administration: foreign policy of, 5, 32, 38, 44, 107, 240, 243
Catholic bishops: and nuclear weapons, 8, 39, 104, 118–119, 120, 122, 126. *See also* Religion and movement support
Center for Defense Information (CDI), 159*n10*
Central America: U.S. involvement in, 12–13, 75, 81, 90, 94, 173, 213; solidarity movement, 90–93
Central Intelligence Agency (CIA), 110, 142
Chilton, Patricia, 94*n4*
Christian right, 2
Church networks. *See* Religion and movement support
Civil disobedience, 13
Civil rights movement: contribution to freeze, 57, 241
Clark, William, 147
Clifford, Clark, 6
Clymer, Adam, 115
Coalition for Arms Control (CAC), 68, 74–79
Coalitions: with elites, 127, 132–134, 136, 141, 154, 158; formation, 64–69, 74, 77–78; in the freeze movement, 74, 241–243, 248–249; maintenance of, 73–74, 76–78; tensions within, 52–56. *See also* Movements as coalitions
Cognitive maps, 99
Cohen, Jean, 20
Cohen, Michael, 159*n6*
Cohen, William, 152
Colby, William, 142
Columbia Broadcasting System (CBS): coverage of the freeze, 7, 102–108, 110–118, 120–126. *See also* Media
Colwell, Mary Anna, 184, 201*n3*
Committee for a Sane Nuclear Policy. *See* SANE
Committee for Nonviolent Action (CNVA), 48–50
Committee on the Present Danger, 6, 118, 123
Common Cause, 68, 70–71, 78
Congress and nuclear weapons. *See* Freeze movement, in Congress
Congressional Digest, 142

Congressional Research Service, 156
Congress of Racial Equality (CORE), 57
Conte, Silvio, 141
Corbin, Juliet, 220
Cortright, David, 94*n3,* 152
Council for a Livable World, 5, 69, 71, 159*n10*
Cruise missiles. *See* Intermediate Nuclear Force missiles
Crumm, Eileen, 159*n4*
Cuban missile crisis, 50
Cycles of mobilization, 2–3, 8, 44, 47–48, 57–59, 181–184, 203, 205, 232, 238, 248–249, 250–251

The Day After, 8, 167
Dean, Robert, 138, 154
Deaver, Michael, 146
Defense PACs. *See* PACs
Dicks, Norman, 12
Doctor Strangelove, 126
Downey, Thomas, 69
Drew, Elizabeth, 41

Economic conversion, 203–204, 207–211, 214–215
Economic Conversion Project (ECP), 208–210, 214
Educators for Social Responsibility, 69
Edwards, Bob, 59*n8,* 201*n3*
Eisenhower, Dwight David, 49
Ekland-Olson, Sheldon, 229
Electoral pathway of influence, 11, 14, 129–132, 136, 143–145, 158, 160*nn11, 12, 13, 14*
Elite coalition shift pathway. *See* Coalitions, with elites
Ellsberg, Daniel, 93
El Salvador, 120
Emergency Peace Campaign (EPC), 48–49, 50, 52–54, 56, 58, 59*n6*
Equal Employment Opportunity Commission (EEOC), 171
Equilibrium arms control policy, 38–39, 41–44, 130–131
Erickson Nepsted, Sharon, 91
European Network for East-West Dialogue (ENEWD), 90
European Nuclear Disarmament (END), 90

ABOUT THE BOOK

How advanced is our knowledge about the dynamics of political and social activism? What lessons can be learned by studying the rise and fall of particular political and social movements? What insights can be gained by applying the different frameworks and methodologies of political science, psychology, sociology, and communications? This original work employs multidisciplinary perspectives to better understand the nuclear freeze movement, a movement that at one time produced a vast national network of activism and the largest political demonstration in the history of the United States.

Incorporating a new, coalitional theory of political and social movements, the authors explore the successes and failures of the freeze movement in its attempts to influence legislation, treaties, and overall public opinion about nuclear weapons. They examine freeze activism in the context of the larger peace movement, its continuing relevance for current and future peace mobilizations, and its implications for the general study of political and social change.

Thomas R. Rochon is professor and director of the Center for Politics and Economics at Claremont Graduate University. **David S. Meyer** is associate professor of political science at the City College of the City University of New York.